FAR EASTERN BEGINNINGS

Also by Olivia Vlahos

THE BATTLE-AX PEOPLE:
BEGINNINGS OF WESTERN CULTURE

HUMAN BEGINNINGS

NEW WORLD BEGINNINGS:
INDIAN CULTURES IN THE AMERICAS

AFRICAN BEGINNINGS

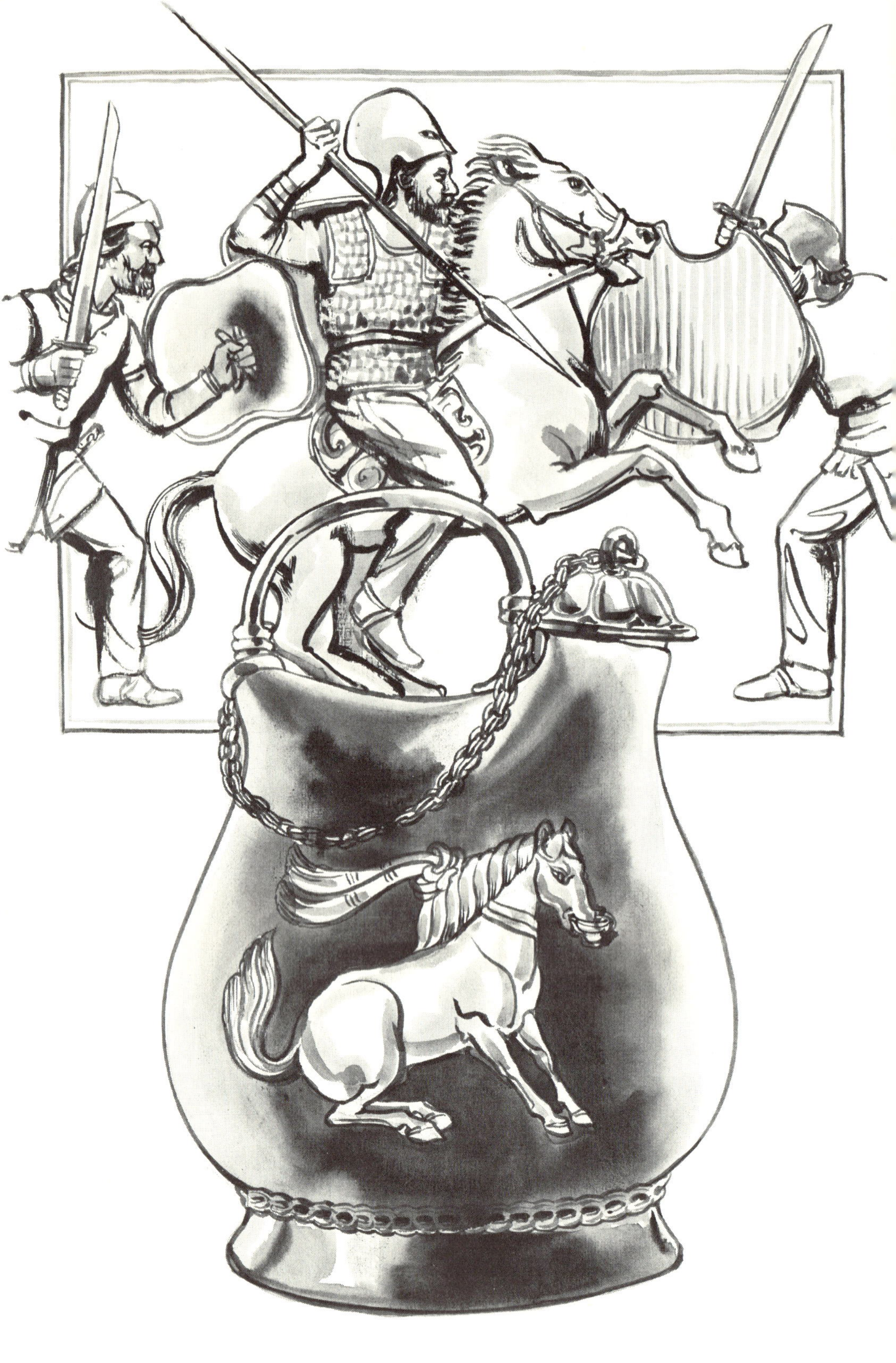

Olivia Vlahos

FAR EASTERN BEGINNINGS

Illustrated by George Ford

THE VIKING PRESS NEW YORK

ACKNOWLEDGMENTS

The quotation at the top of page 89 is from page 288 of Burton Watson's *Early Chinese Literature,* published in 1962 by Columbia University Press, New York. Reprinted by permission of the publisher.

The quotations on page 157 are from *The Wisdom of China and India,* edited and translated by Lin Yutang. Copyright 1942 and renewed 1970 by Random House, Inc.

First Edition
Copyright © 1976 by Olivia Vlahos
Illustrations copyright © 1976 by Viking Penguin Inc.
All rights reserved
First published in 1976 by The Viking Press
625 Madison Avenue, New York, N.Y. 10022
Published simultaneously in Canada by
The Macmillan Company of Canada Limited
Printed in U.S.A.

1 2 3 4 5 80 79 78 77 76

Library of Congress Cataloging in Publication Data
Vlahos, Olivia.   Far Eastern beginnings.
Bibliograpy: p.   Includes index.
Summary: Discusses the history and customs of the diverse cultures found on the Asian continent, from India to Siberia. 1. Asia—History—Juvenile literature. 2. Asia—Social life and customs—Juvenile literature. 3. Ethnology—Asia—Juvenile literature. [1. Asia—History. 2. Asia—Social life and customs. 3. Ethnology—Asia] I. Ford, George Cephas. II. Title. DS33.5.V55   950   76-5855

ISBN 0-670-30739-4

AUTHOR'S NOTE

OF all earth's regions, none is so rich in history and prehistory, in diverse life ways, languages, and lore as the Far East. It is possible to devote a lifetime to the study of one small portion of this intellectual immensity—to one of the Chinese dynasties, one cave excavated in Southeast Asia, one aspect of Buddhism, one of the Confucian Classics. Legions of scholars have done just that. Should any of them open these pages of mine, he or she may well object to the foreshortened record of events, to the simplification of beliefs and ideas so rich and so complex. But I am taking a bird's-eye view of the area: a view of the forest in which individual trees tend to merge into a general green blur. If such a view provides a framework for further study, if it stimulates the reader's curiosity, makes him long to read more, then the book will have served its purpose, and I shall be content. The bibliographies attached supply a good beginning for more specialized study, and I warmly urge the reader to consult them.

For language groupings I have consulted the classifications proposed by W. L. Trager and Joseph Greenberg and recent revisions in the field described by C. F. and F. M. Vogelin.

For the prehistory of Siberia I have depended on the works of Soviet archaeologists, made available in English translations by the Arctic Institute of North America. For the vast materials on Chinese prehistory the masterly syntheses of Dr. K. C. Chang have been my major sources. The most recent and concerted archaeological work in Southeast Asia has been carried forward by Dr. W. G. Solheim and his colleagues, and I have consulted their findings.

For the record of life ways, extant or extinct, I have consulted the ethnographic works listed in the bibliography. These extend in time from the early 1900s—when the great Vladimir Bogoras studied the Chukchi—to today.

Any study of the Far East depends ultimately on that long succession of Chinese historians and philosophers of history—some anonymous, some not—whose writings illuminate and enliven both the evidence of the spade and the studies of living men. One must be grateful above all to Ssu-ma Ch'ien whose lively and eloquent descriptions of people and ethnic groups of Han Dynasty times makes those times seem as contemporary as today's headlines and tomorrow's budget of political gossip.

Sources for quotations may be found at the end of each chapter's bibliography.

Contents

Part I   LAND AND LIFE

  Chapter 1   THE ANATOMY OF A CONTINENT
                        3

  Chapter 2   THE PEOPLE COME   10

Part II   THE OLD ASIANS

  Chapter 3   THE CHUKCHI   29
                      A Double Life in the Far North

  Chapter 4   THE AINU   52
                      Mystery Folk of Northern Japan

Part III   BETWEEN CHINA AND THE SNOWY WASTES

Chapter 5 BATTLE-AX PEOPLE IN THE STEPPES   71
            Warriors, Herdsmen, Conquerors

Chapter 6 THE NORTHERN TUNGUS   95
            From Taiga to Great Wall

Chapter 7 THE MONGOLS   111
            The Winning of Half a World

Chapter 8 THE KIRGHIZ   124
            Transformable Turks

Part IV   CHINA, HEART AND HUB

Chapter 9 GREAT CHINA   141
            A Dynastic Procession

Chapter 10 VILLAGE CHINA   171
            The Earth, the Grain, the Forefathers

Part V   BETWEEN CHINA AND INDIA

Chapter 11 TIBET   193
            The Pillar of Heaven

Chapter 12 EAST BY SOUTH   212
            Crossroads or Source?

Chapter 13 PEOPLE OF THE HILLS   236
            Yesterday and Tomorrow

Chapter 14 HUNTING AND GATHERING FOLK   252
            A Vanishing Link with the Past

BIBLIOGRAPHY   269
INDEX   281

LIST OF MAPS

ASIA AND ADJACENT AREAS   x-xi
LANGUAGE GROUPS OF EURASIA   25
THE ABORIGINAL PEOPLES OF
    NORTHEAST ASIA   39
MIGRATIONS AND INVASIONS: 400 B.C.–A.D. 700
    83
THE HILL TRIBES OF INDOCHINA   239

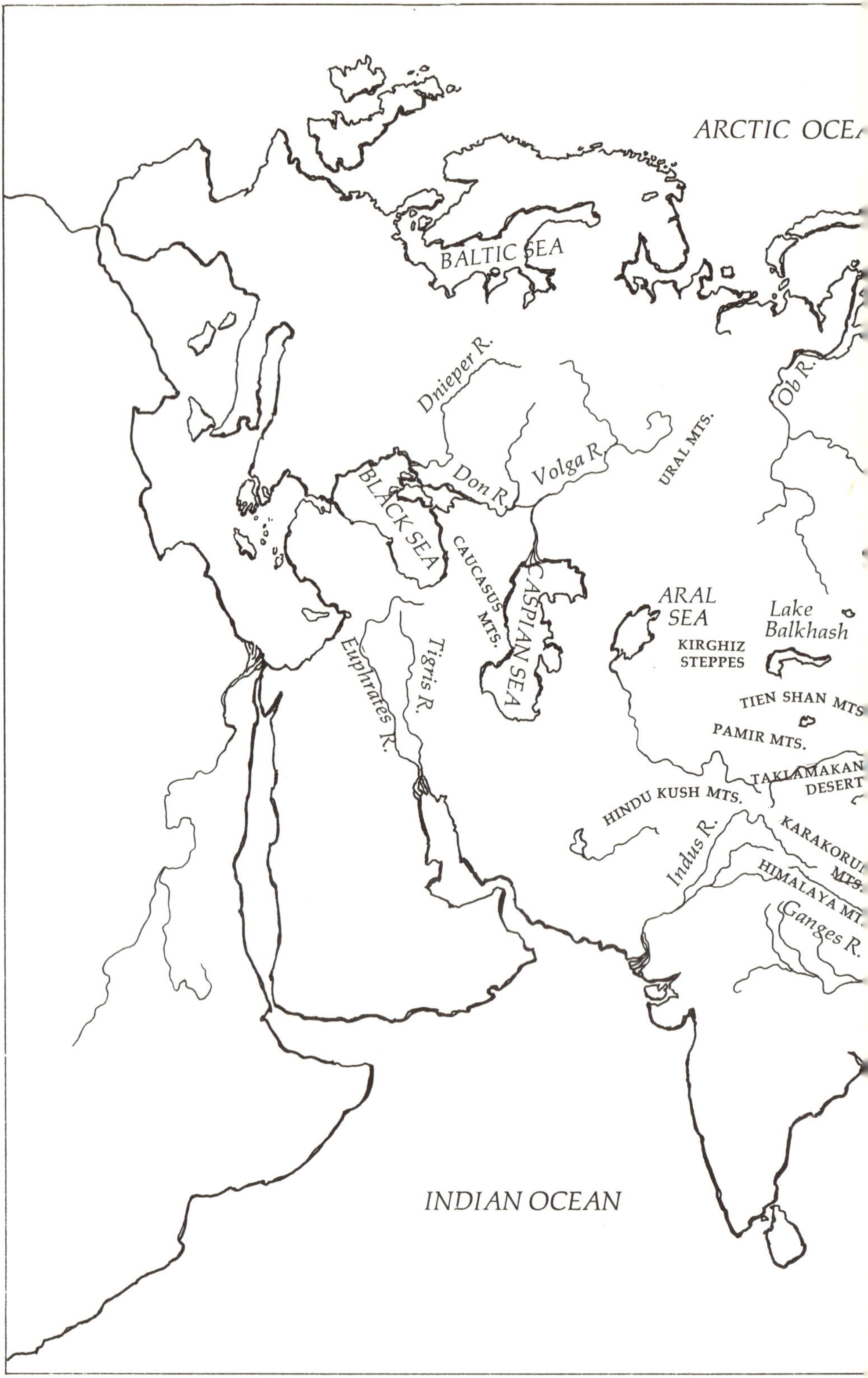

BALTIC SEA
Dnieper R.
Ob R.
URAL MTS.
Volga R.
Don R.
BLACK SEA
CAUCASUS MTS.
CASPIAN SEA
ARAL SEA
Lake Balkhash
KIRGHIZ STEPPES
Euphrates R.
Tigris R.
PAMIR MTS.
HINDU KUSH MTS.
Indus R.
Ganges R.
INDIAN OCEAN

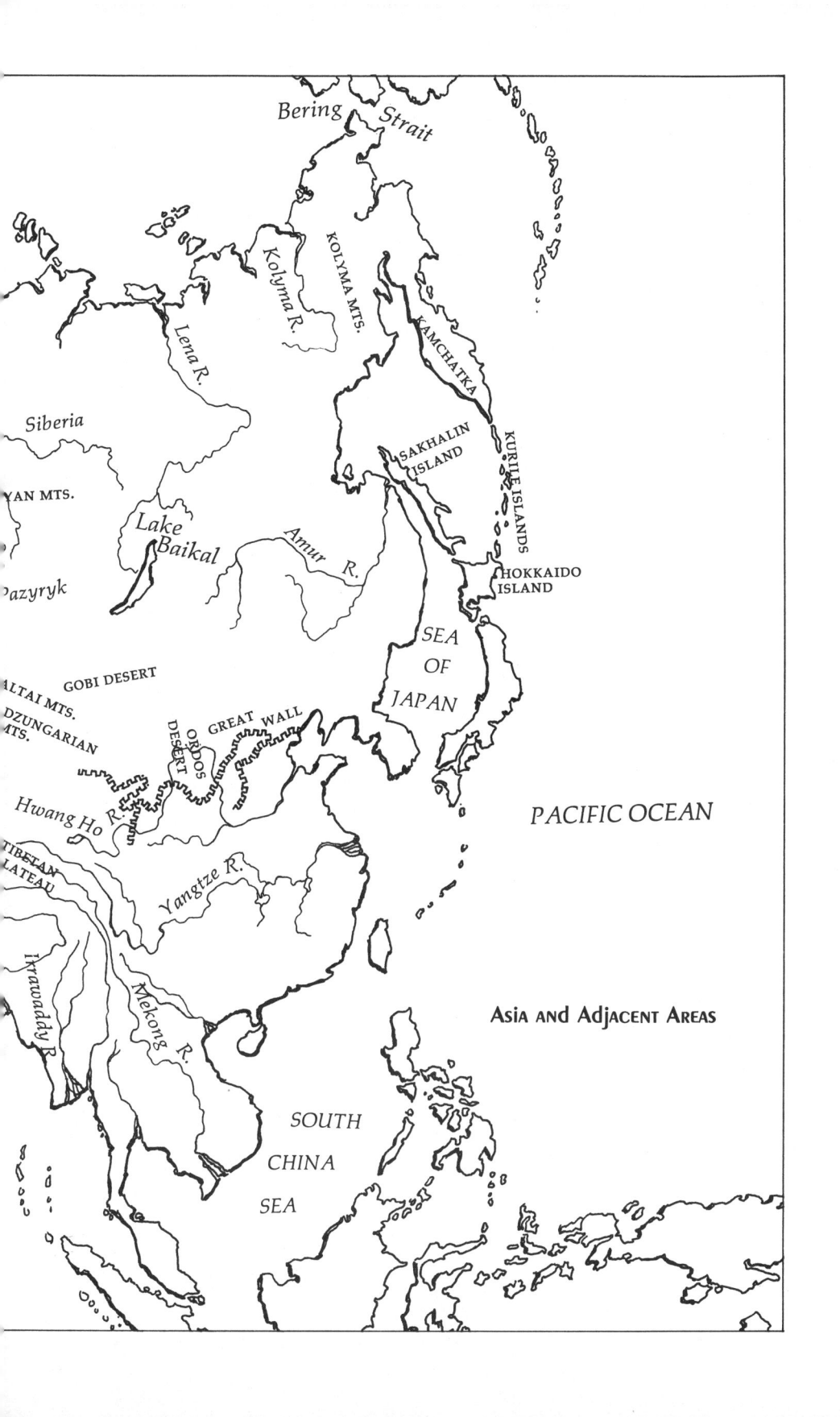

Asia and Adjacent Areas

PART I
LAND AND LIFE

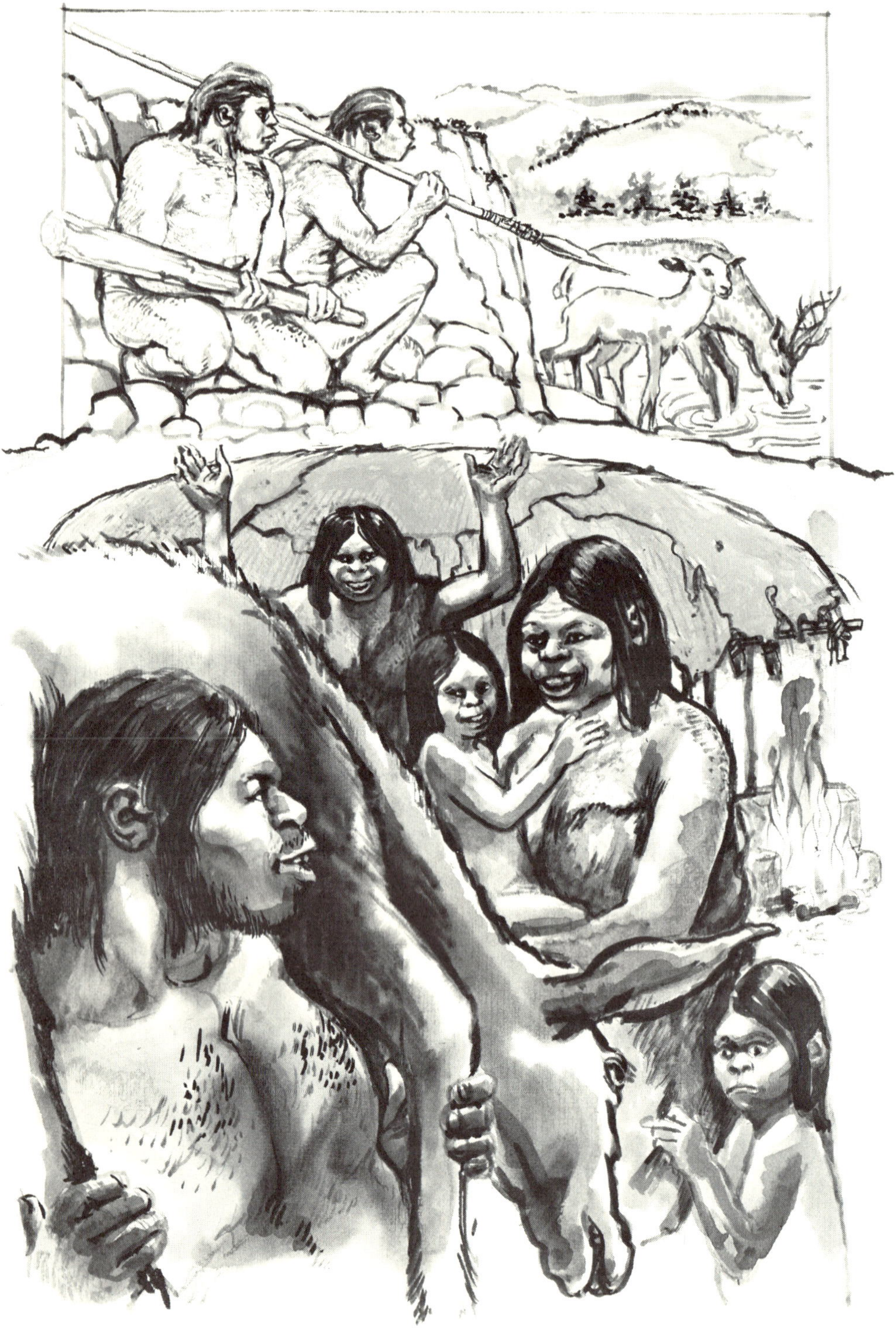

1

THE ANATOMY OF A CONTINENT

"East is East, and West is West, and never the twain shall meet," said Rudyard Kipling in his famous ballad. Certainly the twain did not meet in the geography books and atlases of yesteryear. A map of Europe and of European Russia up to the foot of the Ural Mountains invariably occupied one page, while Asia from the lee of the Urals to the Pacific occupied another. On maps of the world spread flat, it was usual for Asia to appear at the left end of the double page with Europe to the right end and the Americas in the center.

The separateness of East and West, the cartographical illusion of a continent severed by some undefined but perceptible break, has been heightened by the images of Asian peoples, lands, and cultures so different, so exotic as to seem scarcely of this world, let alone of another continent. The face of Asia we call into view is all flat planes and hooded eyes, expressionless, inscrutable. To our mind, the mind of Asia seems mysterious, mystical, closed, following pathways half as old as time. Our favorite picturebook scenery of the East: steamy forest, dripping rain; mountain pass wreathed in clouds; vast, desolate desert bearing double-humped camels, plodding all in line; roof of a temple pagoda, tip-tilted, bright with gilt; delicate garden of raked rock and linear potted tree, spare, austere beyond our comprehension. And the names—with what delicious chimes they ring: Samarkand and Karakorum; the Pamirs, Roof of the World; Taklamakan and Kamchatka—along with African Timbuktu, conjuring up everything most distant in this world, most inaccessible, most remote.

But images can deceive, and often do. The separateness of East and West is as illusory in the hearts and minds of men as on a map. Atlases of today tell a truer story, for they take care to represent East and West as they are: end points of a single continent stretching nearly halfway around the globe. East and West, bracketed by island chains whose peoples eventually conquered in the interior as in the seas beyond, to form the ancient empires of Japan and Britain.

Eurasia is a continent with mountain fingers that stretch east and west, binding, as it were, its far-flung ends to the center. From the mountains, from Himalayas and from Hindu Kush, from Karakorum, from the Pamirs, from Tien Shan and Altyn Tagh rise the highest peaks of our planet. Eighteen top by at least a thousand feet the loftiest elevations of the Americas. Here, pointing nearly six miles skyward, is Mount Everest—Chomolunga in the native language, Goddess Mother of the World. Here, her tall companions, Kanchenjunga and the peak known in the West only as K2. A central fact of life, the mountains have barred land from land and people from people, subdividing the continent.

The mountains ring the lofty plateau of Tibet. So high is this land and its air so thin that rocks may burn to the touch while moisture turns to ice. Its northern plains are treeless, seamed with canyons and wide gaps, where the meltings of perpetual snow gather in salty swamps and basins, sustaining no animals other than the sturdy yak and sheep and their even sturdier keepers. Only along the southern rim where the Brahmaputra rises and flows east before its plunge into India, where the Indus and its tributaries begin their journeys, is farming possible.

Northward of Tibet more sentinels enclose the Tarim Basin, a part of China's Sinkiang Province. Still another step northward in direction but downward in elevation lies Dzungaria, a plain and a pass closed almost shut by Tien Shan, the Heavenly Mountains, and by the Altai. Eastward, Dzungaria leads into the Mongolian Plateau and the Gobi. Westward it points the way to the Kirghiz Steppe and thence to Europe.

Altogether these knots of mountains, basins, hills, and plateaux define the heart of Asia. From them snake out spurs which further subdivide and isolate. Westward from the Hindu Kush range the peaks of the Elburz and Caucasus, Taurus and Pontus, to join across the Hellespont the Balkans, Carpathians, and Alps of Europe. Other spurs push into China and along the arms and islands of Southeast Asia. Northward they festoon the piney taiga and barren tundra of Siberia.

Down from these knots and spurs flow the rivers of Asia. Some of them water interior basins: the Don, the Volga, Amu Darya and Syr Darya—Oxus and Jaxartes of Alexander's time. Some—Tigris, Euphrates, Indus—once nurtured ancient cities. Others like the Ganges are sacred. Still others are among the dozen mightiest rivers of the world: Ob and Lena which pour into the Arctic Sea; Amur flowing out of Siberian Yablonovi to water the northern Pacific; and from the mighty clasping of the Himalayas and Kun Lun flow Hwang Ho, waterer of China's agricultural beginnings, Yangtze, and Mekong. The Thames, Tiber, and Seine may loom large in our European heritage, but they cannot compare in length and size to the mighty torrents of the East.

Rivers of the Far East, even the smallest of them, are often the life blood of the land, for the mountain ranges wherein lie their sources forbid the ocean's moisture-bearing winds. Europe lies open to the rains and climate-moderating effect of ocean current. Asia in the east is closed. Even the summer monsoon, blowing wet and thunderous over the arc of land lying between the Amur and the Indus, cannot penetrate the mountain wall. The wide continental stretch from west to east could alone suffice to guarantee in the interior extremes of heat and cold. Because of the mountain wall, the inner lands of eastern Asia are arid as well. Some of the sandiest, driest steppes and deserts of the world are here: Gobi, Arabia, Ordos, Turfan. In the Tarim Basin lies Taklamakan, so nearly rainless that its sand piles up in dunes, denying passage to the traveler. Here growing things must follow the river, and life confines itself to oases.

If Asia claims the most arid spots on earth, it claims also the wettest lands, the lands where the monsoon blows. The coldest and the hottest temperatures belong to Asia; the highest elevations and at least one very low depression. All these extremes and excesses are to be credited, at least in part, to the mountains which are the distinctive mark and the heart of this vast continent. How those mountains came into being is a story fit to rank with Asia's other wonders, and it is a story just beginning to be fully learned.

Two hundred million years ago, the land masses of our globe had coalesced into a single giant continent which the specialists today call Pangaea (All Earth). Surrounding it was the single world sea (Panthalassa) in which fishes ruled as on land ruled the reptiles and amphibians. There were as yet no monster forms—no dinosaurs, though they were fast evolving —no mammals, though mammal-like reptiles had begun to point the way—no birds.

Then slowly in the supercontinent, on which ancient life went about its business, seams opened, rifts appeared accompanied by lava gushes from the earth's interior. They must have looked, those seams and gaps, something like the great rift system to be seen today in East Africa or the nascent seam of the San Andreas Fault in southern California. And they began somehow, deep in the sometimes molten mantle of the earth, to drive apart the heavy rock plates on which rest the earth's crust. Rifts opened in the crust, waters collected therein, and at last the sea was admitted.

Under cover of the sea, the gaps filled with sediments and with lava flows from the upwelling mantle. The sea floor stretched and spread, towing plates bearing water and plates bearing land. Some plate edges were sucked under others and consumed in the mantle beneath. Some heaved upward, and the sea level rose and fell.

The plates bearing what would be Africa, South America, Australia, India, and Antarctica first broke away from Pangaea, leaving in the still immense northern land mass what would be Eurasia, North America, and Greenland. Then more rifts appeared. The southern land mass broke into daughter continents, and the Atlantic Ocean opened.

Some time between sixty-five and forty million years ago, early in the Age of Mammals, Africa, with what would be the Arabian Peninsula firmly attached, had moved northward, rotating the while in a counterclockwise direction. Slowly, irresistibly, this movement brought Arabia grinding into Asia and merging with it. The Mediterranean, meanwhile, opened farther as another part of the African plate approached what is now Spain. And India, after one hundred twenty million years of surging north, collided with the Asian underbelly. Everywhere plate slid under plate. The crusts above wrinkled, cracked, folded, arched skyward in great thrusts of earth and rock. The shock ripped west and created the mountains of Spain, Italy, and Central Europe, as well as the Atlas Range of

North Africa. It ripped southward into the islands of Southeast Asia and northward into Siberia. But the Urals, unlike the other mountains of the continent, were not an expression of this shock. For they were old as the oldest rocks of Eurasia and owed their beginnings to some earlier cataclysm.

Thus were the mountains of a continent built, knotting and twisting, forbidding the rains, dividing the lands, insuring that the people of eastern Asia, when they came, would create in these mountain-ringed enclaves life ways very different from one another. And yet not so different as one might expect. In spite of the walls, always there were connections, contacts, and a sharing of human events and human lore.

From Mesopotamia, where man first learned to domesticate plants and animals and built the first cities, came ideas and influences moving east and west—to Europe, to India, to China, and to all points in between. They spread northward into the high steppes, the parched grasslands of Central Asia where man domesticated the horse and perhaps there first invented the wheel, and found in both instruments of conquest of farming lands. One such people, speaking a language from which would derive in time all the tongues of Europe, moved westward to the Atlantic. Some elements later doubled back through the Dzungarian Gates into the heartland of Asia and beyond. Other charioteers, speaking Mongolic-Turkic tongues, descended upon the farmers of the Hwang Ho, forging with them the enduring civilization of China. From those ancient times until but a few hundred years ago, the settled lands, East and West, have been bound by that which threatened ever to destroy both—the marauding horsemen of Central Asia.

Whatever the barriers of land and sea, great kingdoms and empires of later times knew vaguely that others existed and coveted the precious things those distant kingdoms were thought to possess. Classical civilizations of the Mediterranean had heard of India and China and had seen their treasures. For, precariously, along the oases of Taklamakan, caravans had carried westward cargoes of silk and turquoise and jade.

Years later, Marco Polo traveled the same routes eastward seeking trade. And it was in search of a quicker access to eastern treasure that Christopher Columbus sailed to the West and found instead the islands of the New World.

The peoples of Eurasia are bound by still earlier ties that go back to the time of the first human migrations out of Africa and into the northern continent. The earliest known hunters in Europe appear to have been, in size and conformation, very like those of the Far East. And though methods of manufacturing stone implements differed, East and West, though languages and religious beliefs almost certainly differed, there are yet evidences of a tenuous exchange of ideas. Populations were few then, and distances vast. The mountains surely loomed and forbade. Yet, in the long run, all barriers have yielded and will yield still to man who must know what there is to find across the next river, on the other side of the nearest hill.

2

THE PEOPLE COME

WHERE did man begin? Fifty years ago, the answer would have been Eurasia. Surely in that vast continent, in its most ancient and inaccessible fastnesses would be found the cradle of humankind. There were compelling reasons for thinking so then.

Earlier—in the 1870s—there had been equally compelling reasons to locate human beginnings in a Mesopotamian Eden and to reckon human antiquity at six thousand years, no more. In the next fifty years, what changes were wrought! Mankind, in the popular view, ceased to hobnob with angels and began to count kin among the beasts. The human span on earth began a lengthening process that still shows no signs of slowing. Specialists fervently sought evidence of earlier forms of humanity and a place of first emergence. Perhaps in Asia.

The changes had begun in 1859—the year Charles Darwin's *On the Origin of Species* was published. Three years earlier an unusual and seemingly very old set of bones had been uncovered in Germany's Neander Valley. The specialists of the day, called in to view the specimen, suggested that it had belonged to an idiot, pitifully deformed, a poor old vagrant who had doubtless crawled into the valley cave to die. Nothing noteworthy, certainly nothing ancient. But in time more bones like those of the creature of Neander Valley began turning up, always in association with the bones of extinct mammals, and the possibility of human antiquity and human change could no longer be dismissed.

Well, then, if the creature *had* to be ancient man, better to keep him as far removed as possible from the gorgeous face and form divine of living men. And, in keeping with the notions of the time, Neanderthal Man was pictured as a hulking brute, bent of back and knee. The first skeletal reconstruction so articulated the neck bones as to suggest a gorillalike slouch. Altogether, the impression conveyed was something more than partly ape. (Today it is totally man, and *sapiens* to boot.)

Even in those times, however, there were specialists who thought the Neanderthal creature more human than the popular image would have him. They wanted to look elsewhere, for a specimen more truly primitive and in-between, more truly a missing link. Charles Darwin had suggested that such a link must appear in Africa. A cradle with warm climate was thought to be essential for hairless, beginning man. And besides, the primates who most resemble man—chimpanzees and gorillas—were there at home. But wait, said the German specialists, what about Southeast Asia? Surely it is and was always an area as warm as Africa. It is, moreover, the home of the acrobatic gibbon. And is he not a more human look-alike than the other apes? (We now know that Darwin's eye was the more perceptive in the matter of similarities, but the German theory had important consequences, nonetheless.)

One of those opting for a Southeast Asian beginning was Eugene Dubois, a young Dutch doctor and antiquarian. Leaving his safe university job, he joined the colonial service in the Netherlands Indies. In his spare time he searched for earliest man. He had been drawn to a particular area in Java by news of ancient primate bones discovered there, and with the luck of the true visionary, he found what he sought. The hoped-for specimen had been named in advance *Pithecanthropus allalus,* Ape Man Without Speech. But since Dubois had uncovered, in addition to a low skullcap, a thighbone almost identical in form to that of modern man, he called his find instead *Pithecanthropus erectus,* Upright Ape Man. Over the long years and after very many discoveries, the Ape Man title has been changed, but *erectus* has stuck fast.

With Dubois's find, controversy erupted anew. Were the bones those of an ape, a man, or something in between? Eventually Dubois himself retired from the fray, embittered, humiliated, convinced he had misidentified the remains, had labeled human what was, in fact, ape. His disbelief was not shared; others carried on, continuing the search for more evidence of early man in Asia.

Western travelers in Asia had long known that the jars in Chinese apothecary shops often contained more than headache powders, that they contained, in fact, bones—fossil bones. These were indeed destined to be ground into powders sovereign for a variety of ailments. For centuries Chinese medicine had prescribed such powdered bones—dragon bones, they were thought to be—and Chinese farmers had long prospected for the raw materials.

In 1901 a German traveler saw in a Peking apothecary jar teeth which were later pronounced human. Soon came the geologists, paleontologists, explorers from the West, eager to find the source from whence local apothecaries were supplied. At last they were led to Choukoutien, a small town twenty-five miles southwest of Peking. Just beyond Choukoutien was Dragon Bone Hill. In the hill was a huge cave complex, and in the caves were the remains of man.

Between 1920 and the onset of World War II, the bones of no fewer than forty individuals were recovered, all from the lowest level of caves in the hill. Their type was named *Sinanthropus pekinensis*—China Man of Peking—although the general resemblance to Dubois's Java Man was noted. In the higher cave levels, the remains of quite modern-looking individuals were found. Clearly, the caves had been occupied over a long period of time as men, selected by necessity, by pressures both environmental and social, became larger and mentally more able.

Back in Java, Ralph von Koenigswald, a paleontologist working in the Dutch survey of the islands, returned to the scene of Dubois's spectacular luck. He dug in earth layers containing the bones of animals which had shared the Ape Man's world. There he found other fossil men much like Dubois's disputed find. But there was more. A deeper level contained still others, older and somewhat more primitive in appearance. No wonder Asia seemed so attractive as a possible birthplace of man.

But only for a time. In the 1920s there had been discovered in South Africa the remains of very ancient creatures, creatures more unlike the early men of Java and China than those men were unlike ourselves. They were little creatures, some graceful, some more robust, but all with the unbridged nose cavity, the protruding muzzle, the small skull of apes. The familiar controversies arose again, and for long the African curiosities were classified with the apes. Australopithecines they were called, Southern Apes. The accumulating evidence of the bones said otherwise, however. At last, the humanness of the upright posture, of the shape of teeth and jaws, and of the ability to shape tools of stone caused specialists to place the australopithecines in the family of man. With this recognition, the probable cradle of humanity shifted from Asia to Africa. For the Southern Apes are old—certainly as old as six million years, and probably more than that.

Strong contrasts tend to highlight unnoticed similarities. With the face of *Australopithecus* in hand, specialists could note at last how very like Dubois's *Pithecanthropus* were all the earliest true men of Eurasia. It could be further noted that, as a group, they resembled ourselves, and reconstructions changed drastically to accommodate the new view. In spite of chinlessness and smallish skulls (at least in oldest representatives), the affinities were too close to permit their being placed in categories other than our own. Their separate titles were, therefore, consolidated. They became, all of them, *Homo erectus*. We are *Homo sapiens*—same genus, same brand of human being, as it were, though the species category differs.

Now, individuals belonging to the same genus, though of different species, may interbreed and produce a hybrid offspring. The offspring, however, will likely prove to be less fertile than its parents if not sterile outright, unable to reproduce. (Consider the mule, offspring of horse and ass.) The name separation of the early true men of Eurasia from ourselves indicates the belief of specialists that just such a breeding difficulty would exist between our two groups, were there representatives of *Homo erectus* here on earth today. But of course, they are not. We are their descendants, much changed and refined, as they were themselves descended from still earlier forms of humanity, forms represented by the australopithecines of Africa.

Since the 1940s many more representatives of *Homo erectus* and many of his living and hunting sites have turned up in Europe, in Java, in northern China, and in Africa. The earth layers bearing Dubois's Java Man have been dated by radioactive rocks therein and by tiny fragments of meteoric glass to about eight hundred thousand years ago. Earth layers underlying this zone, layers yielding the fossils uncovered by Dr. von Koenigswald, are even older. The date of early true man's appearance in Java would appear to be a million years, at least.

There is yet more—more to complicate the picture, more to age it. In India and in China remains of a giant primate have been found. The wear patterns of his huge molars (first rescued by Ralph von Koenigswald from the treasure troves of a Cantonese drug store) seemed to one specialist, at least, to be thoroughly human, so human that, for a time, a giant on the family tree was seen as a distinct likelihood. We now know that the monster—nine feet tall, judging by old and new finds—was simply the largest ape ever, one whose diet (and therefore whose chewing habits) was probably similar to that of beginning man. In terms of time, some of the giant apes may have been contemporaneous with *Homo erectus,* though no evidence of encounters has yet appeared.

Other finds in India (and newly classified older finds) reveal a glimpse of yet another interesting relative. This one had smallish teeth and jaws of a shape altogether different from those of the giant ape or of any other ape for that matter, alive or dead. On the other hand, similarities to the teeth and jaws of *Australopithecus* are quite remarkable. So is the creature's age—something near eleven million years.

Before we start reconstructing an Asiatic "Eden," however, it should be said that representatives of this in-between, this very ancient, primitive member of the family lived in Africa as well and at an even earlier time. It should also be noted that the remains of beginning men, the australopithecines, have not appeared in Eurasia—at least, not in numbers. Ralph von Koenigswald has always believed that some of his Java finds, those at the very lowest levels of the site, much resembled the australopithecines of Africa. His view is becoming more widely shared. Certainly the migration out of Africa had to begin somewhere, sometime. We should not be surprised to find the travel records.

For the moment, man appears to have begun, to have attained size and intellect, to have acquired basic skills in Africa before venturing into the rest of the Old World. Basic skills certainly included a knowledge of hunting (camp sites, kill sites, and bones of animal prey tell us so) and techniques for the manufacture of stone tools. In Africa, the australopithecines had hacked rough edges and points from rounded pebbles, using them and the waste flakes for cutting and scraping meat and hide, perhaps for the fashioning of wooden implements, even for the grubbing of succulent roots and insects.

The earliest travelers into the western part of Eurasia began to produce (or were already using) implements which we call hand axes. Now, if you are a bit of an antiquarian and handy to boot, you might enjoy reviving an ancient craft. If so, please start with a large nodule of stone. Glassy materials such as quartz and flint are most easily worked. Chip at your nodule with a round hammer stone until you have achieved something roughly oval in shape. If it also has two worked faces, a point, and a butt end, you can call it a hand ax. Doubtless it will seem to you a rather crude effort. So were the first hand axes in Europe. In time your techniques of manufacture will improve. So did those of the earliest hand-ax makers. Eventually the hand ax became—at least in our eyes—an object of art as well as use. Perhaps their manufacturers thought so, too.

After long years, later men in the West experimented with still newer techniques of tool and weapon making. Nodules were preshaped for the removal of ready-made knives. Spear points were thinned for the hafting. Mass production of flint blades was achieved. There appears to have been in the West the kind of interest in innovation—perhaps for its own sake—that was of less import in the eastern half of Eurasia. From the first appearance of man in the East until fairly recent times ("recent" meaning close to forty thousand years ago), the favored tool was the chopper, a lump of stone flaked on one face to produce a cleaverlike shape, or a chopping tool, flaked on both faces. To be sure, modifications, refinements appeared over the course of time. Tools found in some sites in northern China and in Siberia reveal a developing interest in the uses to which flakes, produced in the manufacturing process, could themselves be put—as well as an interest in flakes of special sizes and shapes. But the fondness for the good old chopper-chopping tradition remained, especially in southern Asia.

Certainly there must have been reasons for this apparent conservatism of taste and technique. Wilhelm G. Solheim, an archaeologist who specializes in the prehistory of Southeast Asia, believes this may have resulted from a preference for wooden and bamboo tools, the stone choppers having served primarily in the fabricating process. Wood rots, of course. We cannot know for sure what sorts of implements were made with the choppers. The best we can hope for is the suggestion of such a use in the wear patterns of the stone primary itself. Solheim and his students believe they can detect this on the edges of some ancient choppers from Southeast Asia.

Choppers, chopping tools, and their flakes in caches and masses are to be found in the lower caves at Choukoutien. As we have seen, this was for long the home of a northern population of *Homo erectus.* How long? From perhaps eight hundred thousand years ago, some specialists think, until a half million years ago, give or take a few hundred thousand years one way or the other. There has been only one reliable radiometric dating of the cave, and the animal bones do not provide an entirely readable story. It is thought that occupation of the lower caves lasted through a period of cold weather which gradually warmed and then turned cold again. Over the millenniums, the men of Choukoutien appear to have grown in mental capacity as compared to the earlier men of Java. The sizes of their skull cavities overlap the lower ranges of our own.

At some point those men of Choukoutien learned the uses of fire. Whether they could make it or whether they merely sheltered and kept alive what had once been a spark from a lightning-struck tree, the fact remains that their dark caves were alight at nighttide.

The men of Choukoutien were successful big-game hunters, judging by the quantity of large animal bones casually dropped on their living-room floors. It is also possible that they hunted other men. Among the refuse of the cave floors are human skulls, detached from their underpinnings, their spinal sockets crushed and enlarged, doubtless to give easy access to the brains inside. Now, brains of cattle, sheep, and other animals are tasty, and there is no reason to suppose that human brains are less so. But it is just possible—indeed highly possible—that the cannibals of Choukoutien had something beyond nourishment in mind. From what we know of living people who still follow the old ways, cannibalism as often smacks of the memorial service as of the feast. What better way to preserve the kindness of Grandma than by internalizing Grandma herself? What better way to acquire the valor of a fallen enemy than by consuming his substance?

The caves of Choukoutien certainly did not house the only cannibals of the ancient world. All sorts of men have eaten their fellows, sometimes for religious reasons, sometimes not. A colony of later men who lived along the Ngandong River in Java were also cannibals. So have been communities of *Homo sapiens*—early ones of Neanderthaloid features, more recent ones of people like ourselves. The taste for human flesh —or the belief in spiritual power resident in the flesh—has persisted over the long years during which the human form changed, years during which men traveled and spread out, bearing their ideas with them.

In spite of the mountain walls, men of Asia appear to have had some contact with men of the West. Among the predictable collections of choppers, now and then a tool of hand-ax type is uncovered. Evidence of contact is very strong in India, always a midway station. When the bones of early *sapiens* appears in China there appears as well (though not always in direct association) the special sort of flake point, struck from a rounded core, that is associated with Neanderthals of the West. Neanderthal tool kits and the Neanderthals themselves were in Central Asia, some seventy thousand years ago, in what is now the Uzbek Soviet Socialist Republic. At a later time, hunters from that region traveled to Mongolia and settled there. Or so specialists deduce from the apparent western influences in tools and implements. Whatever gaps appear in the annals of prehistory, surely the general picture is one of movement, travel, spreading out, and filling in.

The easterly tide of men and technology funneled slowly, surely into the New World. As the archaeological picture develops for Alaska, for the Great Plains, for the Andes of South America, ties to Asia grow ever more clear. Here, in the Americas, in very ancient sites whose precise age cannot yet be calculated, are represented the familiar choppers and chopping tools of the East, manufacturers as yet unidentified. Here, too —with dates that reveal the time lag in transmission—appear the flake and bone implements, the leaflike points which, in Siberia and northern China, furnished the tool kits of later men.

It was about forty thousand years ago in the East as in the West of the Eurasian continent that these later men, men of truly modern type came into their own. Armed with still better, more efficient tools and technology, they began to move into lands their predecessors had not explored, into deserts, into Siberia, colder then than now. Curiously, the cultural remains of these pioneers (best represented by the Mal'ta and

Buret' sites near Lake Baikal) resemble those of more westerly hunters, the mammoth hunters of western Russia, close to the Arctic Circle, and the mammoth hunters who lived along the Don River in southern Russia some twenty thousand years ago.

The Don men were not cave dwellers but householders and housebuilders. And of what should they build but the bones of the animals they hunted, huge animals, so huge and so abundant as to make settling down worthwhile. Settling down meant digging into the earth for warmth, raising wall struts of mammoth tusks, ribs, or pelves and lacing the whole with the resilient antlers of the deer. Covered with hide and then, perhaps, with earth, such construction must have produced a warm and cozy home, because the general pattern—complete with antler lacings and an added corridor entrance—was favored by the people of Mal'ta and Buret'. The pattern persisted, in fact, until a century or two ago among the Chukchi people of Russian Siberia. They depended on whalebone for house construction. So did their neighbors, the Siberian Eskimos. And across the Bering Strait such house types were favored by groups ancestral to the American Eskimos.

For the people of last glacier times in the Far East, life took on new amenities. Clothing of animal skins, close fitting and warm, came into use, and the luxury and delight of art forms as well. In this the Siberian settlements around Lake Baikal and the headwaters of the great rivers were as much a reflection of the Don settlements as those settlements, in turn, reflected the high fashion centers of Western Europe. Lacking cave walls for the fine paintings popular among the French and Spanish arbiters of elegance, the Don artists nevertheless followed their taste in figurines. They carved in ivory or in stone the shapes of the animals they hunted and, more importantly, of their women, though these figurines apparently aimed at something other than portraiture. Faceless, featureless, with abstracted arms and legs, their swollen torsos—bosoms, bellies, thighs—seem to represent the female principle, the wonder, the mystery of life's regeneration and continuity.

In Mal'ta and Buret' the figurines are fewer and cruder, with less attention given to mystery and more to costume. One little figure depicts quite explicitly the tailored clothing in use in those times and later. The face is engraved as well with the slanting eyes that tell us the true Mongoloid physical type had come into being.

From whence? Nobody is quite sure. Some specialists think the type developed in southern China. Others opt for the far north. The well-padded cheek bones, says anthropologist Carleton Coon, the sunken nose, the scanty facial hair, the double-lidded eye giving the appearance of a slant—all these features offer protection against the harsh cold and evolved as a response to it.

And yet there is the fact that fossil groups of the Far East —where a sequence from early to late can be read—show a sort of family resemblance, perhaps as a result of development in isolation. Certain features of teeth—the shovel shape of the incisors, a frequently absent third molar—have long been common throughout the whole East and are not to be seen among the populations of Europe—fossil or living. American Indians often display those very features, and the origin point of American Indians is most certainly in Asia. But not all the marks of Asia appear on American Indian faces, not the eyefold or the padded cheekbones. Perhaps, as the American anthropologist W. W. Howells suggests, the facial mask and eyefold represent a recent overlay to the basic, early Mongoloid face as represented by American Indians and some peoples of Southeast Asia.

But wait. Not all the peoples of the Far East appear to belong to Mongoloid populations. Some resemble the aboriginal peoples of Australia—known to have immigrated from somewhere in Southeast Asia as long ago as the pioneers who would be American Indians departed from Siberia. And there are still others in the East who appear to resemble southern Europeans, darker of skin, perhaps, but in other ways similar.

On the northernmost island of Japan and the Russian island of Sakhalin lives an ancient people called the Ainu, until recently hunters and gatherers. Over the years and after much intermarriage with the Japanese, the original cast of features has changed. In many individuals, however, the type is still preserved. It is Western rather than Eastern, with a look that is not so much modern European as it is archaic European, faintly Neanderthaloid, certainly different from the look of Siberian hunting folk. The Mongoloid type is short on hair. Ainu people have plenty of it, and not only on the head and face. Some men grow what is near to being a pelt. So admired is hair that women tatoo blue mustaches around their lips, or did in the old days. The mustache is falling into disfavor as a mark of female attractiveness, and lipstick use is on the upsurge.

Our catalogue of faces is not yet complete. The Mongols, from whom the physical type is named, appear once to have constituted a more mixed population than can be seen today. In the hordes of Genghis Khan which so ravaged the great city civilizations of East and West were warriors with white skins and flaming hair. The fact was recorded by Chinese historians. (The Great Khan himself is said to have been so marked.) It must also be noted that, if European looks are to be found in the East, Mongoloid looks are to be found in the West. Some of the ancient inhabitants of northern Europe and Scandinavia appear to have had an eastern cast of feature. Among the Lappish people today—reindeer herders who travel from Finland to Sweden over the northern ice—among Latvians, Estonians, and Lithuanians bordering the Baltic Sea, now and again the marks of ancient mingling appear. Northeasterly, among the Uralic and Samoyed peoples, the marks are plainer still. In central Europe, particularly in Hungary, invasions from the steppes of Turkestan have also left behind something of the face of Asia in the West.

The tale of movement and migration can be read as well in the languages of Eurasia: ties of kinship can be traced and separations plotted. Now, languages, like living organisms, can be grouped according to degree of similarity. For living organisms it is in similarity of form and function that relatedness is revealed. For languages, the similarities are those of sound and meaning. Similar languages, like similar organisms, share a common descent, and the closer they are, the more readily speakers of each can understand words of the other, then the nearer in time their separation. Languages can be located in ever widening circles of affinity. So can living organisms. For them, the widest circle of relatedness occurs in the phylum—a category which indicates a group of beings whose basic plan of organization is radically different from that of every other comparable group. Your phylum and mine is called Chordata. Sharks belong to this phylum. So do frogs and birds and bats and whales. We all have backbones (or a close approximation thereto), internal stiffening, and external bilateral symmetry—which is to say, each half of us is a mirror image of the other half.

The widest frame of similarity into which related languages can be grouped is also called a phylum. Altogether, throughout Eurasia, there are five large language phyla and a few smaller ones. The Indo-European phylum dominates most of Europe, India, Iran, and Afghanistan. Once, anciently, a people speaking Tocharian (an extinct Indo-European language) inhabited Asian land out toward the Dzungarian Gates. Almost certainly other of their language relatives roamed the eastern steppes. Russian is the Indo-European language to have intruded most recently into the East. Speakers of the original mother tongue seem to have been cattle herders somewhere in Central Asia. From that heartland they emerged in their ox- or horse-drawn wagons to spread west, always at the expense of resident farmers. A few speakers of other, older Eurasian languages—Basque in the Pyrenees, Burushkaski in a remote valley in Pakistan, Caucasic near the Black Sea—remain as remnants of pre-Indo-European times.

The remaining language phyla of Eurasia belong to the Far East, and it is with peoples speaking languages of these groups that we shall be mainly concerned in this book. There is not, unfortunately, space to spare (beyond a mention or two) for the Europeans and Indians. And besides, the story of the West and of speakers of Indo-European languages may be found in another of my books, *The Battle-ax People.* So here we must follow the example of the old atlases and sever Eurasia at the Urals and the Himalayas, linguistically if in no other way.

Like a giant layer cake, the language areas of Asia lie one atop the other. The bottom layer seems to have consisted originally of languages of the Austroasiatic and Malayo-Polynesian phyla. The pattern shifted as migrants from other zones entered and settled. Eventually some speakers of Malayo-Polynesian took to their boats, moving out into the nearer islands and finally into the Pacific. Speakers of Austroasiatic languages retained their hold in what is now Vietnam and Cambodia. Here was anciently the seat of empire, brilliant and beautiful, the remains of which can be seen in the ruined temple city of Angkor.

Northward lies the Sino-Tibetan zone. Speakers of its various language groups live and have lived mainly in China and in Tibet. The expanding Chinese empire, however, seems to have forced many Sino-Tibetan groups southward. Among these have been the Burmese, the Karen, and the Miao-Yao. Many speakers of Thai-Kadai (thought by some specialists to constitute yet another phylum) seem also to have moved or

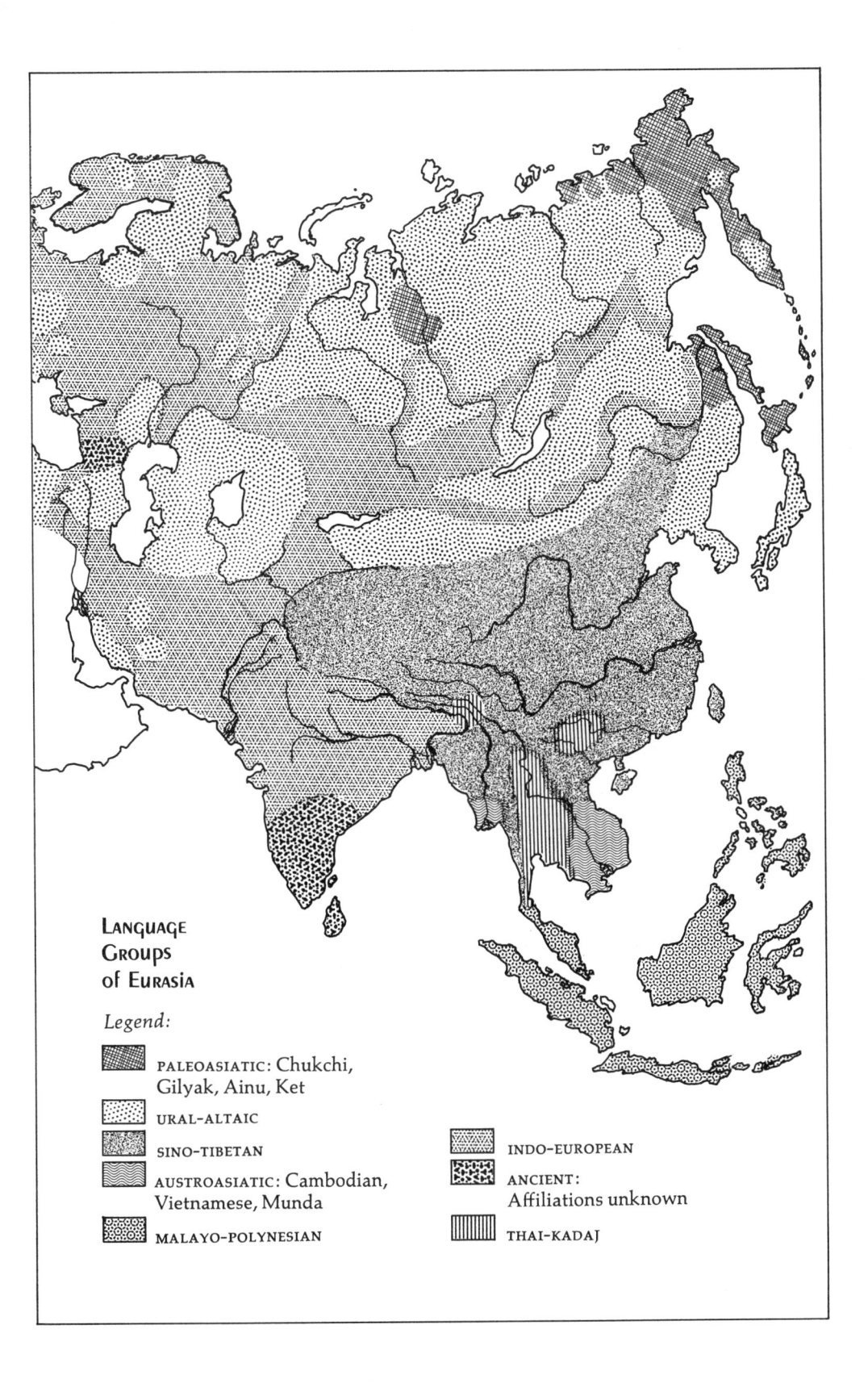

Language Groups of Eurasia

Legend:

- PALEOASIATIC: Chukchi, Gilyak, Ainu, Ket
- URAL-ALTAIC
- SINO-TIBETAN
- AUSTROASIATIC: Cambodian, Vietnamese, Munda
- MALAYO-POLYNESIAN
- INDO-EUROPEAN
- ANCIENT: Affiliations unknown
- THAI-KADAJ

been pushed southward out of China. Some, like the Chuang, remain as ethnic minorities in the homeland.

North of the Sino-Tibetan realm lies the broad band of languages called Ural-Altaic. Its speakers in the West include the Finns, the Lapps, the Samoyeds, the Magyars. In the East, Mongols, Turkic peoples, Tungusic tribes (among whom are the Manchu) belong to its Altaic branch. Some specialists believe that the Korean and Japanese languages might ultimately be located in this phylum, but no one is yet quite certain. Of all the Eurasian language phyla, Ural-Altaic certainly retains the most extensive connections, East and West. Whether by way of migration or invasion (or residential priority), its speakers have established enclaves, not only in the north, but in Hungary and modern Turkey as well.

Most northerly of the language tiers, at the very top of the cake, lies the Paleoasiatic phylum, its territorial coverage much smaller than in other times. Its languages were and are still spoken by people who were—and are still—fishermen, gatherers, reindeer herders and hunters: the Chukchi, Koryak, Gilyak, Yukaghir, Kamchadal, Ainu, the Siberian Eskimo. In their life ways much remains to speak to us of ancient times when people first ventured into northern lands, following retreating glaciers and animals which loved the cold. Perhaps their languages, too, hark back to ancient forms and usages, to a common Eurasian heritage. We do not know. Without writing for its preservation, the word once spoken is lost forever.

PART II

THE OLD ASIANS

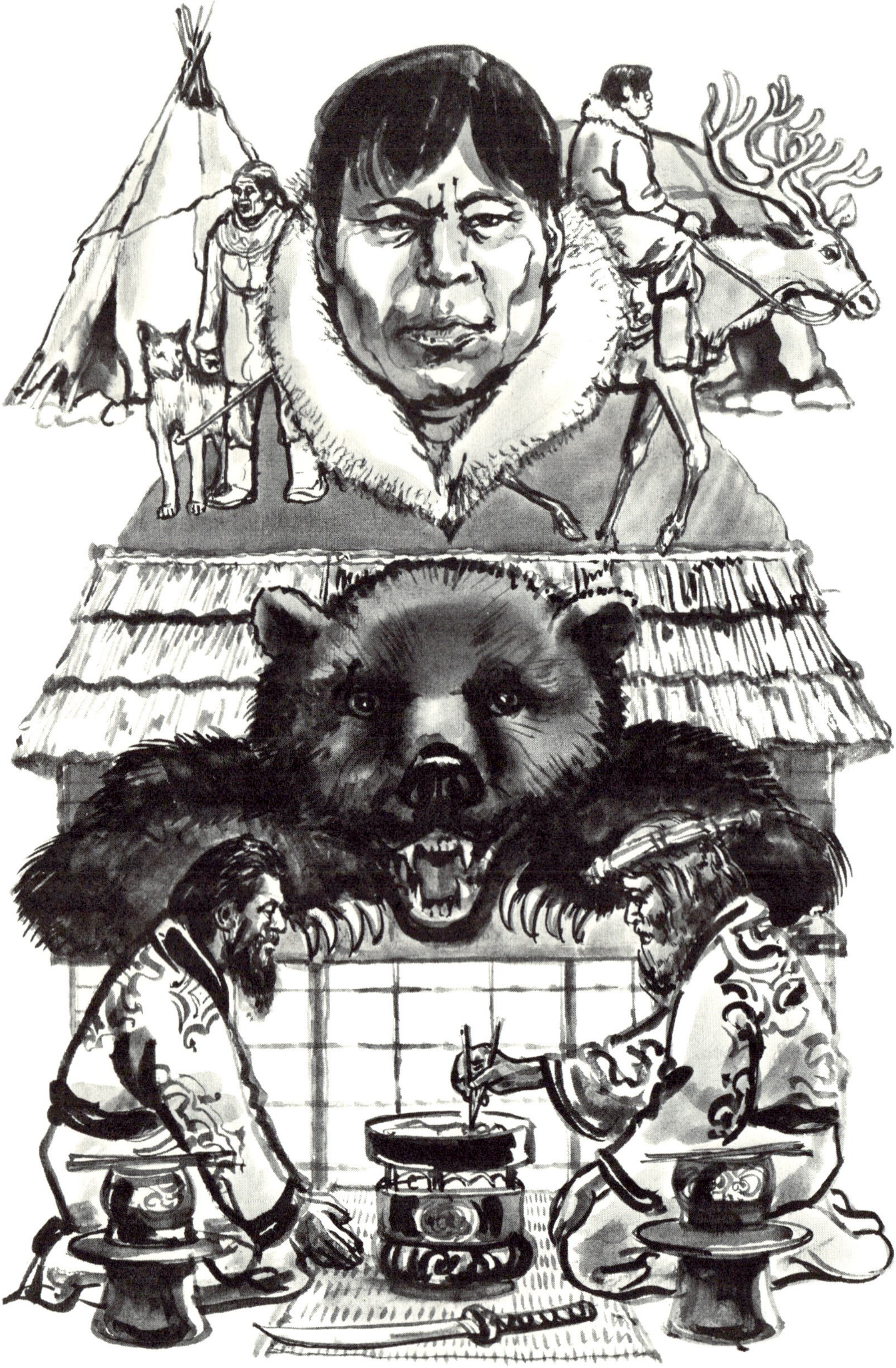

3

THE CHUKCHI
A Double Life
in the Far North

In the northernmost corner of Asia, where the shores of Alaska lie just fifty-six miles across the Bering Strait, live the Chukchi, a sturdy and stocky people inured to the ice-box climate of Siberia. Let the temperature dip below zero; the Chukchi, doffing his hood and sometimes his outer garment, complains of the heat. Constant weight lifting with stones into which finger-holds are conveniently cut, frequent footracing, and furious wrestling (men and women alike) have added muscle and staying power to bodies already tested by a way of life impossible to any but the strong. The Chukchi, says the Russian anthropologist M. G. Levin, are less truly Mongoloid than their neighbors to the south and west, with faces less flat, eyes less almond in shape, beards more pronounced. Some are said to have wavy hair, the fact marked in a popular nickname, the Chukchi equivalent to our own "Curly." Altogether, one may envision features somewhat approaching an American Indian cast—which may itself be close to the ancient Asian prototype.

Among the Chukchi themselves rounded heads ("hummocky," in their term) are much admired. So are red faces ("red as blood, burning like fire") and a well-tuned sense of smell. The model Chukchi is one who can distinguish an old Chukchi camp site from that of a foreign tribe just by its residual odor. Odors of objects brought from another house offend the Chukchi woman in her own home. Indeed, she may faint dead away. But the smells of her own family, the personal, body smells of the dear ones of the house are cherished, and children and adults alike prefer, rather, to nuzzle and sniff one another than to kiss.

Or so it was in the late 1890s and early 1900s when the great Russian ethnographer Vladimir Bogoras (or Bogoraz-Tan) studied the Chukchi, learned their language, lived as their guest. Perhaps not altogether voluntarily, it must be said. The studies were made when, for European Russians, Siberia was a synonym for punishment, and Bogoras was for a time himself a political exile. His observations of the Chukchi may not be entirely outdated even today when the tribe is part of the Union of Soviet Socialist Republics, organized into an administrative unit of ethnic nature called an *okrug*. Bogoras was impressed by Chukchi pride, the strength of their resistance to change, their unwillingness to learn other languages. At that time other Siberian peoples had already become Russianized to some degree. For Russian military forays into the area, beginning in the 1600s, had cleared the way for colonists with their farm animals and newfangled ways of life. In 1900, however, the Chukchi were still very much as they had always been, very much themselves.

Being themselves meant, for one thing, cleaving to the old ways of making a living. There have been two, say the Chukchi, for as long as they have occupied their peninsula, and that has been forever. Always, they say, some Chukchi have lived on the shore and hunted the large animals of the sea—walrus and seal and whale. Always there have been others who have wandered inland—on the bare tundra in summer, in the eaves of the piney forest in winter—tending their herds of domesticated reindeer.

In Bogoras' time, however, Chukchi were beginning to claim priority for the herding way. Did they not, after all, live in rounded "genuine houses" made of deerskin hide, portable and light, suitable for nomadic life? Gone out of use were the old "jawbone houses" of the coast, dug deep into the earth and well covered with sod. Bogoras knew of only five coastal families who still clung to their old-fashioned homes. The others complained that the antique houses—constructed of the ribs and jawbones of whales—were smelly, though certainly warm. To the "genuine house" one did have to add an inner room, rather like a furry box, in order to assure oneself of a comfortable winter's nap. And insulation, true, was achieved at the expense of ventilation. In the inner room, condensed breath of a sleeping family so wetted the common blanket that, in the morning, the damp furs must be taken out of doors to freeze and then be beaten clean of ice before they could be used again.

Other habits bespoke the increasing popularity of the herding way. Chukchi months were (and probably are still) described in terms that catalogued the important events of the pastoral year. Reindeer hide was sought for housemaking, for boots, and for the tailored trousers and tailored shirts worn two at a time. Even the Chukchi of the shore tried to own at least a deer or two, put out to graze in a friend's herd. For the man without at least one reindeer was called *ai'wan,* poor creature, pauper.

And yet, thought Bogoras, in spite of the prestige and security of the herding life, there were many indications that the sea hunt represented the older life way. All Chukchi, whatever their occupation, prized sweet seal, walrus, and the blubber of the whale above all other foods and felt deprived if no taste of these could be had. In every one of their most sacred moments, reindeer herders recalled the life of the sea. Wooden images of the whale hunter's skin boat were given to the dead and hung on the string of each family's guardian figures. In curing, too, the sea was remembered, for the special drum of each religious healer was called his "canoe." Every Chukchi cherished the dog who was then (and may yet be) friend and sacrifice and guardian of man—to be applauded in races, imitated in anger, followed into the land of the dead. For the Chukchi of the shore, respect derived ultimately from a working partnership. Dogs were needed to pull sleds and sledges. For the herding Chukchi, respect remained, affection remained long after the dog had been replaced in the traces by reindeer.

There were still in 1900 many indications that reindeer domestication among the Chukchi was something borrowed, perhaps from the Ural-Altaic-speaking tribes to the south and west, from the Tungus or the Samoyed. Chukchi reindeer, though fat and certainly numerous, were not altogether tame. They had to be watched carefully lest they dash away to freedom. Rounding up draft animals could be a frustrating chore, especially for the family without several sons, and a sled train might be delayed for days while men on snowshoes chased the skittish deer, luring them hopefully with tastes of human urine dribbled onto the snow from a storage pouch. Half-wild Chukchi deer were impossible to milk. The milk-hungry herder could get some only by knocking a doe to the ground and sucking the fluid from her swollen udder.

The wildness was almost admired. Chukchi never cared to mate their does to the strong and well-tamed bucks of their Tungus neighbors. They sought instead to lure wild stags to the herd, calling them "brother-in-law" in countless incantations, inviting them to "marry my daughters." Once such a stag had come, had mated with the herd does, he was quickly killed lest the blessing he had brought escape back into the wilderness. In Bogoras' time, Chukchi were still hunting wild reindeer, ambushing them at river crossings, darting out in the skin boats, surrounding the deer and, after the kill, letting the dead animals drift downstream to the women, waiting there with their skinning knives. Among all the spirit masters of the beasts, it was the Lord of Wild Game, especially of wild reindeer, who received most honor among herding Chukchi, whose rules were most strictly observed, whose sacrifices most carefully offered.

In this kind of honoring, one is reminded of the Yukaghir, neighbors and distant language relatives of the Chukchi, and of the even more distant Ket who lived once along the Yenesei River. Both were hunting folk and tried hard to remain so even when pushed and influenced first by expansive Tungus, then by Yakut cattle herders, then by Russian colonists. An ancient legend likens the Yukaghir to stars in their numbers. Numerous they are no more, but their importance in the northland is still remembered. To the Turkic-speaking Yakut, the magnificent spectacle of northern lights remains "Yukaghir fire."

Long ago the Yukaghir hunted reindeer in the summertime, wandering from water crossing to water crossing, pursuing the swimming reindeer in rafts. Their camping homes were tripods of poles covered with birch bark or skin, a form rather similar to the tepee common among many American Indian groups. In the winter they fished through the ice of rivers and lakes. They hunted birds and small game and the occasional deer lured by a tame decoy or by the hunter himself in antlered disguise. During this season they lived in permanent dwellings of the familiar pit-house type, well insulated with sod.

It is just possible that ancestors of the Chukchi knew just the same sort of residential and economic alternation, moving seasonally between forest or tundra and shore, between the hunt on land and the hunt on water. Gradually the double life may have separated into two distinct life ways. Perhaps it came about with the realization that the sea teems year-round with game—or did in earlier times. Perhaps it came about with the introduction of herding skills so that the summer reindeer hunters were transformed into year-round reindeer herders. Whatever the origin of the divided economy, it is surely true that the herding way slowly gained ascendance. It was an easier and a more profitable way and must have seemed the more so as the sea hunter's prey diminished, frightened off, killed off by American whaling ships in the north Pacific. And so it was that, year by year, family by family, herders increased in numbers.

The growing importance of herding seems to have changed a good deal more about the old ways than its economic pattern. There were, for example, changes to be noted in values. The remaining hunters of the sea considered themselves vastly more hospitable than the herders, more generous, less suspicious of the stranger, and Bogoras agreed with their self-assessment. The hunters frowned on theft and subjected the light-fingered person to a severe tongue lashing. Herders, on the other hand, took theft rather lightly—"I cause this thing to flee," was their pleasant euphemism for pilferage. Such an attitude may well have stemmed from their habit of deer rustling which among them—as among many people whose wealth is on the hoof and in the open—was considered an honorable occupation. Rustling and the threat of having one's own herds rustled demand some military preparedness. And the Chukchi, like most other herding folk, were warriors. They even wore armor—small iron squares threaded on thongs. Bogoras thought the style and perhaps even earliest manufacture had traveled northward from Japan to the Chukchi. (We now know it traveled farther still. Suits of the same type of armor, made with plates of bone or walrus ivory, have turned up on the islands of St. Lawrence and Diomede in the Bering Strait.)

Chukchi warriors fought (and rustled) primarily among other herding folk but were certainly not afraid to challenge Cossack regiments when these appeared on the scene. Sometimes conquered herders were enslaved and taken off to distant camps, where, it is said, they often killed the herdmasters and made good their escape. In Bogoras' time no one could point out to him a real slave. But the descendants of slaves were known and treated with a certain degree of scorn.

Adversaries in battle were often the Koryak who lived to the south of the Chukchi, were very close language relatives, and followed the same divided way of making a living. On the Kamchatka Peninsula were the Kamchadal, also close in language, but already in Bogoras' time mostly Russianized. West on the Chukchi Peninsula's edge were people committed wholly to the sea. These were (and are still) the Asian Eskimo, tied to their relatives across the Bering Strait in both language and life ways.

The relationship of Chukchi to Eskimo of both shores has for long puzzled specialists. There is a certain language affinity. Or so thought Bogoras, insisting that the listener could discover a continuum of speech change as he moved from Chukchi to Asian Eskimo to the Eskimo of St. Lawrence Island to those of Diomede Islands to the Eskimo of Alaska. Modern specialists affirm his conviction. Indeed, some would opt to combine the languages of the Aleutian Islands and the Eskimo languages of America and Asia with Chukchi, Koryak, and Kamchadal into a single phylum. Other old Asian languages would remain, one must assume, in unclassified limbo.

Contemporary Soviet anthropologists believe that Chukchi are latecomers to the peninsula, having migrated northward; believe it was on the peninsula that Chukchi learned the sea hunt from Eskimo already in possession. Certainly it is true that both archaeological evidence and oral tradition seem to indicate a larger Eskimo population in antiquity than exists today and at some point an expansion of Chukchi. Actual events, however, actual chronology are hard to reconstruct. Even oral traditions are contradictory. One myth holds that Chukchi were always sea hunters and also always deer herders. Another suggests that Eskimo taught them the skills of the sea.

The Soviet archaeologist A. P. Okladnikov suggests that all the Paleoasiatic folk owe their origins to late Ice Age hunters who camped around the middle reaches of the Lena River and came late to the sea. His own excavations in the Chukchi Peninsula reveal traces of post-Ice Age people who lived by reindeer hunting and fishing—in a style very reminiscent of the Yukaghir or of the Caribou Eskimo of North America. Influences from the south, perhaps emphasizing sea rather than river fishing, could eventually have mingled with the older, inland hunting style and then have been transmitted across the strait. Whether the Asian Eskimo represent an offshoot of this mingled heritage, flourishing, innovating in isolation, is not yet known.

There is much in the record of living men to suggest that Eskimo were recent arrivals in America. They differ in physical type from American Indians (somewhat or considerably, depending on the specialist at hand). Their languages are usually classified in a distinct phylum. Those languages, however, differ little from one another across the whole of the American Arctic Zone and can be mutually understood. This last is nearly always a mark of recent migration.

There is also much in the archaeological record to suggest recent arrival. Eskimo do not appear to have been the first of the whale hunters on American shores. Old Alaskan beaches reveal the nearly four-thousand-year-old remains of such hunters. Their implements, though made of flaked stone, are somewhat similar in shape and size to the polished-stone implements used by whale-hunting Eskimo and Chukchi before the advent of metals. And yet when the remains are surveyed, the total look is not at all Eskimo.

Soviet archaeologists on the Chukchi coast and Dr. J. Louis Giddings in Alaska have uncovered in a more recent time zone the homes, graves, and tools of people who lived some two thousand years ago. Only the Siberians were whale hunters, but they were artists on both coasts, artists with such a passion for decoration that not a single useful or religious object fails to bear its fantasy, even its nightmare figure. Among the remains in the Chukchi Peninsula sites, archaeologists S. A. Arntynov and D. A. Serveyev found in 1960 a curved object somehow reminiscent of an Australian boomerang. Living Eskimo in the area could not relate it to their own tool kits. But both Chukchi and Yukaghir of the Kolyma lowlands produced similar throwing sticks used today in herding but also, oddly, in the hunting of partridge, ducks, and geese.

About 700 B.C., midway in time between the first Arctic whale hunters and the artists of the Old Bering Sea, there lived on the Alaska coast in a site now called Choris a curious and interesting people. They made pottery with linear markings, perhaps produced by cord binding. (Dr. Giddings sees Asian influence in the design.). They lived in large, oval pit houses. Hearths and refuse mounds give evidence of their diet: mainly caribou (the American term for wild deer of the north) with some seal and game birds for variety's sake. It was the particular sort of caribou bones retained in the houses that impressed Dr. Giddings. They were shoulder blades, and most of them had been cracked in the fire—but not in the cooking process. The cracks were made for very different purposes which had nothing whatever to do with extraction of marrow but very much to do with telling the future. We have ourselves used bones in divination. The children do, at any rate, whenever the family has roast chicken for dinner. Here are the rules of the game. Two players grasp a particular part of the fowl's breastbone (the "wishbone") and pull. The one with the head of the bone remaining on his piece wins and, as winner, expects to receive the wish he made while yanking at the bone.

Now the shoulder-blade game, the divining game played by the Choris diners, has a name: scapulimancy. It represents a way of foretelling the future by fire cracks in the bone. Scapulimancy was known perhaps four or five thousand years ago to the Chinese who used for the purpose first the shoulder blades of sheep and later the carapaces of turtles. Scapulimancy was known and used by the Chukchi in Bogoras' time and also by the Tungus both of whom employed the shoulder blades of reindeer. Eskimo on both sides of the Bering Strait do not know, nor have they ever known, this form of divination. But there are American Indians to the south of the Arctic Zone who do and did.

There is yet more to the Choris site. The deer bones found there appeared to Dr. Giddings and other specialists to have belonged to animals smaller and lighter than wild caribou. Indeed, they conform to the bone sizes of herding reindeer of Siberia. Dr. Giddings wonders if the people of the beach at Choris might have been herding folk with animals imported from Asia. Not Chukchi and not Chukchi deer, surely domesticated in a much more recent time. They were other folk, southerly folk, perhaps, filtering through the peninsula, moving by boat across the strait, bag, baggage, and deer. We may never know for sure.

It was not until A.D. 500 or later that what Giddings calls "the utilitarian look of modern Eskimo" began to turn up on both shores. This may provide a possible confirmation of Bogoras' belief that Eskimo came late to or developed late on the peninsula and formed a wedge between Chukchi and other Old Asians on the Siberian side and earlier migrants over the strait.

The Aboriginal Peoples of Northeast Asia

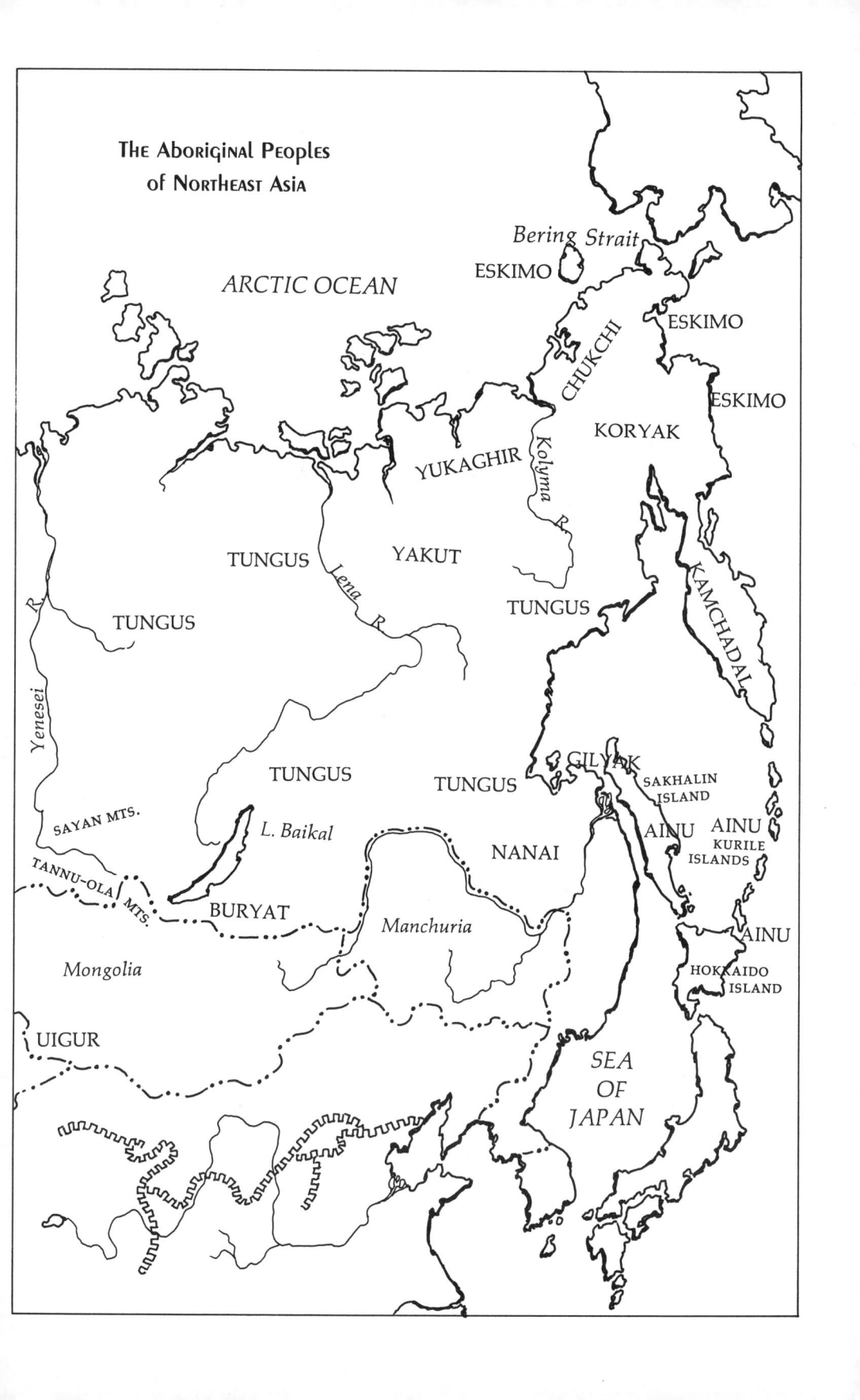

The ethnologist Waldemar Jochelson, a friend and colleague of Bogoras, was especially sensitive to the ties between Old World and New. Of the Paleoasiatic peoples, he called the Chukchi, Koryak, Yukaghir, and Asian Eskimo "Americanoid," believing that all represented a reverse migration, a backwash from the frontier, a return from the New World. Certainly the echoes of common origin are very strong. It is more than a matter of similar dog-drawn sleds and skin boats and house types. There are the beliefs, the techniques of hunting and healing, the social conventions—not only among Eskimo, but especially among Indians south of the Arctic Circle—which now and again remind one of Siberia.

Whatever the routes of travel, whatever the pathways of ideas and men, they are certain to be of a more complex nature than any one explanation can reasonably accommodate. There must have been homeward journeys over the Beringian land bridge. We know from the evidence of living men that, even after the bridge disappeared into ice-choked waters, the to-and-fro travel between continents was continued at a brisk pace by boat.

The archaeological picture in Alaska—where in some inland spots the earth layers go deeper and are the more easily read than on the shore—indicates the passage of many peoples through time. The earliest immigrants, it appears, bore the cultures of Ice Age times. These were to change as their bearers created life ways amenable to new demands, and their adaptations, in turn, would influence each group of new arrivals out of Asia. In both continents, all possible variations of time, circumstance, and invention have been played on the common, on the original theme, on the ancient Ice Age inheritance. But outlines of that heritage remain. It is the heritage of the hunt, man's first life way and his longest-lasting one.

Now the hunter, unless he inhabits a zone of unfailing natural abundance, must live in small groups of people who travel often as the game moves on. The hunting band may be composed of a core of relatives or of members only distantly related, if at all, drawn together merely by the wish to hunt where the hunting is good, to hunt with people who are congenial. Bands tend to have a shifting membership, and sometimes economic cooperation needs a bit of a boost. This may be supplied by a fiction of common family. Thus all men of father's age might call one another "brother" and be addressed by all the band's children as "father." (Of course, each child knows his real father and loves him best.)

Such conventions were not for the Chukchi sea hunters of Bogoras' time. They lived in permanent villages of semisubterranean houses and later of tents, and the house groups might or might not be related. No matter. The Chukchi did not extend the terms "father," "mother," "sister," "brother," "son," "daughter" to anyone other than those of the house and the blood, the unit anthropologists call the nuclear family. Peripheral relatives were called something like "parent's sister" or "parent's brother," roughly equivalent to our own "aunt" and "uncle." Some peoples consider the offspring of mother's sister and father's brother equivalent to one's own sisters and brothers and think the offspring of father's sister and mother's brother as kissing kin, more or less. For the Chukchi, all were simply "cousin." Eskimo of both continents and we ourselves use the same system of family titles. It is called, wherever found, Eskimo Kinship Terminology.

Any Chukchi was glad to give or receive help from cousins, whether located in father's or mother's side of the family. Indeed, the unit of closest cooperation among the sea hunters was the group of brothers and cousins who labored together in the skin boat built or bought by one of their number.

Herding Chukchi used the same kin terms but liked to travel only with relatives, particularly relatives in the male line, for they were considered "soft to one another," particularly close. However much father's brother's sons were separated in title from the nuclear family, their special ties were reknit constantly in ritual when, with the blood of sacrifice, family designs were painted on family foreheads and cheeks. Thus were they made of one blood and of one fire, too. Among the Chukchi in Bogoras' time fire was a symbol of the family. Its coals could be shared only among members of the line.

The ties of male relatives were reknit whenever one of their number suffered injury or death at the hands of enemy groups. Such injuries, such deaths must be avenged by surviving kin. Families with many young men to count on were proud and ruthless in their behavior to outsiders, secure in their numbers. Ties of brothers and cousins were continually reknit in labor, for the herds required much tending. The herdmaster—grandfather or eldest of a band of brothers—tried to keep his group together. Sometimes he failed. For all the ties of blood and fire, a young man grew restless, particularly if he was not to be the master's principal heir. He and the master might come to blows as he grew older and the awe he had felt as a youth began to thin. Afterward he would leave to become "assistant" to some other herdmaster. In any case, he would have to do so at least temporarily in the camp from which he hoped to win a bride to bring back to his own camp. The assistant who chose a master without sons, however, might find his fortune made for him.

Among herding Chukchi, the herdmaster might well name a daughter to be his principal heir, to receive in time, not only the herds but the sacred objects of the house. Such a girl never left her hearth for her husband's, never transferred her family allegiance. It was, on the contrary, her husband who would become attached to *her* fire, bound to *her* family by the rituals of blood.

For all that, women's lot among the Reindeer Chukchi was hard, harder perhaps than that of their sisters of the shore.

For often they did men's work as well as their own. What with erecting and dismantling the "genuine house," what with beating the damp bedding and processing the skins, surely women's work was sufficiently strenuous. In the season of insects, however, when the herds, driven mad by stings and bites, had to be watched constantly and protected in the smoke of smudge fires, then women went out to take turns on sentry duty. Like the men, they spent days and nights without sleep, without rest, eating on foot and in hasty snatches. On returning to camp, however, they found no one to give them dry clothing, a warm meal, and a furry bed. They were, instead, expected to help the other women to provide such comforts for the men. Bogoras saw many a woman, vainly trying to do both jobs, fall senseless to the ground, overcome with sleep.

Women, said the Chukchi of both economic persuasions, are inferior beings. They then proceeded to contradict themselves in action. Two images of femininity were admired: the blushing, bashful beauty, pale from long seclusion in the house, blear-eyed from concentration on fine needlework; and the hardy amazon who could not be wooed, who could be won only if the ardent swain could defeat her in a foot race or wrestling match. From Bogoras' descriptions, one may suppose there were infinitely more amazons in "genuine houses" than shrinking violets. He saw none who were unwilling to contend with their husbands, even with blows in the offing. Doubtless it was their participation in men's work that made Chukchi women masterful to some extent, but it was surely a command of ritual that gave them real importance. Men were no more familiar with the sacred objects of the hearth than they were with the construction of the "genuine house" or the cooking of the evening meal. When a wife died, all the guardian figures, the fire boards were put away. Incantations of protection had to be stilled until the next wife came to recall them.

Women were not forbidden to be healers and healers of

power, too. Indeed, the Chukchi woman's position could not have been too low, for sex change was possible, and men now and then became "women." They might do so in various degrees, some merely affecting female coiffeur in order to confuse evil spirits. Others made the change entirely—clothes, name, work, manner, the use of the female dialect. Bogoras describes several whose bashful, blushing, feminine faces sat on the bodies of giants. The change was thought to come about at the behest of the spirits. "Soft Men" were thought to make the most powerful healers. Often the call was dreaded, resisted to the point of suicide. Yet, once made, the change was forever. In the manner of many Indians of California and of the Great Plains, the Chukchi Soft Man took a "husband," though that individual played second fiddle to the spirit who was the real "man of the house." The sorrow of the Soft Man was his barrenness, his inability to produce babies. "Some can," the Soft Man mourned. "Why not me?" Over and over Bogoras was told of Soft Men who had managed to create the necessary organs. On the other hand, women who had become men told no wistful tales and mourned not for their childless days. For they could have children, not of their own bodies, of course, but by their "wives." All was accomplished through the Chukchi institution of group marriage.

If the words bring to mind images of proto-man, like other innocent primates uninhibitedly sharing the sexual wealth, discard such images for they do not fit the Chukchi case. Neither does the image of the American wife-swapping party, a recent suburban addition to our sexual folkways. For the Chukchi, group marriage was neither orgy nor occasional spice to a jaded connubial diet. It was, quite literally, another way of reknitting the social bond, of achieving order and predictability in life. This is not to say that the Chukchi were high-mindedly above sudden onslaughts of passion. Indeed, Bogoras describes them as bumptious to the point of coarseness, fond of lewd jokes and body references. Adultery was not at all unknown, and a whole body of legend prescribed the proper punishment: removal of the erring wife's nose. Bogoras, however, observed no missing noses nor any hint of drastic retribution. Adulterous spouses simply extended reciprocal rights to the other parties, and jealousy disappeared.

Ideally, groups were formed on a much more orderly basis and with very practical ends in view. Distant relatives living in widely separated villages or camps were preferred to neighbors. Even to the lively Chukchi, a local group marriage smacked altogether too much of promiscuity. Nor were groups disparate in age and wealth approved. Young folk with an eye on the main chance often invited older established couples to form relationships. They were invariably, though politely, refused.

When a group of the proper membership was formed, its members went from camp to camp, sacrificing dogs and reindeer and anointing one another with blood. Then were they members of one fire, closer than kin of the male line, bound to avenge, to entertain, to befriend; bound to cherish the group's children, all of whom would be considered cousins and forbidden to one another as prospective mates. It was in group marriage that the barriers of distance were overcome, that the obligations and protection of kinship were extended afar so that strangers became relatives and possible enemies, allies. Every man of the group was thus provided with a warm home away from home, and every time he visited, the ties of friendship and kinship were renewed.

Many of the world's people have used wife exchange as a means of making men brothers. Underlying this custom is the belief that brothers are socially interchangeable in marriage as in all else. If a man dies, his brother should become husband to his widows—a custom anthropologists call the levirate. Often wife sharing is practiced while brothers are still alive. If brothers may share, why then, men who share must *be as* brothers, must assume fraternal ties. Chukchi seemingly never adopted the initial premise, though they cheerfully made use of its corollary. Real brothers might inherit one another's wives, all right, but certainly could not make free with them while brother lived. Neither could brothers join the same marriage group. It was the extension of brotherly ties (however fictitious) that counted among the Chukchi, and wife sharing made the tie strong.

Both custom and intent call to mind the Eskimo institution of wife lending. Often interpreted as something of a crowning ultimate in hospitality, anthropologists L. Hennigh and R. F. Spencer say otherwise. Noting that host and guest address one another with special kinship terms, they suggest that wife lending, like Chukchi group marriage, might have served to create and reinforce bonds between scattered hunting people who surely needed all the help they could get.

The realities of the hunter's world, and those of the hunter turned herder, are different from those of the farmer, the city dweller, the manipulator of machines. To the hunter, all things—rocks and trees and beasts of land and sea—have will and intelligence not too different from man's own. All things have names and territories and voices. And so it was that Chukchi quarry had to be induced to yield its meat to Chukchi need and, for the yielding, deserved thanks and recompense. Herders poured water over the wild deer they slew and placed soft willow branches beneath its hind quarters. The sea hunters gave their prey a drink of fresh water— exactly as the Eskimo of Baffin Island do to this day.

For the whale and sometimes the polar bear, the thanks went on for five days, along with feasting and entertainment, all for the benefit of the slain animal. Bits of his bones and flesh were taken as his representative and enthroned on the inner house canopy of the boatmaster. Never were remains left alone lest the whale be lonely, lest he fail to use his influence in luring his fellows to the harpoon.

All living things were thought to have Masters, great spirits responsible for their well-being, spirits who must be noticed and placated by man, even as each slain animal, each felled tree must be thanked. Only the birch tree could be used without ceremony, for the birch, alone among trees, lacked a Master. Bogoras never learned why this was so.

The most sacred rituals of the Chukchi were tuned to remembrance and thanksgiving. Those of the shore men most often involved family prayers, offerings, and sacrifice. Thus were honors paid to the great spirits of the sea. Herding folk, with more wherewithal for celebration, could afford to elaborate the rituals, provide more song and drumming and dance, and invite a crowd to share in the festivities.

Not all the spirits of the Chukchi universe were giving and good. The population of bad ones ran very high. These were the *ke'let* who subsisted on their "seals"—the bodies and souls of human kind. There were thought to be *ke'let* of every sort and for every evil thing. Like the great Masters of the universe, they were personified, given form and dimension. Among the *ke'let* who brought disease there was, for example, the Cough Spirit, a tiny old man who drove a white deer and tied captured souls to a long string. There were the Spirits of Syphilis, miniature beings who pitched their tents on human bodies. Red and skinless, they were, hung about with long black capes, and always hungry. All the *ke'let* lived in an underground world from which they emerged to hunt. And, as they could assume human or animal disguise, no one was safe from them by day or night, at home or on the march. However much the staunch dogs might bark, some *ke'let* would manage to steal under the tent covers. Often the fearful one, unable to sleep, would murmur,

I make myself into a small stone. I enter the stone. It is lying on the seashore. Every wind is blowing upon it. Every wave is washing over it. I am safe!*

In Chukchi belief there was no such thing as natural death. There were only murders by the *ke'let* or by men who could command them. And survivors had to know by what means a loved one had been slain. Each corpse before its exposure on the tundra—surrounded by the meat of sacrifice, many deer antlers, and a ring of stones—was opened with a knife and its entrails carefully examined for the telltale signs of murder. Even the suicide must be so examined.

Now, among the Chukchi, a voluntary death was highly honored. Suicides were said to dwell among the northern lights. And yet they were also, in some curious way, a kind of sacrifice to the *ke'let,* an appeasement offering. The man or woman who requested death of his relatives said, in the metaphor of the hunt, "Since I become for thee like thy quarry, like thy quarry treat me." He could not be refused. The wish, once said, could not be unsaid. However painful the act, however much in dread, the surviving spouse or children must kill the death seeker. For the *ke'let* were everywhere, heard all, and would sure come for some other offering were the suicide denied his wish.

Between the Chukchi and their enemies stood only the healers, each one able to call, to command certain of the spirits of evil to do his bidding. "These are my people," said a healer to Bogoras, "my own little spirits. They will not leave me but will seek me out all the time as a fawn seeks his mother." If these spirits could be forced to do good for others, they could

---

*The sources for quotations may be found in the reference notes at the end of the bibliography for each chapter, keyed to the page numbers on which they appear. For the source for this quotation, for example, see page 271.

also play the tyrant to their possessor. He might be forced to take another name, to change sex, to run away. Though Chukchi tradition abounds with stories of the poor orphan who becomes a healer, defeats his enemies, and grows rich, Bogoras discovered that young people most often dreaded the "call." So did their parents.

In our world, the sensitive adolescent, the dreamer, the different child is considered a likely candidate for the commune, the drug subculture, or a life of poetry. Among the Chukchi such a one was certain to become a healer. For months or years he would struggle against the call—always a dangerous effort. He would fall, become disoriented, prone to slumber, refusing food. At long last—unless some sympathetic or perhaps jealous female put in his food the circumventing blood or tissues of childbirth—the healer-to-be would succumb, and, surrendering, "take the drum."

The proper word for healer is "shaman." Among anthropologists the word describes the expert directly in touch with the great powers, unseen and unknown. Such a one has spirits at his or her command and may kill or cure with the aid of these spirits, may give advice, may lighten the troubled soul, may foretell the future. Often this is accomplished while the shaman is in trance, a psychic state which can be gained through rhythmic drumming and dance, through deep meditation, or through drugs. For this purpose the Chukchi used the mushroom we know as the fly agaric.

Shaman is a Tungus word. Doubtless much of the present art has been transposed northward to the Chukchi. Spirit possession, the "throwing of the voice" (what we call ventriloquism), the speaking in strange tongues, the sleight-of-hand tricks, the special performance in the inner room, the sucking cure by which the shaman pretends to remove some foreign object from the patient's body—all these have become part of the role known generally to shamans in Siberia. Many of the selfsame techniques were common among shamans of the New World and, secretly or openly, are practiced still. For however much a matter of performance, manipulation, or trickery, shamanism works. It works well in cases of mental distress. But it serves in all painful situations for those who truly believe.

In 1929, rehabilitated by the Revolution, Vladimir Bogoras went to Leningrad, there to become teacher to Chukchi children sent from Siberia to learn the new thought—as in America Indian children were once sent to missionary boarding schools. One of his students was the grandson of a famous shaman. For this spiritual connection, the boy was much mocked by classmates. At last, converted, reborn to grace, he announced to all, "Shamanism is the opium of the people." Hearing the comment, Bogoras mourned, privately, of course, and with scholarly restraint. How sad, he thought, that old ways must die before they could be fully understood. How sad that simple people, politically innocent people, must fade as civilization comes near.

He may have mourned too soon. What Cossack armies could not accomplish, what missionaries and the demand of fur tribute could not enforce, the new Soviet government could not achieve so easily, either. After 1850 the connections with Alaska, always strong, were reinforced to include White American traders. They were connections not to be broken until the 1950s, until the Cold War between the United States and the U.S.S.R. had finally set in.

In a vain effort to impose some degree of centralization, Czarist administrators had tried to organize the Chukchi into clans and to appoint a Chukchi king or, at the very least, Chukchi chiefs. The Chukchi not only failed to recognize such leaders, but failed as well to understand the very concept of leadership. For were not all Chukchi equal? Some were richer than others, of a certainty, but of what importance was that? The Soviets had little greater success with the concepts of

Communism and Revolution, and State (as W. Kolarz reports) was defined by the Chukchi as "a White man." In 1947, in the June 2 issue of *Pravda,* a writer complained, "In the minds of the Chukotka people old times are still surviving."

Even today, in the midst of praise for the new, modern collective farms, meant to reunite Chukchi herders and hunters in a single economic unit, there creeps a hint of cautious dismay. Almost plaintively scholarly studies concede the lure of the old nomadic ways, note the difficulties involved in persuading hunters and herders to settle down, to exchange their "genuine houses" for snug frame cottages.

Surely change must come. The twentieth century presents its bill of particulars, and no people can remain entirely exempt. But it would seem that the Chukchi are not, in their phrase, "soft to die." Patiently they drag their feet. Slowly they perform the necessary cultural addition and subtraction, changing, in the process, just enough to remain essentially the same.

4

THE AINU
Mystery Folk
of Northern Japan

An air of hushed expectancy hangs over the knot of tall thatch-roofed houses. Nearby is what appears to be a cage made of stout saplings, so adorned with the wooden curls of shaved-stick figures, so closely hemmed in by clustering men, that one cannot see what is inside. The elder of the house, magnificently bewhiskered, approaches, and the men move back and sit in a circle. Now is revealed the occupant of the cage: a young bear, almost a cub. Now can be seen, too, a woman who leans her head on the cage and weeps bitterly. "This is my child," she cries, "and he leaves me to go far away."

The elder, turning to the cage, solemnly addresses its occupant:

> *O, thou precious little one, we worship thee; pray hear our prayers. We have nourished thee and brought thee up with great pains and care,*

and all because we loved thee so much. Now as thou art grown big, we are about to send thee to thy parents. When thou comest to them, please speak well of us and tell them how kind we have been to thee. We beseech thee to return to us once more, that we may again entertain thee.

Quickly the door to the cage is opened. Hunters, standing nearby, slip two ropes over the bear's head and, since he is a large cub, another over his hindquarters. Thus protected from biting teeth and raking claws, the men urge the bear to rush this way and that, and all the while the festive crowd dances about him ceremoniously. All the while they sing, reminding him of how much they have loved him, giving him messages for his spirit parents in the mountains and for *Metot-Ush Kamui*, the Master Bear.

Suddenly the bear snorts and rears. A blunt arrow has caught him in the side. Another and another comes until he is made weary and frantic. Quickly then the men place the bear's neck between two heavy logs. On these the villagers press and lean, squeezing the bear's life away.

A sharp knife at last "sends the dear little one home." Blood gushes forth, and the men hasten to catch it in special cups, lest it touch the contaminating earth, and to drink of the cups while yet the fluid they contain is warm with life, with the vital essence, the force which imbues all things.

The body of the bear, addressed in the tenderest and most reverent terms, is passed from hand to hand through the sacred east window of the house in which he had been reared. Deftly, women skin the body and cut the head free. It will then rest on its folded skin, the chief guest of the feast to come. Gifts and offerings of food—even of its own cooked flesh—will be placed around it. And all the while it will be entreated to speak well of its hosts when it returns home. Later still the head will be placed on a special rack outside the home along with many sacred shaved sticks. There it will remain, long after skin and ears and snout are gone. The bleached bones, no longer bear-like, will be addressed as Divine Protector.

Men who thus honor the bear were and are the Ainu, once a hunting, gathering, fishing folk who early occupied all of the Japanese islands, Sakhalin, and the Kurile chain. Now they are a remnant few to be found only on Hokkaido, the northern Japanese island, to which even the Sakhalin Ainu migrated after World War II when their land fell to Russian ownership. On Hokkaido the Ainu reenact for tourists the ceremonies and dances of their past. The bear ritual in its original form is no longer presented. We have seen it through the eyes of the Venerable John Batchelor, in 1888 a member of the Church Mission Society of London. At that time, he had lived eleven years among the Ainu and was to remain for yet another thirty.

In truth, the bear sacrifice may be the thing best known about the Ainu. Over the long years it has been mentioned and described by ships' captains, travelers, visiting divines, and officials of every ilk. In 1890 the episodes of the ritual were captured in paint by the Japanese artist Tomeoka Tessai. In 1933 they were filmed by Neil Gordon Munro, a Scottish physician who, like Batchelor before him, lived for many years among the Ainu and held them in love and respect. Even then the ritual had been much modified. Even then it was the elderly Ainu who alone remembered and honored the ancient ways.

In that other life, in those older times, the Ainu honored and feasted, not only the bear cub brought up in an Ainu home, but also the wild bear, full-sized and formidable, hunted and killed in the mountains. They were not alone in so doing. There seems to be something about the bear which has always inspired the hunter with awe. Perhaps, as some North American Indians say, it is because the bear walks often on two legs like a man, indeed may be a man, a powerful shaman in bear disguise.

The Reindeer Chukchi believed so. Never, they cautioned their children, may one speak ill of a black bear or plot against him. For he can hear over long distances and will surely punish. The Chukchi of the shore feasted and honored the slain polar bear exactly as they honored the whale. The Ket, a people of the Yenesei River, considered the bear a gift to the living from kinfolk dead and gone. It was necessary among them to conduct an elaborate recognition ritual so that the bear soul could be given family identification, so that thanks could be properly addressed. The Yukaghir called the bear simply "Grandfather."

Far away in space and time, other men have paid homage to the bear. In one of the European caves of late Ice Age time, there has been found a large, earth-mounded body of a bear, headless, its clay body pocked with arrow wounds. One may imagine such a figure draped with the skin and head of a real bear, newly slain. In flickering torchlight it would have looked like a living creature, crouched in fear or in sleep. One may imagine the hunters reenacting the kill, releasing their arrows, dancing, shouting now in triumph, now in supplication.

Were there really cries and prayers echoing through the cave? That we cannot know. But dancing there surely was—the footprints of the dancers can still be seen. And certainly a real bear skin and head were used. The hole for a supporting stick is there in the neck of the clay model. And beneath the figure its discoverer found the skull of the last bear to be an object of honor or of rage.

Awe of the bear can be more plainly read in the cave remains of still earlier people, the Neanderthals. They placed the heads of giant cave bears in niches and on covered shelves of stone. Shrines we must call them. Sometimes the long bones of the leg were inserted in empty eye sockets. Meaning what? We perceive only the reverence, perceive that the bear was a being to whom deference was due and must be paid.

There is something about the Ainu bear sacrifice and about the Ainu themselves that recalls long-vanished hunters of the European Ice Age rather than Siberian contemporaries. Certainly the Ainu differ in looks from the peoples around them. They are hairy while their Japanese and Tungus neighbors are smooth of face. Ainu hair is often curly ("the hair of the gods," they call it); Tungus hair is straight. Ainu have wide, high-bridged noses and wide mouths; the others generally do not. The specialist in physical anthropology discovers that Ainu teeth (their incisors are not shovel-shaped as are those of other Far East peoples), earwax (sticky, not crumbly), and finger ridges (more whorls than loops) are European in type. And there is the matter of eye shape. Even though Ainu are today intermingled with Japanese, culturally and physically, the original eye form lingers on. It is not almond shaped, and the lid is not double folded. "People of the same eye socket," say Ainu of Ainu—drawing thus the contrast with neighbors.

How came they here? Could the Ainu be living representatives and descendants of European Neanderthals? The occasional appearance in Asian archaeological sites of implements similar to those of European Neanderthal manufacture has stirred not a few specialists to speculations of Neanderthal movements toward the East. Do the Ainu perhaps represent a later Ice Age intrusion from the West, a movement along the edges of the northern pine forest, around the Urals, and over the Amur river? The Japanese islands were once attached to the mainland, and a tenuous land bridge remained until some three thousand years or so ago.

A number of Ainu physical characteristics appear among the Gilyak of northern Sakhalin Island and, less strongly, among the other peoples of northern Siberia. Ainu language is related to Gilyak, though distantly. Affiliations with Chukchi are even less distinct. Yet Ainu is classified as one of the

Paleoasiatic languages. Noting the similarities in looks and language, some specialists have declared that no west-to-east migrations occurred at all. The Paleoasiatics hark back, they say, to a time before the formation of the Mongoloid type. Ainu, they continue, moved down the Kurile chain into the Japanese islands. There, in relative isolation, they mixed less with incoming true Mongoloids and retained more of the ancient face and physique.

Not less of a mix, but more, insists still another group of specialists. The mix they have in mind involves a dollop of Mongoloid added to a basic genetic brew mostly Australoid in character. Now, the Australoid type is most strongly represented by the aboriginal peoples of Australia and others in the Pacific and in Southeast Asia, the presumed homeland. Nose shape, craggy face, and wavy-curly hair remind us vaguely of Ainu, it is true. But Australians tend to be tall and stringy. Ainu are short, stocky, and broad of chest and shoulder. Australians are very dark, almost black, indeed, in the north of their island continent. So are their relatives on the Asian mainland. If there was at one time a movement of people and looks from south to north, a good deal of skin bleaching must have occurred along the way.

The equation Ainu equal Australoid plus Mongoloid seems to be based in large part on cultural similarities. And it is true that many of the old Ainu ways remind us of Southeast Asia. Ainu hunters poisoned their arrow heads, a practice unknown in Siberia but familiar still among hunting peoples of Southeast Asia. Ainu clothing was made of the woven fibers of elm-tree bark, dyed, appliquéd with elaborate designs, and worn in a long robe called *attush*. It is cold on the island of Hokkaido. Snow falls from November to May. Yet the Ainu did not wear furs tailored after the Siberian manner. They clung to their fiber clothing, sewing furs to them as to a lining.

It must be remembered that ideas need not be imposed on

people by an incoming throng. Ideas may be passed along by visitors, traders, curious wanderers; by bearers who have no intention of settling down to stay. Ideas catch on when their receivers are ready for them, when the climate, so to speak, is right. Sometimes ideas catch on for no apparent reason, even when the climate is not exactly right. The Chukchi, for example, used to enjoy describing a giant "worm" with sinuous red-striped body which lived in the aurora borealis near villages of the honored dead. This worm was said to hunt wild reindeer, killing them with pressure in the coils of his giant body. Now, some small snakes are to be found on Hokkaido, but none are to be found in Siberia. No living prototype exists there for the celestial "worm," which resembles in description nothing so much as the huge anacondas of Southeast Asia.

Another example of the traveling idea is to be seen in the thatch of Ainu roofs which must surely have come from the south, probably via China. It was erected over pits of the time-honored pattern. Yet the most ancient Ainu word for house, says Dr. Munro, is *kenru* which refers, not to a pithouse, thatched or no, but to a tripod frame covered with bark or skin. To Dr. Munro, this recalls other times when the Ainu, like Yukaghir in Siberia, were nomadic hunters. Certainly the word, like the house type, has for very long been in disuse. Whether the traditional Ainu way represented a southern veneer over a heritage basically Siberian in character or a quick wintertime addition to a culture more southern in origin may never be made plain. It is worthy of note that the Ainu of Sakhalin Island made use in winter of semi-subterranean homes dug into the hillsides close to shore.

In some ways less mysterious, in other ways more, and in all ways important were the mutual influences of Ainu and Japanese. Japanese oral tradition holds that the islands were created especially for themselves by the Sun Goddess, who sent down her son, Jimmu Tenno, to be the first emperor. This was thought to have occurred in 600 B.C., a date obtained by counting back 1200 years from earliest dates to appear in writing. The number 1200 figured importantly in ritual cycles. Landing on the island of Kyushu, Jimmu Tenno miraculously crossed the strait on a turtle's back to establish his rule in southern Honshu.

The Ainu must certainly have been then in residence on all the Japanese islands. Tradition mentions great battles of Japanese with barbarians. And in the eighth century A.D. such references appear in writing. Epic battles between the Ezo or Emisu (Ainu?) are recorded. Generals complain of the drain on resources occasioned by constant strife. But gradually the records indicate a retreat and finally an assimilation of the remaining barbarians on Honshu. Others moved north to join their relatives on Hokkaido.

Hokkaido had early been reconnoitered by Japanese travelers but was left politically untouched. Nominally under the control of one or another of the great Japanese clans, its people kept to their own ways, trading now and then with the outsiders. In time island resources—furs and gold, fish and meat—became more valued, more sought. Demands for trade, rules for trade, rules for land usage, and rules for behavior were presented to the Ainu. Boundaries of land allocated to Japanese settlers were expanded. Ainu were forbidden to intrude within. Forbidden to them, too, were farming, the wearing of straw hats and garments in the rain, the use of Japanese language and Japanese writing. They were not, however, restricted in the practice of their religion or in their daily life. They were merely to be kept strictly apart, to be welcome only in trade, in all other ways to be scorned and belittled. In 1456 they revolted and remained at war with the Japanese on Hokkaido until the founder of another important clan made peace.

For long there was quiet and order on Hokkaido. Then again the Ainu were harassed and exploited, this time by independent traders admitted by the ruling Japanese clan. Again the Ainu went to war. Finally in the early 1800s, the central

Japanese government, startled by Russian interest in the area, took charge of Hokkaido and, with somewhat lesser confidence, of Sakhalin and the Kuriles.

Ainu policies were sharply reversed. Japan's "primitives" were to be weaned, and quickly, from their old ways. They were to be Japanized as soon and as completely as possible. Buddhist temples and missions were established. Farming was encouraged. With the sudden influx of colonists from the southern islands, hunting and the old fishing methods became impossible, whether actually forbidden or no. Some of the old Ainu rituals, rooted in hunting, fell into disuse; others were abolished. The tattooing of women became unlawful, and for a time Ainu men were even forced to cut their hair. Remember Samson with his shorn locks, shorn equally of his strength? The Ainu suddenly became a race of Samsons, for hair to them was the very special mark of man's estate, not to be shaved or cut save in mourning or for the sake of ritual. The years passed, and the Ainu, some of them, have gradually learned to live comfortably without their long hair, doffing with it the old ways as well.

For something over two thousand years Japanese and Ainu have confronted one another. In the beginning it must have been on equal terms, or very nearly so. That the confrontation was most often hostile need not have prevented the flow and counterflow of ideas. Think of the influence of American Indian cultures on American ways. Some of our most important foods—corn, potatoes, tomatoes—were domesticated in the New World. Certain items of clothing—the moccasin, for instance—can be traced to Indian originals. American personality ideals (the "strong, silent, type" celebrated in movie westerns), certain political ideals (a leader must be one among equals, not divinely chosen), even a few bad habits (chewing gum and smoking cigarettes) have been borrowed from the first Americans.

This same kind of mutual influencing seems to have occurred in Japan and nowhere more pointedly than in the area of religious belief. The oldest Japanese religion is Shinto. It has been described as having priests but no theology, ritual but no dogma. In its shrines are celebrated quite simply the wonder and mystery of life and of the pure-hearted man who can receive these mysteries with gratitude. Mystery and awe dwell ever in special places of greatest beauty. They dwell in the utensils and tools which faithfully serve human life. They dwell also in certain animals.

At Nara, an ancient city near Osaka, there is a Shinto shrine and a park which is the habitation of sacred deer. In the fall of every year the deer therein are captured by men especially trained for the task. Thrown to the ground, the deer are given a ritual drink of water, then their antlers are removed. It is said that the antlers might be dangerous to visitors, that someone could be gored. This is an explanation tuned to the world we inhabit today, a literal, practical world with little room for mystery or wonder. Surely the antlers meant something more once and perhaps still do for the priests and keepers of the shrine. For the branching tines and horns are always reverently arranged on an altar, in offering and in remembrance. (One remembers the Chukchi habit of adorning with antlers the meat-encased bodies of the dead exposed on the tundra. It was a sort of living memorial, for the antlers were thought to rise at night and troop in solemn parade around the dead.)

The deer of Nara has *kami,* is *kami*—something which is close to "god" but not quite, close to "spirit" but not quite that, either. There are *kami* of every sort in every environment: the *kami* of the home—parents, fire, cooking pot, and the beer a-brewing in its cask; the *kami* of special places; the craft *kami* which guard the artisan's skill and inhabit his tools; the national, the great *kami,* ancestral to the living ruler, which must be thanked and honored in his person.

The Ainu also recognize beings of power and call them

kamui. All things in Ainu belief have vitality, an essence which does not die though its vessel be broken. In Ainu belief, as among the Japanese, there are kinds and grades of *kamui*: the great ones, creator *kamui* of the skies; the humble helpers of greater *kamui*; the power spirits of animals; the personal *kamui* which may possess and be commanded by a person sensitive to them; the evil *kamui*; the *kamui* of pestilence and horror—always, it is hoped, to be restrained by the *kamui* who are giving and good.

Unlike the Japanese, Ainu have never built elaborate shrines or temples. There is no connection of high gods with a ruler and a state. The Ainu never knew a state of their own and never had rulers higher than village chieftains who, when it comes to that, could not rule at all. Instead, they advised, mediated, besought the *kamui*, entertained, and were generous. Would that all chiefs everywhere were so!

An Ainu's home was his temple, and the hearth his altar. Here, in the very center of the house, dwelt *Fuji-Kamui*, the ever-living spirit of fire—mother, nurse, and protector of all Ainu. And the Ainu Fire Lady at some time entered Japanese tradition and was celebrated as Fujiyama, the majestic volcano of Honshu. So thought the Venerable Mr. Batchelor.

Fuji-Kamui of the Ainu hearth was likewise a never dying flame. Never must she be extinguished. No unclean thing could be allowed to sully her flames, no evil deed contemplated in her presence. Knives could not be pointed flameward nor bare feet exposed. Even the pot, hanging from its tripod, must not boil over. In view of these manifold prohibitions, Ainu women were often forced to kindle an "assistant" fire at the other end of the central hearth, one humble enough to see to the necessary but contaminating business of death and birth and cooking spills without taking offense.

Upholder of the World, *Shiramba-Kamui*, also had his deputy and representative in every Ainu home. From the northeast corner of the room this assistant communed with *Fuji*. Through the sacred window came the sun's rays to seek *Fuji;* there flowed as well the thoughts of *Shiramba-Kamui,* brother of *Fuji,* from his fence of offerings outside the window. Some say the sacred window faced ever upstream. On Sakhalin it is said to have faced the high sacred mountains. As these lay mostly to the east, it was to the east that windows were there oriented. Whatever the direction of the sacred window, no visitor might peer within or in any way block Fuji's communion with her fellow *kamui* lest she be thus prevented from interceding for the family within.

Because house was also temple, the etiquette of entering and departing, of greeting and farewell was solemn and elaborate. Men fluttered their hands, stroked their beards, coughed in the prescribed way. Women cried on one another's necks and moaned, waved their arms, and covered tattooed lips with tattooed hands. Batchelor calls it a kind of dance, graceful but tedious. There were seating positions around the hearth prescribed for every family member and for visitors of every sort. The meal itself was a kind of sacrament. *Kamui* and ancestors were "fed" choice morsels and always drops of drink—beer until its making was forbidden by the government, sake thereafter. Drops were scattered with the mustache-lifter, a long, carved wand intended to keep whiskers out of the cup.

The officiating priest was always the eldest man of the house. (He might have several houses with a wife in each.) It was he who offered the libations and addressed the *kamui.* It was he who carved the curled-shaving prayer sticks, now messenger, now offering, now representative of a *kamui* itself. It was he who inserted these sticks, or *inau,* at hearth or prayer fence or place of special beauty. It was he who offered the curing prayers when someone fell ill and purified the sufferer with water and fire.

On Sakhalin Island, a woman had close connections with

the seashore as well as with the fire and might herself become a healer. On Hokkaido, the lady of the house did not address the *kamui,* offered only one prayer and that a brief formula from which she might not stray. "Our wise ancestors," said the Ainu, "feared that women might turn their prayers against men." She was, nevertheless, in old age addressed as Fuji and was supposed to have the connection of her sex with that august female *kamui.*

If the Hokkaido Ainu woman could not address the *kamui,* she could be possessed by one—most frequently the spirit of an evil snake. In the throes of possession she suffered headaches, eyeaches, paralysis, bad dreams. Everyone—friends, relatives, neighbors—gathered round to cast out the snake and, in the midst of loving attention, the afflicted one poured forth her anguish. Ever after she was believed to have the power of long sight, of foretelling the future.

In spite of a role somewhat restricted in scope, each Ainu woman was believed to have mystical connections with *Fuji*—the mother spirit of all. Never did she appear before the hearth without her secret girdle, the mark of her identity about which men were supposed to be unaware. Men counted their descent, father to son, in unbroken line. Family signs were carved on all the most important prayer sticks. Women, too, counted descent and did so with their girdles. These were made in some eight different styles to represent various powerful beings of the sea or water or land. Each woman inherited her style from her mother, and she was forbidden to marry any man whose mother wore a girdle of the same style.

Among other peoples of the world, both men and women are included in kin groups, in lives of descent, whether these are reckoned along the maternal line, to be led and represented by mother's brother, or whether they follow paternal descent to be led by father, his brother, or his eldest son. Some folk reckon descent through both lines simultaneously. The Ainu were different, perhaps unique, not in following two lines of descent, but in maintaining one for men only, openly reckoned and honored openly; one for women only, reckoned in whispers and honored in secret. It was a secret so well kept that, of all the students of Ainu life and lore, only one foreign person learned of the girdle-descent. This was Dr. Munro. He learned because of his medical skill and because of his respect for all things Ainu. His female patients revealed the secret—a reckoning of descent that may recall a time when living women, like the female *kamui,* were more honored than in later times.

Ancient people on the Japanese islands, people known to us only by way of their archaeological remains, seemed to pay honor to the female principle, for they furnished their graves with little goddesses of clay. Their contemporaries on the mainland seem to have made no such figurines though the uses of pottery were known there. Even so, the clay work of the islanders, at first used as cooking pots, later in art, may be the world's oldest. Sites containing early and crude samples of the new technique have been radiocarbon-dated to 7500 B.C. Much of the later pottery is marked with lines as if, in the shaping process, it had been pressed with cord-bound paddles. And so it is called Jomon—"cord-marked"—and the period of time during which it was in use, the life style which produced it, these are termed Jomon as well.

Whether the early pottery makers came from the mainland bearing their skills or whether the craft was home-invented and home-grown, we do not know. Their predecessors or ancestors on the Japanese islands had been hunters, using a technology of ancient times. Their first tools had been the familiar choppers, later giving way to carefully fashioned flakes and blades. The Jomon people also made tools carefully ground and polished. Now, tools of this sort are usually associated with people who farm, who have need of axes of heavy, dense stone, and who have the extra time required for the tedious grinding techniques involved. The Jomon people were not farmers. They had domesticated dogs and hunted the deer and boar, but mainly they fished. The bones and shells of swimming fish and mollusks raised large dump heaps near their round or rectangular pit houses.

Sometime around 300 B.C. a new people came to the islands. They were rice farmers and had tools of bronze and iron, some of it in Chinese style. They made their pottery on wheels. It was thinner and finer, perhaps, than Jomon ceramics, but it took its artistic inspiration from the older forms. The new people and their pottery are called Yayoi from a major archaeological site near Tokyo. Like the Jomon, they placed figurines in the graves of their important folk. And these graves were not the simple ones of Jomon times, but large, sometimes huge, mounds, richly furnished with winged objects which had, perhaps, religious meanings, and with mirrors, swords, and bent pendants of jade. The Jomon people had earlier carved ivory and also jade into just such comma-shaped "jewels."

Slowly, as the archaeological picture reveals, the Jomon folk were pushed northward by the Yayoi. Once Jomon pottery and shell mounds had extended throughout the islands as far south as Kyushu. By A.D. 700 they had retreated to northern Honshu and Hokkaido. But the pushers may themselves have been pushed. Just before A.D. 300 the great tombs were being filled with different trappings: horse equipment bearing dragon and phoenix designs, horse masks, armor, many weapons of iron. The figurines, too, depicted warriors and their horses and many varieties of fabulous beasts. Not too long after A.D. 300 the Japanese state with its variously blended folk was consolidated, and history, written with characters imported from China, was launched.

Who were the variously blended folk: horsemen and tomb builders and fisherman-potters? Professor Namio Egami believes the horsemen were intruders from the mainland plains and steppes, probably Tungusic in appearance. Designs on the burial equipment of later Yayoi times are echoed in Korean burials of the period. From here, perhaps, the horsemen had embarked for the Japanese islands. After the consolidation of peoples, after the formation of the Yamato Dynasty—sometime in the fifth century A.D.—Japanese kings designated themselves overlords of the Korean peninsula as well as of the islands. Historical annals of the mainland record the visits during that time of five royal personages seeking confirmation of their claims by the Chinese emperor.

Other Japanese specialists deny the intrusion of steppe warriors, but most are united in tracing true Japanese origins to the Yayoi. As to where *they* came from, no one is agreed. A southern origin in rice-growing lands is often suggested. Traces of words and forms suggesting Malayo-Polynesian influences are to be found in the Japanese language, so some specialists believe.

But what of the still older Jomon people? Who are they? Whence did they come? Some Japanese scholars have called them ancestral to present-day populations, holding that Japanese, truly so in looks and language, have always inhabited the islands, receiving from time to time influences from the mainland but remaining essentially themselves. Others, like Professor Susumu Ono have thought it was the Jomon people who were the southern migrants, not the Yayoi. It is to this earlier migration that he traces Polynesian word influences in Japanese. Many believe that Jomon potters, whoever they were, whatever their origin, simply became extinct during their long retreat from the incoming Yayoi. Certainly, they hold, the sensitive Jomon artists could have no connection with the embarrassingly primitive Ainu, whose ancestors are presumed to have come from Siberia, island-hopping down the Kuriles.

Yet this is precisely the view of some Japanese and most Western scholars: that the Jomon people, whatever their original home, were ancestors of today's Ainu, ancestors who, in the long retreat north, lost or relinquished their ancient arts. To prove their point, these specialists point to the curved and spiral designs which adorn Ainu mustache-lifters and carved wooden bowls and appliquéd robes, all very like the incised designs on late Jomon pottery, Jomon carved ivory, even carved wooden objects of which some few survive. The pit houses which Ainu used to occupy are nearly identical with those of Jomon times. In Jomon houses as in those of traditional Ainu, the northwest corner is marked with a shrine. Traditional Ainu boats—made of planks sewn together—resemble those made in Jomon times.

A series of skulls from Jomon burials has been compared with a series dating from late Yayoi tombs. The Jomon skulls differ markedly from those of the great tomb period but resemble rather closely the skulls of Ainu from recent times. As Professor Carleton Coon points out, "This does not mean that the Jomon people were the only ancestors of the living Ainu, but it implies some degree of genetic relationship."

There is yet more. It is just possible that the earliest pottery in the New World—discovered in a shell mound on the coast of Ecuador—owes its shape and form and very existence to Jomon originals. This first American pot—dated to 3000 B.C.—is already sophisticated in style. (No early crude experiments have yet been unearthed on American shores.) It is cord-marked and is in shape identical to pottery styles found on the southernmost Japanese island and dated at the same period. American anthropologists Betty Meggers, Clifford Evans, and Emilio Estrada believe skills in pottery were borne by Jomon fishermen blown off course and carried by prevailing winds and tides to the New World.

If these fishermen were ancestral Ainu, why then, some of the ancient Asian blends and mixes—in looks, in life ways—found their way across the Pacific, as across the Bering Straits, and into the New World.

Part III

BETWEEN CHINA AND THE SNOWY WASTES

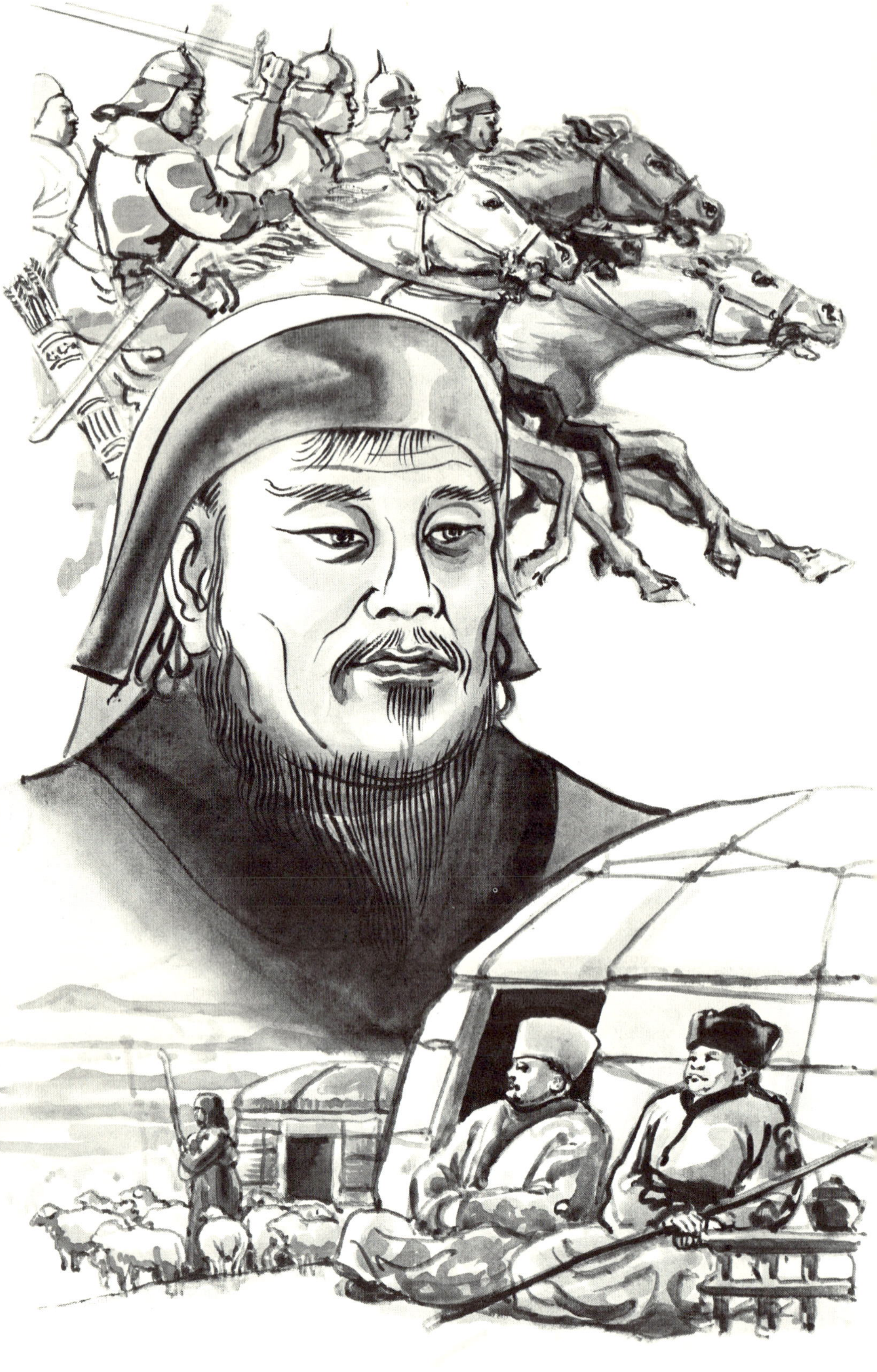

5

BATTLE-AX PEOPLE IN THE STEPPES
Warriors, Herdsmen, Conquerors

THE wide-stretched ends of Eurasia are bound, not only by mountain chains, but by a great mottled highway of desert, semidesert, and steppe—that treeless expanse of green scrub carpeting wind-blown soil. Winding around and between the mountains the highway terminates, east and west, in grasslands: in the Manchurian Plain, in the prairies of southern Russia, and, beyond the Carpathian mountain barrier, in the plain of Hungary.

In older, colder, wetter times, there was, over the highway, less desert and more grass. The northern piney forest narrowed, leaving here and there pockets of steppe, but the way was still marked and people traveled it. During middle Stone Age times the travelers came and, some twenty-five thousand years ago, later hunting folk wandered there, following the great grass eaters—rhino and bison. In sites uncovered along the way there have been found the tool kits of the travelers. They are of the same general type as those of western hunters. Like their colleagues in the West, the easterners felt the need to commemorate in rock paintings the forms and the vitality of the animals on which existence hinged. Alike, too, was the style in which the animals were rendered, graceful, natural, larger than life. The easterners preferred to paint in red, the hue of life. Professor A. P. Okladnikov describes for us the oldest of these paintings, found on rock faces overlooking the upper Lena River, not too far from Lake Baikal. Here, hard by the old Russian village of Shishkino, can be seen two wild horses and a bison bull, in static poses yet somehow solid and dominating. The artist exaggerated the organs of procreation as if to call attention to the need for fertility, for strength and life, never more manifest than in the act of sexual joining. Artists in the West were wont to express the same concerns, the same need.

In time the trees retreated northward following the ice. Rains diminished, and the long drying up began. New tools and techniques were learned to meet the demands of a changing environment. Some animals disappeared and were replaced by newer prey. So it is that we find, superimposed on the great bison-bull of Shishkino, a reindeer stag with magnificent branching antlers. The stag (and also its cousin the elk—our American moose) was to remain a powerful theme among people who roamed the belt of steppe. However the life ways changed (and they did: the record is plain in the rock annals of Shishkino); whatever other animals, domesticated animals, in time rose to importance, the wild stag retained its grip on human imaginations. It was to figure in the mythologies of many later peoples, peoples such as the Lapps, the Tungus, the Samoyed, peoples who would take to reindeer herding as a way of life. But horse nomads, too, herders of cattle and sheep all across the steppes, would continue to find in the stag their favorite decorative theme. Only horse and rider as a unit would rival the stag in artistic popularity. One group of pastoral nomads destined to roam the plains and plateaus of northern Iran, just south of the Sea of Aral, would call themselves *Saka,* which meant in their Indo-European tongue "stag."

Just how the life ways changed, the exact sequence of learning events which enabled men to tame and herd the animals they once had hunted is not yet plain and may never be so. The progression from plant gathering to plant domestication is somewhat easier to read. The earliest farm villages seem to have been built in Southwest Asia along the "Fertile Crescent," stretching from the Mesopotamian highlands through Palestine and into Egypt. This was some ten to twelve thousand years ago. In northern China along the Hwang, the Yellow, and the Wei rivers, plants were domesticated a bit later, as was also the case in eastern Europe.

The domestication of animals is usually thought to have followed hard upon the beginning of farming. Wild animals during seasons of drought were drawn to farms and to the water on which they were based. Or so the theory goes. They lingered then to be tamed and to be exploited. It makes a tidy sequence. The realities of domestication—could we but see it plain—might be somewhat less tidy; might, indeed, have been different for each potentially tamable animal species. Realities of domestication might even have been different for the same species at different times and in different places. The gentle reindeer, it seems clear, was originally attracted to man, not by his grain, but by his salty urine and by the protection his very presence offered against wolves. The record of reindeer domestication is recent enough for the sequence to have been recorded in the varying lives and habits of reindeer herders of the North: hunters, some of them, who merely followed and guarded the deer from other predators; others who harnessed the animal in draft in addition to slaughtering it at need; still others who rode the animal as one might ride a horse, tended it with care, and used its milk in many dairying operations.

There is some indication in the rock paintings of the Sahara and Arabian deserts that wild cattle and sheep there may have been trapped and penned by hunters who were slowly transforming themselves into herdsmen. The archaeological picture of animal domestication in Eurasia generally, however, suggests for cattle, goats, sheep, and perhaps also the horse, a possible progression from byre and barnyard to herds and open spaces. Apparently marginal gatherers all across the steppe became marginal farmers, scratching for a living in soil too far from streams, too deprived of rain to be very productive. More and more they turned their attention to the barnyard animals which had accompanied the spread of farming techniques. And as more skillful farmers, expanding out of their river basins, pressed the marginal folk for land, those folk became ever more dependent on animals which, after all, could survive with scanty pasture and, stripping that, could be driven to yet another stand of grass. Other folk, hunters living still farther from the settled fields, may have learned to herd the animals of the wilderness without experiencing even a brush with farming ways.

At least part of the sequence from settled farming to nomadic herding can be glimpsed in archaeological sites in southern Russia. Here along the Dnieper River some six thousand years ago were settled communities of farmers who grew grain and raised livestock—cattle, sheep, goats, pigs. Here we see for the first time the bones of domesticated horses—meant for the table, it would seem, or for pulling sledges. Much is represented in clay models, for the Tripolye People (as they are called) recorded thus everything about their lives—the kinds of houses they built, the way they ground grain, the hair styles preferred by the lady of the house. The time span of the culture is long—as much as two thousand years—and through it all we can trace a shift in emphasis from farming to stock breeding. In the Tripolye remains, dating to the year 2000 B.C. or thereabouts, there appears quite suddenly a new, a different type of pottery. Soon thereafter the sites were abandoned, overrun, perhaps, by people who were true pastoral nomads. Or so suggests Dr. E. D. Phillips, the noted student and chronicler of nomad movements in Eurasia.

The sort of people who might have overwhelmed Tripolye villages in their later days have left *their* remains in a site close to the Black Sea and the modern town of Usatova. Here, with the bodies of important persons, were interred less important persons—slaves, perhaps—and also very many horses, clay figurines, copper weapons, all intended to equip, serve, and comfort their owner in the world beyond. The graves of VIPs, slab-lined and arranged so as to include the sacrificed in subsidiary channels, were heaped over with large barrows. How could they be missed?

Farther east and north in a pocket of steppe, where the upper Yenesei and its tributaries approach Lake Baikal, other groups of sites reveal a series of cultures much like those of southern Russia (even in pottery styles) and nearly as long in time depth. Here, too, can be read the gradually increasing importance of stock. Horse and cattle bones appear in the graves of men whose skeletal features identify with those in the graves of Tripolye and Usatova. Remains of camel appear, domesticated here perhaps for the first time.

Sometime around 1100 B.C., the farmers and stock breeders of the upper Yenesei and the Altai highlands received an influx of immigrants whose pottery and weapons are reminiscent of the first Chinese civilization already in flower to the south. Metal objects are skillfully wrought. The shapes of knives and daggers speak of southern influences, but the bold and beautiful heads with which the handles are decorated bear witness to steppe connections and the dominant animal themes of nomad art. These people left behind their bones (thought by specialists to be more Mongoloid in type than those of their predecessors), and they left their art. On rocks and cliffs they painted fantastic creatures half beast, half man, and strange human masks. The fascination with the face appears also on carefully carved upright stones. Alongside the faces are also scratched doodles of various sorts—lines, stick-figure stags, geometric signs. The most important doodle of all appears on one stone: a four-wheeled wagon, horse-drawn. It tells us that here, at this time, the way of the nomad, cut off from the farming fringes, had at last become possible. For there were here in existence the preconditions for nomadic life: the wheel, the draft animal, the portable home. People of the Mongolian steppes today still use similar shelter—the lath-framed, felt-covered yurt.

It was the wheel that first opened the inner reaches of desert and steppe—that made possible the nomad's way, with his wide swings through open land. And the wheel, like herding itself, seems to have been an invention of the steppe fringes among people who had options and knew how to use them.

For long the wheel has been credited to the inventiveness of city people, people who were part of the earliest Mesopotamian civilizations. Its first appearance there is as a pictograph: two circles attached to a sledge. The pictograph is supposed to have been drawn some time around 3000 B.C., though no one can say for sure. Two or three centuries later, city folk of the area were already burying persons of rank right in their carts and wagons. Later still, the two-wheeled cart was used in the area as a battle chariot, drawn by onagers, the domesticated native ass. The ideas of wheel, wagon, animal in harness are thought slowly to have diffused northward.

Not so, says Professor Stuart Piggott, a specialist in the prehistory of Europe. Is it likely, he asks, that a people lacking suitable timber altogether (and Mesopotamian land, being flood plain, was short of hard wood) could or would produce the first solid wheels? Look to the north, he says, to that stretch of wooded hills and plain between the Black and Caspian seas and south of the Caucasus. Here can be found the wherewithal of wheeled vehicles as well as strong animals to draw them—cattle and also horse, native to this region but not to Mesopotamia.

In Soviet Georgia and Armenia, Russian archaeologists have uncovered over twenty-five wagon burials, burials of chieftains, dating back to 2500 B.C. And now that radiocarbon datings earlier than 1500 B.C. all appear to need the addition of hundreds of years to bring them into line with other age scales, the wagon burials of the southern Caucasus may be a great deal older than the dates originally assigned. Certainly it is true that pottery models of wagons from southern Russia have been found in contexts older than 3000 B.C.

Whatever the center of invention, the wheel very quickly accelerated vast movements of peoples. Tribes of herdsmen began to roll westward into Europe—and eastward, too—between and among the resident farmers, wherever there was a spot of graze. The wheel revolutionized warfare. The light, spoke-wheeled chariot gave an army definite advantages over infantry. Some nomad tribes began to use it as an instrument of conquest. One after another, the kingdoms of the Middle East and of the Indian subcontinent fell prey to nomad charioteers.

Very quickly the wheel altered notions of prestige, and the change has been permanent. From chariot to late model sports car, the glamor of the wheeled vehicle has never dimmed. The owner of a modern Rolls-Royce would, of course, never consider using it as his coffin (modern cemeteries are much too crowded and expensive, in any case, to accommodate that sort of passion), but he might well understand the feelings of a nomad chief who refused to leave his wheels behind. Whatever the feelings involved, wagon-and-chariot burials became, early on, obligatory for Very Important Persons. What started out as an imitation of Mesopotamian grandeur quickly developed into a structure and style unique to herding peoples of the steppes. Graves of nomad chiefs, often reminiscent of the ancient pit house, were furnished with luxuries acquired in raids on settled lands, adorned with art in the animal style and with the socketed "battle ax" which has given the life way a name. These chiefly graves have been found across the steppe from end to end and in many time periods.

Such burials have been found in northern China, associated there with the sudden growth of cities and the reign of the kings of Shang—around 1500 B.C. Royal tombs were dug wide enough, deep enough to accommodate, not only beautiful grave furnishings, not only dogs and horses in quantity, but human company by the score. Some of these were evidently charioteers, for their vehicles were buried with them. This is, as far as we now know, the first appearance of the wheel in China. Bronze casting, too, appears for the first time in the royal graves and cities of the Shang Dynasty, and already highly sophisticated in form and technique. Here also appears, and for the first time in China, pictographic writing used for the description and elaboration of prophecy cracks burned in the shoulder blades of oxen and sheep and in turtle carapaces. All else in Shang royal tombs and cities is of a piece with what has gone before. The lines of development can be traced from their village beginnings. Perhaps the antecedents of the beautiful bronzes, the pictographs, the wheeled carts will yet be found among the farming communities which preceded the Shang. Or perhaps the idea of the wheel, the use of metals were brought by nomads, tribe learning from tribe, slowly across the steppes. Wheels, yes. Writing, no. It is hard to associate record keeping with people forever traveling light and traveling far.

The gifts, or at least the manner of their delivery, may

have proved in the long run a mixed blessing. Shang armies were soon equipped with a new war machine, the means of conquest and, through conquest, the means of expansion. Of the barbarians, at whose expense Shang China grew, some had apparently received horse and chariot from the West. Many more had not and would not for a long time to come. Nevertheless, the nomads grew in strength, in influence, and in confidence. Earliest Chinese records refer solemnly to the tributes delivered to court by various wild tribes, but there may have been a good deal of wishful thinking involved.

In 1100 B.C., the Shang Dynasty was overthrown by that of the Chou, a house which originated in Shensi Province, in one of those fingers of steppe which reach into the very center of China. There are in Chou remains elements strongly reminiscent of the nomad life and style. The animal themes in art, the quantity of beautifully made horse gear—masks and harness ornament and chariot poles—all are very like themes and gear to be seen in the western steppes. So are the royal burials with their evidence of great parades preceding the actual interment. Such parades were common among steppe people who demanded, each one, his right to view the body of his chief and to rage at his loss.

Some specialists have suggested that the Chou represent the first of those nomad incursions destined to disrupt and enliven Chinese history from first to last. Others see in the Chou the rise of a people who developed under the influence of two ways of life—Chinese and nomad—and took the best of each.

Having risen to power, the Chou found themselves challenged by nomads on their flanks. In steppe and mountain, marsh and forest, hostile tribesmen seemed to be everywhere. We begin to read in the developing record of history the names of tribes on the fringes of civilization. We hear of a people called Ti: the Red Ti, who dressed all in that color; the Ti who preferred to wear white; the Giant Ti—just how large and in comparison to whom we are not told. We hear of Tung-i in the northeast and of a people in the west called Jung. One early Chou ruler, after a conflict with the Jung, is said to have brought back four wolves and four white stags as tribute. In the ninth century B.C. the records tell of another noble who took a thousand horses from the Jung. A Chou poet from the state of Wei sang triumphantly:

> *We struck the Hsien-yun*
> *And drove them to the great plain.*
> *We sent for our chariots in majestic array*
> *And walled the northern regions.*

That the conquest was not all one-sided we learn from the records as well. Great lords on the empire's marches were not at all loath to seek barbarian alliances in furthering their own political ambitions, and some were willing to marry barbarian women as a pledge of good faith. Ssu-ma Ch'ien, the Grand Historian of the Han Dynasty (he lived around 125 B.C.), tells of one King Hsiang who did just that and then, when his grand design had been achieved, renounced his barbarian queen. He underestimated her resolve, however. Making alliance with the king's hostile stepmother, she called in her father's chariot hordes. Together the two ladies watched as King Hsiang was slain.

Sometime around 900 B.C. the nature of the struggle between farmer and nomad, plow and plain, began to change. Indeed, the very nature of nomadism itself had changed. It was a change which began early in the western steppes and, spreading eastward, replaced the charioteer with the horseman. Man and mount became as one. Draft animals were then hitched only to large conveyances (the old covered wagon remained a staple vehicle and portable home for supplies, for families, and for the traveler less athletic than the iron-kneed equestrian). Riding astride revolutionized men's clothing. Very shortly the tunic was out and pants were in. Pants, the great protector of chafed knees, were of course nothing new to old Asians of the far North who had been wearing tailored garments since before the last glacier's retreat. And it is possible that the idea of pants came down from the northern forest and tundra to horsemen of the steppes.

Everywhere across the steppe region and into plowed lands, chariot brigades gave way to mounted warriors. Cavalrymen of the western kingdoms were armed with lance and spear. Steppe nomads used bows made of laminated horn, resilient and strong. So perfectly trained were steppe horses that the archer's hand was freed for the bow. So secure was his seat that he could deliver arrows rearward over his shoulder in what has come to be called "the Parthian shot."

Mounted warriors were in the armies of the Middle East sometime around 1400 B.C. There is good evidence in the tombs of the Shang that China had encountered mounted riders by 1200 B.C. But the possibilities of cavalry did not catch on for a long time—not until the nomads were themselves mounted and clamoring behind the long walls begun by local marcher lords in the fourth century B.C. to keep them out.

The archaeological record reveals the increase of mounted riders east and west sometime after 800 B.C. Old settlements in Central Asia and the Altai were apparently overrun around that time by new people. The graves reveal new styles in pottery and metal goods, much more emphasis on horse gear, suited not for harness, but for riding astride. Bones of the newcomers themselves reveal a western origin.

Mounted cavalry has the twin advantages of mobility and surprise. A strike force can be in and out of a settlement, loot in hand, almost before the victims know what has happened, certainly before they can mount an effective defense. Given enough such attacks, a farming community might well prefer to pay the nomads protection tribute in grain or even to become grain-raising serfs to nomad overlords, themselves entirely divorced from the soil. Such arrangements were certainly well known and used by nomads of more recent times. History attests to it. There is little reason why earlier nomads should not have exacted similar tribute.

Mounted cavalry makes possible lightning raids on other cavalry as well, quick victories and precipitous retreats. Typical of the horse nomads, says Dr. Phillips, was the rise of tribe over tribe, of royal tribes exacting tribute and fealty from their nomad neighbors. Typical, too, were the shifts in strength, the rebellions, and the battles for supremacy, battles which often ended in headlong flight by the defeated tribe. In its line of retreat there inevitably loomed other tribes who must be fought and pushed aside. And so it was that each power struggle on the steppes sent a series of shock waves rolling east and west.

Middle Eastern history records many of these struggles. One involved a people called the Cimmerians who, around 800 B.C., traveled the southern Russian plains and points west and east. It may have been some of their outliers or allies who overran the Altai settlements. By the late 700s the Indo-European-speaking Cimmerians were driven by related Scythians out of their homelands. They fled into Anatolia, attacking villages and kings, destroying along the way. Eventually they were penned up, one group in Anatolia, another on the Crimea where they disappear from history. East of the Scyths roamed tribes of Iranian Sakas and east of them, near the Dzungarian Gates, a shadowy folk known to the West as the Massagetae (the Chinese would have another name for them). Allied to the Massagetae were the Sauromates, forebears of the later Sarmatians, who would drive the Scyths into a Crimean refuge as they themselves had driven the Cimmerians. For

**Migrations and Invasions
400 B.C. to A.D. 700**

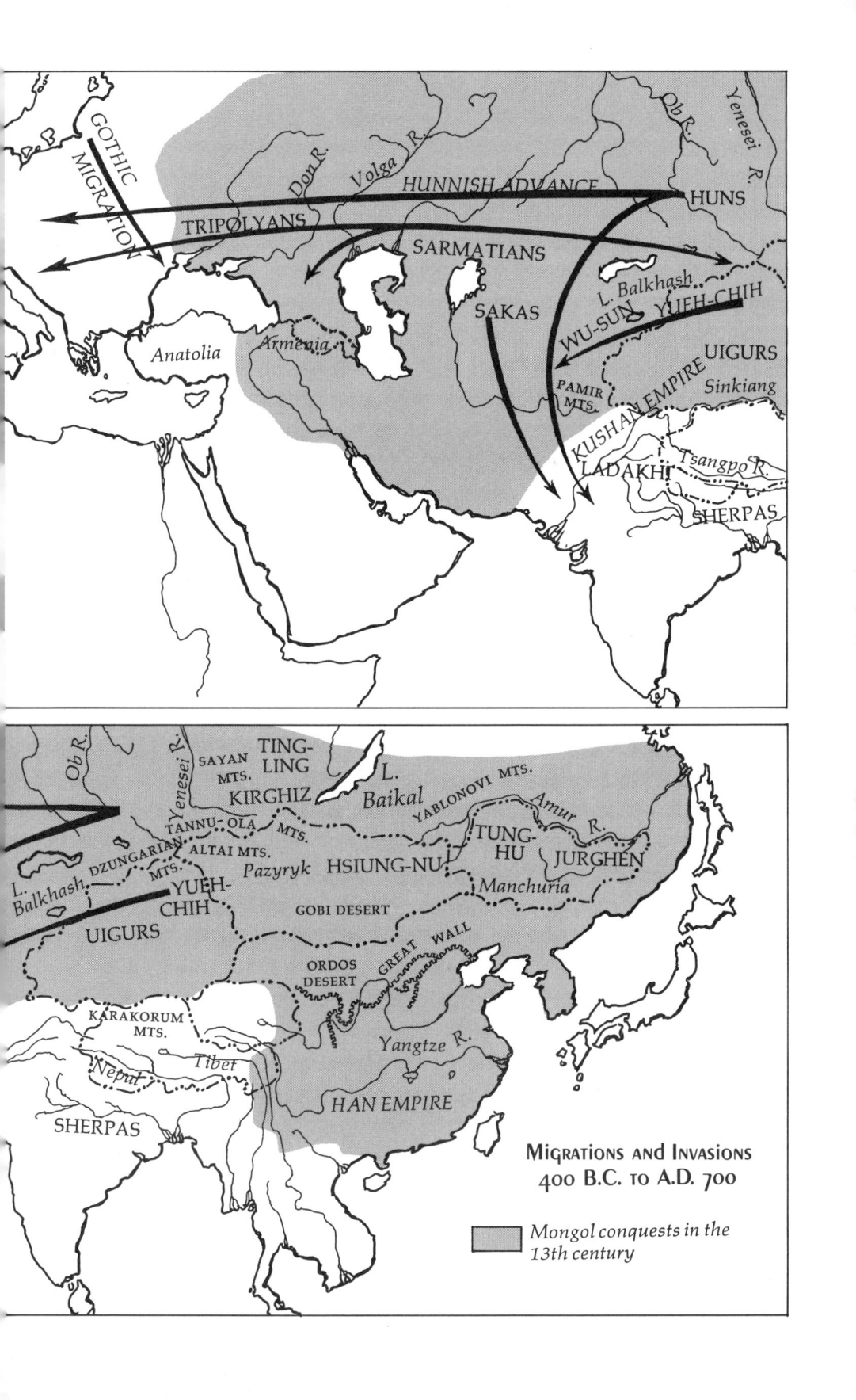

Mongol conquests in the
13th century

nearly a thousand years these tribes would truly wander the breadth of the steppe, contesting with China at one end and with Rome at the other. It is they who are credited with the invention of armor made of iron scales and of the stirrup which gave the mounted rider a steadier seat.

In Scythian times (fifth and sixth centuries B.C.) the animal art of the steppes was brought to its finest expression. Borne by a chain of wanderers, it traveled east. In the Altai region called Pazyryk where modern Russia, Mongolia, and China meet, there have been found tombs very like those of Scythian chieftains farther west: deep pits lined and roofed with timber, divided into outer and inner rooms, one for the sacrificed horses, the elegant wheeled bier and work wagon; one for the chief and his sacrificed wife or companion. Clothing, felt rugs on walls and underfoot (all bearing beautiful appliqué designs), grave goods, fanciful masks worn by the horses, indeed, the horses themselves, all are preserved in ice. For the tombs were early filled with seepage which, in this region of permafrost, froze forever.

The art styles to be seen in the Pazyryk tombs were Scythian, enriched by Chinese influences. They appeared sometime after 500 B.C. in the Ordos and Gobi deserts. Soon after that they reached Pacific shores. Rock drawings along the Amur River give testament to the change. For long the fishermen of the region had recorded on the cliffs artistic evidence of a system of thought, a focus of interest somewhat different from that of the forest hunters to the north and west. In spite of their daily calling, they did not turn to the fish for inspiration. Their drawings, instead, depicted water fowl, sometimes elk and deer, sometimes snakes—all drawn in curiously static fashion without the sense of motion characteristic often of the hunter artists. And the Amur people had a veritable fascination with masks, strange masks ornamented with curls and spirals reminiscent of the Jomon pottery masks across the sea in Japan.

All these themes, says Professor Okladnikov, linger in the legends of Tungus fisher people living in the area today, people who speak of Fadzya, the old woman who is mistress of the hearth and of the great elk who rules the sky.

Between and among the wild-fowl forms and the masks, superimposed on them are newer themes—figures of mounted riders, speeding figures, figures in motion, hunting, herding, waging war. Here the record of contact is clear—Amur people with nomads of the steppes and with the warrior way of life. And the mounted warriors sped on. By A.D. 400, so holds Professor Namio Egami, the way of the horseman, complete with all its trappings, had spread to Japan.

What of the people among whose shards and bones we have irreverently wandered? What languages did they speak, whence did they come? Without samples of writing, the specialist can provide only educated guesses about language groups. He is on somewhat safer ground with skeletal evidence. Even there, however, the evidence is not always easily interpreted. The archaeologist inevitably encounters in each skeletal population a range of individual differences, whatever the general continuities in nose shape and head length and size of eye opening. Still, differences *between* two populations can often be noted and newcomers to a given population identified. The spread of style in art and artifact is easier to read. And when, in time, the written record becomes available, it can be extrapolated backward through the years, can cast light (however dim) on unreadable artifacts, can relate people to events.

We can say with certainty that tides of people moved for centuries over the steppe corridor, leaving behind their physical features and their cultural creations. Mixed farming and stock breeding spread early, borne by people of mostly Europoid looks. The original intrusion was augmented at the time of mounted nomadism, and eventually the western groups in farther Asia acquire names and a history of sorts, first in the ancient Chinese documents dating back to Shang Dynasty times, then vividly and clearly in the records of China's Han Dynasty (206 B.C.–A.D. 220), in the works of Ssu-ma Ch'ien, the Grand Historian. Mentioned in his works are the Ting-ling, the Wu-sun who inhabited lands around Lake Baikal and the Altai Mountains, and the Yueh-chih, who lived farther to the west. Ssu-ma Ch'ien describes well the life ways of these people (all much alike, he says). Their wanderings, their dependence on their herds for food and shelter, their skilled archers, their daring battle tactics, all are noted. He says nothing whatever about their appearance. It is only in documents of later times, particularly in those of the T'ang Dynasty (A.D. 618–907), that we hear of blue-eyed, blond Wu-sun and Ting-ling and learn that the Yueh-chih, though much mixed in ethnic character, probably included people with Western faces.

Perhaps it is these people whose chiefs fill the tombs of Pazyryk. Here we can be sure of looks, for the bodies, like their furs and felts, were frozen. They are of mostly Europoid type although several are Asiatic. One chieftain, magnificently tattooed, looks wonderfully like an eastern Turk or Mongol of today. The Yueh-chih historically wandered in lands around the Dzungarian Gates and the Tarim Basin up to the foothills of Nan Shan. One of their subject groups were the Tocharians (*T'u-hulo,* sometimes *Ta-hi* in the chronicles) who spoke, it is known, an Indo-European language. Some scholars believe the Yueh-chih are one and the same with the Massagetae described in the histories of the West. There remain to this day in the Pamir Mountains refuge, herding peoples whose Iranian languages remind us that western battle-ax people once ranged the East.

Up to the fifth century B.C., the traffic in ideas and the major intrusions of steppe people were moving from west to east. After 500 B.C., the trend was decidedly reversed.

When the Han Dynasty came to power in 206 B.C., after

having overthrown the lords of Ch'in who had, in their turn, displaced the Chou, they faced a new and powerful nomad enemy, the Hsiung-nu. In Chinese, the word translates as "fierce slaves"; its Turkic original we do not know. Ssu-ma Ch'ien quotes the adviser of a Han king as he describes the Hsiung-nu:

The Hsiung-nu move on the feet of swift war horses, and in their breasts beat the hearts of beasts. They shift from place to place as fast as a flock of birds so that it is extremely difficult to corner them and bring them under control. . . . From the most ancient times the Hsiung-nu have never been regarded as a part of humanity.

The Chinese may well have considered the Hsiung-nu outside the realm of human ways (which, after all, were Chinese ways), but human they were, and for the first time in Ssu-ma Ch'ien's records we hear human stories about them. We hear of Tumen, chief of the Hsiung-nu. He had come to power at about the same time that Kao-tsu, the first Han emperor, came to power in China. Earlier, Tumen had led his people far into the deserts of Mongolia to escape the attacks of Ch'in armies, and then, hearing of the civil strife in China, came back in strength.

We hear, through Ssu-ma Ch'ien, of Tumen's son, Modun, whom the father disliked and wished to disinherit. To accomplish this end, he sent Modun as hostage to the Yueh-chih, then attacked that tribe, knowing it meant his son's sure death. But Modun escaped and made his way home. There he was greeted with honors and given a command. What, after all, could the old chief do but put a good face on the situation?

Modun, too, hid his anger and waited. Meanwhile he trained his men, sometimes with great cruelty, to obey without question. They were to shoot at once anything at which he directed a whistling arrow—be it his own favorite dog or horse or wife. Eventually, the arrow was launched at Tumen, a whole flight followed, and Modun became Shan-yu, or Khan of the Hsiung-nu.

The other nomad tribes, supposing Modun to be young and weak, tested him. He feigned submissiveness. Then, striking swiftly, he defeated first the Tunghu in the east, then the Yueh-chih. These went caroming off to the west, pursued by Modun's Wu-sun allies. In their flight, the Yueh-chih would defeat several Iranian tribes and establish in what are now the Turkmen and Uzbek republics of the U.S.S.R., the kingdom of Kushan.

Han rulers alternately placated and attacked the Hsiung-nu. Three kings of Han were to send royal princesses to marry barbarian chiefs. Kao-tsu, moved by the tears of his wife, appointed a substitute daughter, and apparently Modun never discovered the deception. In later years, when he was old and lonely and Kao-tsu long in his grave, Modun proposed marriage to the imperial widow, presumably as lonely as himself. The cruel and indomitable empress was enraged by Modun's barbarian effrontery, and only the wisdom and exquisite tact of her advisers prevented her instant declaration of war.

Kao-tsu's son, King Wen, always a man of his word, did send his daughter to yet another Shan-yu. With her went a very reluctant courtier (made eunuch for what crime or whim we are not told). He warned the king that no good would come of this uprooting and made good his prophecy by transferring his loyalty to the Hsiung-nu at the earliest possible moment. King Wen's grandson, Wu Ti, sent a princess (though not his own daughter) to the old chief of the Wu-sun, hoping thus to drive a wedge between them and their Hsiung-nu overlords. The pretty princess wrote a poem which somehow found its way home though she did not:

My family has married me
   In this far corner of the world,
Sent me to a strange land,
   To the king of Wu-sun,
A yurt is my chamber,
   Felt my walls,
Flesh my only food,
   Kumiss to drink.
My thoughts are all of home,
   My heart aches within.
O to be the yellow crane
   Winging home again!

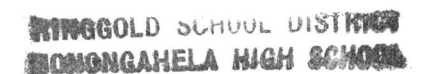

The Han had a long time in which to try all expedients in their dealings with the barbarians, for the Hsiung-nu lasted as a tribal confederation from about 200 B.C. to A.D. 300, longer than did the Han Dynasty itself. In their heyday, the Hsiung-nu extended from Korea to the Altai. For the first time, a nomadic horde was organized into something close to a state. Profiting from the Chinese example, Modun and his successors strove for unity among the diverse tribes, organizing the territory into units, dividing political responsibility, and seeking the best advice. He had it in plenty. Many Chinese officials deserted to his cause. Many others were captured and, while captive, were persuaded to serve. It is easy to understand why.

> *If a battle is going well for them [said Ssu-ma Chien of the Hsiung-nu], they will advance. But if it is not they will retreat, for they do not consider it a disgrace to run away. Their only concern is self advantage, and they know nothing of propriety or righteousness.*

The Chinese soldier was instructed to die rather than retreat, and the honorable general, bested in battle, was expected to be a suicide. Should he, in spite of orders, return from defeat in one piece, he might find himself under sentence of death back home.

Eventually, with the help of wily ambassadors and the expenditure of many royal princesses, the Chinese managed to effect with diplomacy what they could not with force. They split the Hsiung-nu into antagonistic groups who were opposed by other hordes, those of the Yueh-chih and the Wu-sun as well as by the imperial armies, until at last they were spent. By A.D. 220, as the weakening Han Dynasty fell in a flurry of barbarian activity along the walls, many Hsiung-nu had themselves become members of the Chinese gentry in frontier areas around Tunhuang, that contested area now on the edge of Sinkiang Province. Indeed the rulers of one group of Hsiung-nu, mindful of the many Chinese princesses in their line, considered themselves for a time at least the proper successors to the fallen Han.

Out in the steppes, other Hsiung-nu clans joined with tribes of various origins to form a new horde, that of the Huns, a mostly Turkic-speaking group. These new contenders did not try their strength against China but instead moved westward, conquering and amalgamating as they went. They added as allies the southward-trending German tribes. By A.D. 434 the Huns threatened Rome. Europe was not overrun only because Attila, the Hunnish leader died. His German allies then revolted and defeated Attila's disheartened army which ebbed to the Black Sea region and was eventually lost to view.

In the hub of Mongolia and Altai, new groups of nomads consolidated, confederated, and grew strong. This time they were Mongolian in heritage. The Chinese called them Juan-Juan. They had their day and were eclipsed as Turkic-speaking hordes in their turn rose to prominence. The Juan-Juan fled west and became known in Europe as the Avars, Slav-conquering, Slav-ruling. The Turks, following hard on Avar heels, established their own states as far west as the Caucasus.

By A.D. 745 this Turkic empire had been appropriated first by the learned and sophisticated Uigurs, oasis-dwellers, converts to Nestorian Christianity, then by the wild Kirghiz who now included the Turkicized Ting-ling. The skill of Kirghiz ironsmiths became well known, and the Kirghiz established trade ties with China, the Arabs, and Tibet.

Earlier tribal conflicts in the eastern steppe seem to have pitted tribesmen of largely Western origin against Turko-Tatar speaking nomads whose origins lay in the lands around Lake Baikal, and in the Taiga to the north. Later power struggles were in the nature of a family fight.

The Turko-Tatar languages (one large grouping in the Ural-Altaic phylum) include the Mongol (from the Chinese *mengu*, sometimes *tata-mengu*, the *tata* representing yet another Chinese generic name for barbarian), the Turkic (from *Tu-chueh*, originally intended to name a nomad political confederation), and the more distantly related Tungus. Their speakers are (or were before western dilutions) look-alikes. Certainly language similarities would indicate a separation into isolated groups not too far in the past.

For long, control of the eastern steppes swung between Turks and Mongols. The Turks who displaced the Juan-Juan were displaced in their turn by the Khitans, who most specialists believe to have been at least a partly Mongolic group of tribes traveling on or near the borders of Tung-pei (Manchuria). In A.D. 905, the Khitans invaded China and returned, bringing with them, so it is said, sixty-five thousand captives who were forced to build a Khitan city with all the comforts and amenities known to civilized folk farther south. Then, not content with a part of China at home, they craved the Chinese all. Recrossing the Wall, they established in northern China from the tenth to the twelfth centuries their own rule and their own dynasty, that of Liao.

By this time, Turkic-speaking folk in the steppe hub had

become quiescent, subject to Mongol overlords. All their martial energy was playing itself out on western stages. The Khazar Khanate, the Bulgars, Magyars, Ghuzz, Patzinak, and Seljuk, not to speak of the later Ottomans, all were Turkic tribes which, at one time or another, threatened, dominated, or held the balance of power in the West. In time some embraced Christianity; others converted to Islam. After the rise and fall of Khitan, all the power struggles of the East would pit Mongol against Tungus.

The peoples of Tung-pei had long been known to the Chinese. Through them we hear first of the ancient, almost mythical Sushen; then of the Tung-hu, opponents and later confederates of the Hsiung-nu. We hear of the Hsien-pi, the Mo-ho of the sixth and seventh centuries A.D. The Chinese chronicler credits the Mo-ho with ferocity, says they hunted with bows and poisoned, stone-tipped arrows, adds, with some distaste, information about their hygiene. It appears they washed with urine and allowed the bones of their dead to be cleaned by wild animals (all customs which were shared by more northerly folk).

The Mo-ho may have outraged Chinese sensibilities; they nevertheless managed to build a state which they called Po-hai. It was dissolved by invading Khitan Mongols, but the urge to ride and rule, once realized, can never be entirely extinguished. Statehood rose again in Tung-pei, impelled by the wild, Tungusic-speaking Jurchen tribe of the North. By 1123 the Jurchen had replaced the Khitans in Tung-pei, had taken over much of northern China, and had styled their new-founded dynasty Chin. The Jurchen emperors, however, had the bad sense to rule despotically and with cruelty. Worse yet, they discounted the threat of nomads beyond the walls, a threat to which they should have been acutely sensitive. One Jurchen emperor saw fit (so the story goes) to execute with particular torture three important Mongol chieftains. Their kinsman, a young man named Timuchen, swore vengeance. He took the name Genghis Khan.

Through superb generalship and a compelling personality, Genghis Khan confirmed his own clan leadership, drawing to his standard other clans of the Mongols and then other nomad tribes until he had collected a horde of consequence. His men were superbly trained and superbly led, but his concerns did not end with the military. Like Modun before him he set out to unify the Mongols and their allies. Toward this end, he examined the religions of East and West and gave their priests the freedom of Mongol encampments. Lamas bringing the Tibetan form of Buddhism were given particular encouragement. Many years later this encouragement would have important consequences. Genghis Khan had his scribes make use of Uigur Turkish script rather than the ideographic writing of China. To his court he brought Persians, Turks, Christians from the West, anyone skilled in the art of statecraft, hoping thus to lessen the nomad's inevitable dependence on Chinese bureaucracy. He also favored trade and traders. (In the South, cut off from the old overland routes, the Sung Dynasty was forced to place its faith in shipping.)

Eventually the empire of Genghis Khan and of his sons stretched across Asia from southern Russia to the Pacific, from Palestine across northern India to Tibet. At one point it seemed that all Europe must surely surrender to the Mongol hordes. But then their khan, the son of Genghis, died, and his armies, like those of Attila long before, withdrew to the steppes of southern Russia. There they remained for two hundred years —the once-powerful Golden Horde, weakening, fading slowly into oblivion.

The Mongolic Yuan Dynasty in China was eventually overthrown by a resurgent Chinese dynasty, that of the Ming who held power until 1644. In that year armies of the Manchu (a southern Tungusic tribe), in concert with their Mongol auxiliaries, made themselves masters of China. They made themselves masters as well of the Mongolian and Turkic tribes of their borders and beyond. Having learned well the lessons of the steppes, they divided the tribes, intervened in petty steppe conflicts, offered princely titles to nomad chiefs, and became their liege lords. While their dynasty prevailed (and it lasted until 1911) there were no further incursions from the steppes. And, forgetting their Tungusic tongue, their Tungusic ways, the Manchu became in time more Chinese than the people they had conquered.

For the nomad, lured by the riches of settled lands, is ever fated to lose, to give over that which made him strong in the beginning. However much his leaders exhort him to honor the good old ways, the hard life, the simple food, the traditional religion, in the long run he cannot. Thus does the civilized nation—if its numbers and skills are great—conquer those by whom it has been conquered. Thus does the flypaper swallow the fly.

6

THE NORTHERN TUNGUS
From Taiga to Great Wall

Long, long ago when man became human, when he learned to speak and, in speaking, fell heir to past and future, he learned as well the reality of death. Pain, the herald of that end, could now be described and, with description, came experience, anticipation, dread. But to be human is also to be curious, to be adaptable, to be inventive. To be human is to seek or to create meaning where there appears to be none at all and, in meaning, to survive.

And so it is that, for all people, the world seen and the world unseen take particular forms, shapes, intentions, are activated by particular laws. And always there are some individuals more learned in these laws than others, more skilled in dealing with the special reality a people over its long history has come to see. These specialists are in touch with the powers of life. They are for a people its teachers, healers, protectors.

They are shamans, and their profession must surely have existed since human time began.

We know there were shamans practicing during the last Ice Age perhaps fifty to fifteen thousand years ago. Their images can be found among the painted herds of animals which adorn ancient caves of southern France and northern Spain. Dressed in bird masks or animal skins, dancing among the thronging beasts, theirs are images of power. On the cliff walls of Shishkino are also creatures half man, half beast. And in a tomb of the steppe people at Pazyryk was found the felt appliqué image of a being with the body of a griffon, the curling horns of a stag, and the face and arms of a man. Was this meant to be the shaman in his power guise, enlarged and emboldened by the strength of his animal helpers?

Among the Evenki and the Eveni (Lamuts)—both Reindeer Tungus of Manchuria and points north—there is (or was as late as the 1930s) a belief that each shaman's ancestor, the one from whom he had acquired his lore, lived in the other world as a creature half animal and half man. Every Tungus had three souls, but one of the shaman's souls found its home in a spirit beast, a double who lived and served and died with its owner.

Some professional secrets, apparently, like the profession itself are as old as time. But others begin in a particular shaman's specialty and spread abroad. One "school" of shamanism seems to have developed in the particular knot of piney-wood taiga, mountain, and steppe occupied by Turko-Tatar and Samoyedic-speaking people before their scattering, their separation from one another. The Samoyeds seem to have been first to depart and the others thereafter. Tungus, in their own journeys toward the sea, then developed shamanistic specialties peculiar to themselves. It is no accident that Western scholarship has used "shaman," the Tungus word, to describe all healers and teachers of a certain sort. The word, along with specific concepts and techniques, has been borrowed by many Siberian neighbors of the Tungus. Among the Ainu, whose religious leaders were all family elders, the specialist who could heal or harm was addressed by an Ainu term which meant "the double-lived one." What he did, however, was described with the Tungus word, *e-shaman-ki*, performing the work of a shaman. The Chukchi have adapted for their own use the Tungusic word for storytelling. Among the Tungus, storytelling is part of a shaman's business. It is thus that he teaches the lore of the tribe, the virtue of the good old ways, and he does it as entertainingly as possible in order to make the lessons stick.

He tells his listeners of the construction of the universe, of the ordering of the three worlds lying one atop the other, layer-cake fashion, and explains that spirit people live in the top and bottom layers much as do Tungus in the middle zone. He speaks of the sky, a great deerskin sieved with holes through which shines the light of stars. Men may, if they are adventurous enough, climb into the upper layer through the north star's opening. "But don't do that," he warns. "I'll only have to go bring you back again. Just look," he says, pointing to the constellation we call the Big Dipper and Russians the Great Bear. "There is the heavenly elk pursued by hunters. See the ski trail they have left behind." To us, this is the Milky Way. "The elk," he continues, "will not suffer himself to be killed. Frightened out of their wits, the hunters forever change places and so are frozen in the hunt for good and all."

In complex states of every sort, the religion of priests often differs from that of the ordinary folk who come to worship at temple now and then but must concentrate on the dailiness of life. The priest, released as he is from toil, has time for thought. His religious world is therefore more intricate than that of the layman, riddled with contradictions to be argued learnedly among his fellows. For the priest is an organization man, holding his authority by virtue of his membership in a trained and select group. The shaman, on the other hand, must have personal contact with the other world or be no shaman at all. He functions on his own, an individualist from first to last. Even the spiritual free lance, however, blessed with some leisure, generous patrons, and the occasional company of his peers can give his time to speculation and to the construction of a complex shaman's universe. And so it was with the shamans of the Reindeer Tungus.

The shaman's universe, like that of the ordinary Tungus, was divided, but its worlds lay flat as the horizon is flat and joined the way countries join, not as stacked boxes are joined. The shaman's universe lay outside the layman's universe but was magically connected to it by the great river of life. Whirlpools in earthly rivers could suck the unwary into the great river, which flowed from the east and turned north through the shaman's universe. Each of its tributaries was owned by a particular shaman. There dwelt his spirit helpers and, around its pools, the human souls of those yet to be born, of Tungus who would in time be his special care. In the most distant part of the shaman's universe dwelt the Creator who, with the aid of water fowls, had produced the universe in all its layered and bounded manifestations; who, with the aid of the dog, had caused human beings to appear. In that most distant world lived, too, the Creator's older brother, the jealous one, bringer of sickness and disruption to the lives of men.

Juggling two conceptions of cosmic reality—one a set of stacked boxes and one a string of magical zones—perplexed the Tungus shaman not at all. It should not perplex us, either. We do not see the curve of our earth or feel its movement in space, and so we daily orient thinking and action to a stationary world, one which lies flat and on which we can progress geographically from point to point. Yet all the while we *know* that our earth is really globular, know that straight-line travel on its surface will bring us inevitably back to our place of departure. We *know* that we are in motion: that earth orbits sun, that sun swings in its own great arcs, that universe itself revolves and whirls. We *know* that our orientation is "up" as well as "across," and we inhabit the two realities simultaneously. So did the Tungus shaman who could follow in his mind the travels of his spirit helpers as they ranged at his bidding the two realities, the two worlds horizontal and vertical.

In a nearby zone of the horizontal shaman's world lived the shaman's spirit ancestor, his predecessor on earth. And it was to this ancestor and to other celestial personages that the shaman sent his animal soul and his spirit helpers (themselves in animal guise) to learn how to cure the sick persons in his care. The quest was always begun at night in the shaman's tent, a special one built for the healing act. It was guarded with wooden images of spirit helpers—mainly elk, wild deer, and bear—and by a fence of young larches planted upside down to symbolize the great life tree. Another tree was placed inside the tent, its crown thrusting through the roof hole. Up this tree would climb the spirit helpers in their quest for ghostly advice.

The congregation arrived with the patient to be treated, threading their way around the many images, seating themselves timidly around the small, dim fire. The shaman was helped by his human assistant into a special robe—armor against enemy shamans—and then given his drum. The drum was at once weapon, shield, and boat on which to sail the great river of life.

The shaman sounded his drum softly, slowly. Then came the spirit beings one by one, on cue. As each approached, the spectators trembled, for they could hear its cries and groans. Indeed, they could all but see its form as the shaman dramatically described its appearance and mood and then, yawning wide, took it into himself. Once assembled and internalized, the spirits were then sent forth, each on a separate errand into the nether world. The shaman himself enacted their journeys.

Drumming, singing, dancing until he fell entranced to the tent floor. Tungus shamans did not travel by means of drugs. They did not use the hemp of the Mongols or the mushroom sought by the Chukchi. The insistent rhythm of the drum, the tinkling iron ornaments of the shaman's robe, the urgency and fear of the assembled throng—these were force enough to send his soul flying and his body tumbling to earth.

He revived as the spirits returned with their messages, as they described the exact nature of the evil spirits harbored within the patient (always animal spirits—wolf or ferret, wolverine or stoat) and revealed the identity of the enemy shaman who had sent these evil ones. Then was begun the second phase of treatment. The evil had to be lured forth with the meat of a sacrificed reindeer or hounded forth by one of the shaman's allies: the goose who probed, the bear who rent. Once out of the patient's body, the evil could be trapped (horror among the vulnerable spectators!) and sent back into the nether world pursued by the shaman's own spirit troops, bent on revenge. This accomplished, the shaman could relax. He was free to smoke and tell stories, free to divine the future for those who remained. This he did with the shoulder blade of a reindeer, holding it over the flames and noting the pattern of cracks and fissures which appeared.

Was it all hocus-pocus? To us, yes. To a few shamans themselves, perhaps. To most of them, no. To the people themselves, most certainly no. Believing made it so, made of ventriloquism the voices of spirits, made visible the shaman's second self, made possible the climb up the tree of life. If the shaman failed to cure, then one of the helpers was to blame. Surely each had his weakness as well as his strength and his own malice, too. And if the patient died, would not his soul be conducted by the shaman himself to the other world, there to await rebirth?

But not all patients died. There were cures, many cures,

particularly in cases of mental and emotional distress. A damaged world can be reconstructed, after all, only with its own building materials, with its own symbols and images. And the shaman helped the process along. In this he functioned (as all shamans still in practice continue to function) much as does the psychiatrist in our world. Modern specialists, some of them, have begun to see the connection and to treat with respect their colleagues of other cultures.

In the days when the Soviet Union was concentrating on another kind of reconstruction, a social reconstruction among its tribal wards, when it hoped to make of every Tungus a model Soviet citizen, indistinguishable from the Moscow man in the street, then the shaman was seen, not as a sort of healer or psychiatrist, but as an enemy of change and a champion of bad old ways. He was, after all, a highly influential figure among his people. He was also an indispensable part of the clan system. And clans were rich in reindeer, or rather, some members of clans were rich in reindeer while others were poor. So it seemed, at least, to the Soviet specialists on the scene. The clan system, moreover, was thought to be incompatible with the collective farm system. According to the Soviet ideal, cooperation should be based not on the family but on economic comradeship. Sentiment should be vested not in the family but in the state from which all blessings flow.

Long before the appearance of the Russian State (Soviet or Czarist), however, long before the appearance of the Manchu State or even the Chinese dynasties in their stately alternation, the Northern Tungus clan was the means of organizing a far-flung and wandering people, of binding them together and making them one. Czarist Russians, unlike the later Soviets, found the clan a convenient tool of administration and plumed themselves on its introduction. At that time the Reindeer Tungus along the disputed Manchurian border were wont to have two things to say about their clans. When speaking in

Russian to a Russian, they would say, "Before the Russians came, we were wild people and knew nothing of the clan." When speaking in Tungus among themselves or to one who had troubled to learn their language, they would say, "We always had our clans, and we lived by our clans, but nowadays clan organization is dying." So we learn from the great Russian ethnographer S. M. Shirokogoroff, who lived among the Tungus of Manchuria and of the Baikal region in Siberia from 1912 to 1918.

The clan, whenever it is used as a means of organizing larger family relatedness, has a quite specific meaning. It includes all those people who believe themselves related through a common ancestor (in the Tungus case, always a male ancestor) and bear a common name. The believing part is important, for the exact way in which clan members are affiliated may not be directly traceable—not in the way a family line, a lineage, can be traced. (Remember the Biblical "begats"? "Terah begat Abram, Nahor, and Haran; and Haran begat Lot." That's a lineage.) Because clans include many lineages, the exact links among these are often unclear. Adoptive members, even outsiders can easily be incorporated, and the clan grows. Some Tungus clans in the old days numbered as many as a thousand members.

The fact that actual blood ties may be thin makes all the more necessary their constant affirmation. And so it was that Tungus clansmen were bound in the nether world, bound by spirits good and bad which were attached to each clan. It was in the management of these spirits that the shaman figured. And he had to belong to, had to be part of the clan. No outsider could deal with a clan's spirits. No outsider could neutralize their danger and command their aid. There were, therefore, no female shamans among the Tungus. Women marry out of the clan. Even though when ill they return to the shamans of their own clan to be healed, they may not remain with their original clan.

To marry out of the clan is a prime rule among the Tungus. Yet, with the family groups always on the move, in touch with clansmen and often no other folk, how did a young man find a bride? Clans solved the problem by traveling in clan pairs which exchanged their young people, preferably on a brother-sister basis. ("You give me your daughter for my son, and your son can have my daughter.") Generations of exchange usually resulted in everyone's being married to a kind of cousin—what the anthropologist calls the cross-cousin, child of one's mother's brother or father's sister. And since the clan as a whole was responsible for providing each young man with the many reindeer or horses needed as presents to the bride's parents, responsible for providing the dowry for each young girl, clan partnership kept the wealth circulating, but always in a predictable round.

But what if, in one year, the clan elders were presented with a hundred marriageable young men for whom the partner clan could supply only fifty suitable brides? In such dire circumstance, Shirokogoroff tells us, the clan with surplus males would have to scout out another friendly clan, not too far away, or, failing that, would have to split itself in twain, split into two exogamic, outmarrying units. It was a matter not to be taken lightly, for the spirits in such an emergency had themselves to be divided, and who knew whether they would agree to that? Only a trial separation would discover whether the groups could live and travel apart as two separate clans.

Decisions of this sort were made in clan council. Here came the elders, men who were heads of individual families and all unmarried men over twenty-five (though they usually remained silent). Here, too, were bidden women, those who were widowed and continued to act as family head until sons should succeed to authority. They exercised as much influence as any man there present.

It was the clan council which chose its temporary war leaders, the chairman for each meeting, sometimes a chief.

Clans did not necessarily have elected, permanent leaders. The clan that did tolerated no bossy behavior on the leader's part, no independent action without benefit of advice from the council. Harsh words were never permitted in meetings. There were no heated arguments, no disputation. Each speaker waited his turn for recognition and then presented his opinion quietly, without arrogance, without flattery, and with perfect candor. This, says Shirokogoroff, was the Tungus way.

Here in council it was decided whether feuds with other clans should be prosecuted, whether misbehaving members needed punishment, and how the general welfare could best be achieved. All herders of the Northern Tungus were required to help provide bridewealth and dowry. And a general reapportionment of deer or horses took place inevitably in case of epidemic or other natural disaster. The individual family which had lost its deer could not be allowed to starve. What with gift giving and reapportionment, every family of a clan was, in the old days, pretty much like every other. There existed no Tungus words for rich and poor. These were borrowed in later times from the Chinese.

Each clan maintained with the help of its shamans long oral histories, records of battle and conquest which dimmed into the usual travelogue—how they moved from west to east, from south to north, or in the other direction. Only a few of the Southern Tungus tribes in what is now Manchuria claimed to be aboriginal in the area. And only the Nanai (or the Goldi as they are sometimes called) harked back to an island home somewhere in the East.

There are stories of travel because the Tungus *did* travel, late and soon. The facts of language similarity bespeak a point of origin, a home common alike to the language ancestors of the Mongols, the Turks, and the Samoyeds. Some have thought to locate that common home in Mongolia. Others, like Shirokogoroff, have pointed to northern China around the mouth of the Yellow River. From there, he believes, the Tungus were pushed by expanding Chinese into Manchuria where they displaced, in their turn, the Paleoasiatic folk native to the region. Some then moved even further northward, mingling with Yukaghir en route.

Other Russian specialists discount such a beginning for the Tungus, a beginning in steppes and plains, and think instead of a taiga origin somewhere around the headwaters of the Yenesei and Lake Baikal. From here the Tungus are thought to have spread north and east, funneling slowly into Manchuria. Perhaps it was the pressure of herding folk and the influx of nomads from the West that started the Tungus travels, perhaps not. In any case, those travels cannot have begun too anciently. The dialects of the Southern Tungus—Manchus, Nanais, and others south of the Sungari Basin—and those of the tribes of northern Manchuria and Siberia differ from one another a good deal. But the various dialects of Northern Tungusic peoples are close enough to be mutually intelligible.

Whenever the Tungus moved east, it was as hunters that they moved, hunters on skis, for the winters are long in the region around Baikal, and the snows are absent only a month or two in the year. Those Tungus who penetrated to the ocean shore seem to have mingled with Paleoasiatics, taken up fishing as an additional means of livelihood, and learned a new fund of lore. Still, hunting ways and the hunter's world remained in the ascendant.

Those Tungus who traveled south into fertile lands fell under Chinese influences and became farmers and pig breeders. Others, under the influence of steppe folk became horsemen and warriors. Again, the old hunting ways were not forgotten. Some horsemen, so Shirokogoroff tells us, hunted to feed their horses as well as themselves. Unlike the resourceful reindeer with his diet of lichens, horses are unable to forage for themselves during the winter. If their owner lacked fodder, what else should a horse be fed but meat? And since, like the Reindeer Tungus, Tungus horsemen were freed by their womenfolk of most herding cares, there was time aplenty in which to indulge the passion for the hunt.

Yet, says Shirokogoroff, for all this love of hunting, Tungus did not kill unnecessarily, not for sport alone but for need. Game had to be shared amongst the hunter's clanspeople and nothing of it eaten by himself. His own hunger had, perforce, to wait upon their successful hunts in turn. The forest which was home to the game was likewise carefully protected and shared. No fire could be left ablaze on the hunter's departure to start a later conflagration.

Some animals—bear and tiger in particular—were treated with elaborate respect. As they were thought to abhor iron and therefore guns, the careful hunter tried to leave such weapons at home when in their particular territories. They would not kill the unarmed man who spoke kindly to them, though certainly the bear was thought to be more reliable than the tiger in this respect. Tungus women in the old days were quite content to pick berries in the same meadow where a bear was also berrying. In this special relationship with the bear we are reminded of the Ainu, the Chukchi, and other hunting folk farther north.

Should a bear be killed, its meat was cooked by men, not by women, and the meat consumed in a thanking feast. Its head and bones were ceremonially displayed on a framework especially constructed for the occasion. Some Northern Tungus believed—and perhaps believe to this day—that man was created from parts of a bear. There were other stories in which hero and bear wrestle and the man wins. Around the headwaters of the Yenesei old men used to say it was thanks to the bear that domesticated reindeer were given to men, and this is how it came about:

A young girl met a bear, and the bear said to her, "Take

me home with you." Once inside the house he said, "Kill me. Place my heart beside you. Spread my fur in a dry ditch and hang my intestines on a bent tree. Don't be afraid." Being an obedient girl, she did as she was bid and then went to sleep in her house. Next morning, there were reindeer everywhere, grazing patiently and tamely in the yard. Over the bent tree could be seen the halters with which the deer could be led or ridden, forever after the servants of men.

In other of the old stories, the bear was sometimes identified with the Creator. He bore a god's name and asked for a god's sacrifice of reindeer shins.

Some specialists might read in the connection between bear and deer (never between bear and horse) a slow transition from hunting to herding, a slow taming of the gentle deer for use, first as a decoy to lure wild deer, then as draft animal in imitation of the old Asian dog-driving folk. But some Northern Tungus also ride the reindeer very nearly as one rides a horse (the saddle is placed over the animal's shoulders, not on his back). Further, they milk their deer as the steppe folk milk their cows and mares. These two ideas—riding and milking—could have been transmitted to the Tungus only in an area where life ways met, where the ranges of deer overlapped with those of cow and horse. That area, so a number of specialists believe, lies in a region near the upper reaches of the Yenesei, an enclave surrounded by the Sayan and Tannu-Ola mountains. Here live a people who, well into the last century, spoke an archaic Samoyedic tongue and whose reindeer skills and reindeer usage seem to have been the most advanced in the entire complex. From this center, it is said, reindeer herding and driving (but not riding) spread west with the Samoyeds to the people of the Urals and on further to the distant Lapps.

Maybe this sequence is true for the West, say other specialists, but the reindeer complex in the Far East had yet another home. This they locate in the valley of the Manchurian

Nen River, another spot where steppe and taiga meet and where reindeer domestication (or at least the riding and milking aspects of domestication) could have begun. Marco Polo spoke of reindeer riding in this area. Chinese writings of the fifth century A.D. noted reindeer milking among the people of the Nen Valley and also the drawing of vehicles by reindeer in harness. It is certainly true that the Reindeer Tungus of the region and in nearby Siberia appear to have as many elements of the complex and as large a vocabulary of terms dealing with it as the people of the Sayan Range. These two peoples alone ride their deer and use them for packing and sledging as well.

Among the Northern Tungus, pack trains of reindeer are driven by women, the most important woman riding astride at the head of the line. Women are the milkmaids and draw from every doe in season a cup or two of liquid, very thick, but not especially fat. The women know every deer of a herd by name and expect each one to come at call. Sometimes they come all too readily. During the brief summer when flies abound, deer often rush into the nearest human habitation to lie, doglike, by the fire. Since habitations among the Tungus are (or were in the old days) tepee-like tents covered with birchbark, built to accommodate no more than eight people at a time, a cuddly deer can often preempt all the space. And once inside he is hard to evict.

To this day among the Tungus no animal means so much as the deer. Those groups which have taken to horse and cattle herding retain their former affections and try to keep at least one deer as part of a woman's dowry. Just thirty years ago deers were used in sacrifice—breast split in the old manner and heart stopped with never a drop of blood shed. In the absence of deer, horses were substituted but were never thought to be entirely suitable in a ritual way. A horse was sometimes made to serve then as "placing" for the clan souls but never, it was thought, with the same majesty as that with which the large white reindeer bore clansmen to the other river world.

Tungusic-speaking people stretch now far to the north, into Sakhalin Island, among the Yukaghir, and alongside the Chukchi. The reindeer complex on its way north lost some elements—lost the knowledge of milking, lost riding, until the complex reached the Chukchi who had trouble keeping their large, partly wild herds intact and could scarcely tell one deer from another.

The ideas of civilization, spreading northward from China, moved as slowly and were modified en route—modified to function in an environment little suited to settlement, adapted to peoples grown fond of distance and motion, accustomed to take what they themselves could not produce. Coalescing into waves of conquest, nomadic folk engulfed China periodically and then ebbed back into the hinterland.

Tungusic tribes of southern Tung-pei were responsible for summoning several of those waves, formed confederations, kingdoms, dynasties, and themselves grew rich and powerful and forgetful of their beginnings. Yet behind lay always the hinterland. And between them and the roving bands and clans of hunters and herders stretched an unbroken cord of relatedness in language and belief. As Owen Lattimore perceptively points out, the difference between the Reindeer Tungus and the Jurchen or early Manchu soldier was one of degree, not of kind. The adventurous herder, hearing of great doings in the South, could come to take part in them without experiencing too great a culture shock.

Nurhachi, founder of the horde last to conquer China from its frontier, was a descendant of men loyal to the old Jurchens, and he called his dynasty Chin in memory of that older Tungus dominion. (In 1636 it would be renamed Ch'ing, or "Pure"; the name Manchu came into being even later.) Nurhachi was, it would seem, a leader for his time, a man who knew well the forest nomads and their ways, knew the steppe warriors and their ways, and made best use of each. Indeed, he and his descendants recruited actively among the Reindeer

Tungus. Chinese immigrants were barred from much of Manchuria. Local leaders and headmen were honored and the old traditions carefully preserved, even as the Manchu dynasts themselves tried (however unsuccessfully) to maintain the forms and beliefs which set them apart from the ruled.

In 1911 came the Chinese Revolution. The powerful and absolute dowager empress had died in 1908. Her child-successor abdicated, and China was proclaimed a republic. Suddenly the Tungus were exposed to a Chinese culture which had itself undergone rapid change. Some Reindeer Tungus were pushed northward into Russian Siberia, there to join their fellows. They, too, then came under pressure to change, to modernize, later to Sovietize. A gap has opened between old ways and new. It is wide and deep, and there is no bridge. To cross, one must leap the chasm and, having leapt, cannot go home again.

7

THE MONGOLS
The Winning of Half a World

ETHNOGENESIS—the emergence of a culture, of a language, of a life way, a set of beliefs distinct from those of neighbors and kin—is a piecemeal and long-range event. It is no surprise, therefore, to find that the people who became Turks, Tatars, and Tungus for long retained ties of common heritage even after differences in dialect had widened into language gaps, and the common speech had been lost. For all their dizzying shifts in enmity and alliance, they yet shared the nomad's common scorn of town and field and of the settled, farming life. They shared as well a common desire for the luxuries that could be wrung by hard warriors from soft townsmen. And there was more. Similar beliefs and family arrangements continued to relate the people of steppe and forest fringe and taiga —so long as they remained well beyond the orbiting influence of civilization.

Legend, as recounted by Marco Polo, points to a Mongol homeland somewhere south and east of Lake Baikal. The Mongols—or one group thereof—were first mentioned in chronicles of the T'ang Dynasty (around A.D. 800) as Meng-u or Meng-wu. They were described then as living along what is now the Inner Mongolian-Manchurian border and as traveling with the Shi-kien, probably a Tungusic tribe. Later Mongols were to retain something of the connection. Genghis Khan, whom we met in Chapter 5, was the son of a Tungus woman, stolen from her intended husband by Yesugei, chief of a small Mongol tribe. When Timuchin (the young Genghis Khan) was ready for a bride, Yesugei took him to the Tungus, his mother's people, to look for one. It was the sort of bride shopping approved by both peoples. The grandson of Yesugei would also take a Tungus woman to wife. The particular Tungus tribe in question was that of the Merkits, mentioned in the journals of Marco Polo as a stag-riding people. In the 1920s the Merkits were still intact and were described by Shirokogoroff. By then, however, they had given up reindeer riding and taken to horses instead.

Buryat Mongols, who live around Lake Baikal, once claimed that Tungus shared with them the same spirits and were subject to the same taboos on that account. Among both peoples—Mongols and Tungus—spirits belonged to the clan, and the in-marrying wife was forever something of a stranger, religiously if in no other way. Only when a new clan member, strong with clan spirits, inhabited her womb could she participate in family ritual.

Mongol shamans, like those of the Tungus, belonged to their clans and managed clan spirits. In life the shamans were clan defenders and in death, ghostly intercessors for their relatives on earth. The clan, with its membership counted always through males, father to son, was everywhere in steppe and forest the core of loyalty, one might almost say, of patriotism.

As among the Tungus, the continuity of Mongol clans depended on marriage out, on marriage into other clans, and the knot was tied similarly by a transfer of property from groom's herd to that of the bride's father. A man might, and often did, take many wives, and when he died, these could be inherited by his brother or by his son and heir (excepting, of course, the heir's own mother). This custom of the steppe folk more than almost any other shocked the Chinese and later-appearing Europeans who could not see it for what it really was: a kind of welfare system for widows and orphans. But, of course, not all women among Mongols and Tungus needed protection. The woman who preferred to manage her late husband's estate and bring up their children singlehandedly was allowed to do so and was much admired for it. Nomad society did not encourage the shrinking violet. Among the Mongols, girls learned, like their brothers, to ride and shoot as well as to milk the animals and care for the home. Those with good advice to give were heard with respect. Timuchin was said to have counseled often with his mother and his senior wife, mother of his four royal sons. The wives of these sons were equally strong-minded and served from time to time as regents of the Mongol Empire during its dizzying alternations of rule.

Mongols of both sexes wore clothing similar in cut to that of the Tungus: baggy trousers and boots, a long, heavy robe crossed in front and tied. They were not, however, dependent on animal skins but had learned to roll and pound sheep hair into woolly felt—a universal material for apparel and also for shelter. The bark or skin-covered tepee favored by hunters of the far North and by the herding Tungus had, among the Mongols, evolved into a rounded hut of greased and white-limed felt, bound to a folding, latticework frame—a frame (as Harold Vreeland puts it) rather like the folding gates we use to keep our toddlers from falling downstairs. Such houses are still in use today throughout the steppes. As indicated earlier, they were once called yurt, a word which also came to mean one's territorial domain. In order to avoid confusion such homes are now called ger. The ger can be folded, loaded into a covered wagon and moved in a trice, and it was always so. In other times, however, some ger—the large and important ones—were mounted permanently on special wheeled platforms and pulled by teams of oxen, as many as twenty to a platform.

In the center of the ger is a perpetual fire. Nothing sharp must be pointed at the hearth, no refuse fed to it. For it is the symbol of the family to be shared with each son as he marries and is inherited at last by the youngest remaining son, the Lord of the Hearth.

Mongols were once, like the Tungus, hunters and, in medieval times, retained this interest. It was through hunting that men were trained for war, and their mettle was tested, their abilities gauged in the yearly grand surround. As among the Tungus, animal models were honored and slain in sacrifice. The wolf among wild things was accorded pride of place. Some said the first Mongol was wolf-born. Others claimed the Mongols were descended from a bull-prince, son of the highest spirit. In celebrations, honor was paid to the horse, thought to be supernaturally wise, to the reindeer (in rock drawings associated with the sun), and to the soaring eagle, personal guardian of Genghis Khan.

But the Mongols, hunters though they remained, depended for sustenance on domesticated animals and on a great variety of them. In this (as in much else) they were like the Turkic-speaking people of the western steppes rather than the Reindeer Tungus. Herds and flocks were mostly sheep—ever hardy in dry lands—sheep, which produced milk, meat, hide, hair; bones and sinew for the making of implements; dung to be burned for warmth. There were also cattle or, in the colder zones, yak. There were camels for hauling packs, for wool, and for milk. There were horses which meant to the Mongols mobility and prestige but which provided as well the wherewithal of conviviality. Mare's milk, fermented and beaten, yields kumiss, a nourishing drink once called (by Justice William O. Douglas and his wife) "a cross between buttermilk and champagne." Distillation transforms kumiss into the heady ariha, the liquor which turned many a Mongol tippler into a habitual drunk. Advised Genghis Khan, "Get drunk only three times a month. It would be better not to get drunk at all. But who can abstain altogether?"

Variety in the Mongol herding complex found echoes in social life. Basic themes of the steppe pattern took on the elaborations one might expect from nomads in constant contact with Great China and interaction with one another. We can trace the path of change in Chinese writings about the nomads, in writings the nomads themselves caused to be written once they had come to dominate the world scene, and in life-way studies undertaken by social scientists of this century.

Buryat Mongols of Lake Baikal, for example, were last to become converts to the Buddhism espoused by most other Mongols and, as late as the 1920s, followed religious forms as they had been during the Mongol heyday in the thirteenth century. Buryat tradition created a world (so we are told by anthropologist Lawrence Krader) in which everything came in threes. The human self resulted from a fusion of body, breath, and soul. Soul itself was triply divided and triply ranked: good, better, best. So were the spirits, the *tengeriner* (in number ninety-nine), triply divided, subdivided, and ranked. The sick man cured by a shaman in control of the spirits received a life extension of three or nine years. The bride fed her new fire three times and thrice anointed with animal fat her new father-in-law. And the Great Khan of the Mongols on his accession received from his vassals nine obeisances.

One remembers, of a sudden, how important in Western custom and lore is the number three. In proverbs and descriptions: three on a match; third time's charm; tall, dark, and handsome; three wishes; going down for the third time. In organization: beginning, middle, end; first, last, and always; ready, set, go; morning, noon, night. In religion: the god-trinities of the Greeks, the Germans, the Norsemen, the Christians. How much of this stems from a spread of ideas out of the steppes or from a time when nomads of varying persuasions were in closer communion?

Some notions, purely home-grown, were to be found only among the Mongols. Children of arid country, they had a nervous respect for water and a positive mania about thunder. Utensils were never washed in water, and customary law forbade the display of washed clothing on the plain. (The tidy housewife, threatened by her peers, soon learned to leave garments dirty.) One might not in summer draw water in gold or silver vessels or wash one's hands at a stream. Kublai Khan (grandson of Genghis Khan and himself Great Emperor of China around A.D. 1270) is said to have made use of a special birch-bark talisman whenever he crossed a stream.

Ordinarily, death punished the violater of running water, for such a one had recklessly invited thunder's wrath. Yet not all Mongols were so frightened or so cruel in consequence. Rashid-ad-din (the Persian chronicler of Mongol history) tells how Ogedai, son of Genghis, saved a poor Moslem who had chosen to bathe, all innocent of the consequences. While soldiers carted the culprit away, the Great Khan dropped silver in the stream and at court next day announced that the Moslem had dropped it while crossing the stream. Surely, whatever the slight to religion, surely one was permitted to retrieve lost silver, was one not? Case dismissed.

However inflexible the general tenor of Mongol customary law, religions of all sorts were welcomed in the camps of Genghis Khan and those of his sons. Even so, Mongols of early empire times adhered in the main to the old beliefs and to their old ministrants who were the clan shamans. The clan shamans of the Tungus were self-appointed and trained through apprenticeship. Those of the Mongols in the Great Khan's time and among the Buryat in recent years were organized into schools subsidized by the clan in which each shaman leader had his band of disciples, nine in number. Shaman schools foreshadowed the Buddhist monasteries of later times. First built in Mongolia around 1530, these came at last to monopolize all learning, both sacred and profane.

Mongol shamans of the old days were good and bad, white and black. And their familiar spirits—kept in close check by the good shamans, served in fear by the bad ones—were likewise white and black, good and bad. Blacksmiths, too, in their magical calling were classified good and bad, white and black, along with *their* spirits. The white-black dichotomy came in time to distinguish, not only good and bad, but also high and low in terms of social rank. Thus Kublai Khan, and only he, owned a herd of white mares. In the Ordos Desert to this day is preserved a shrine to Genghis Khan. It consists of what are called White Tents, originally erected at the time of his death and guarded by the Ordos tribesmen who wander thereabouts.

Among some Mongol groups, white and black was applied to inheritance. Ordinary commoners were described as "black-bone people" (as, in later times, during the ascendance of Buddhist lamas, the laity would be known as "black men"). Ranking of descent and titles applied, not merely among clans, but within clans as well. Each was arranged in a tight pecking order. Each clan had its aristocratic, its white-bone lineages whose eldest sons maintained the right to lead and the right to rule. The lines of white-bone younger sons faded off eventually into the clan's pool of black-bone commoners whose ranks were augmented from time to time by conquered and enslaved folk. If one had to marry outside one's clan, one also had to marry inside one's bone. Young men of high rank sought wives among the white-bone lineages of other clans. Still and all, there was hope for advancement. The clan commoner who distinguished himself in battle could hope to lighten the bone color of his line.

Clans were organized into neat series of interlocking boxes. There was, at bottom, the extended family which lived and traveled together in the grazing circuit. Next came the collection of extended families related in the lineage. Then followed the many lineages which constituted the clan. And clans themselves used the presumption of distant kinship in order to cement themselves into a tribe. In whatever box, at whatever level, the tradition of obedience to the decrees of the leader was strongly pressed, required, demanded. It had to be. The single family, offended by an unfavorable ruling at law, could easily decamp. And wholesale decampment could be the end of order altogether.

The myth of kinship, once established as fact, can be used to cement many alliances, and it was so used among the Mongols. Through the myth, sets of related clans were bound into the tribe. And the leader, unable to conclude an alliance through conquest, sought to promote one by counting kin among the nearest friendly tribes.

Allied tribes created hordes, and allied hordes (bound likewise by the presumption of kin) made nomad empires, short-lived or no. The eternal jockeying for power among contending units, the constant involvement in persuasion, negotiation, battle, from the time of the Hsiung-nu, had produced exceedingly able leaders. Also, adds Owen Lattimore, success in besting peers tended to convince the Mongols that they could beat anybody in the world. It was a belief translated by Genghis Khan and his sons into the Will of Providence. Each prospective Mongol antagonist was duly put on notice, thus: "We are destined to conquer. Submit, and we shall be lenient.

THE MONGOLS 119

Oppose us, and only God can predict the consequences." The consequences extended, of course, to total annihilation of a people, with the occasional exception of men skilled in needed crafts.

In the long run, Mongols as a people, as a life way, make little sense without Genghis Khan. Indeed, there were no Mongols before him. The Juan-Juan, introduced earlier, are thought to have been led by men speaking a Mongol language. Later there were the Khitans who hailed from Tungus country, Mongol also, it is thought; they were not so called in the old Chronicles. Early in the twelfth century, records mention the Naiman, Keraits, Tuman, Buryat, Oirat, and other tribal groups speaking similar languages. By A.D. 1207, these were Mongols, all. Even though all did not fully participate in the conquests, there began at that time a sense of community, of common kind and common heritage which persists to this day. There were even some Turkic groups, affiliated with or subject to the Mongols, who came to count a distant kin with the descendants of Genghis Khan.

The Mongol conquest of half a world began in the familiar steppe context of conflict, alliance, and subjugation. Yesugei was poisoned by his enemies, who then sought to kill his children as well. Faced with the destruction of family, with the loss of clan leadership, his by inheritance, the young Timuchen learned early the uses of guile. By the time the four sons of Bourtai, the Tungus woman who was his principal wife, were men, he had consolidated tribal alliances in what are now Inner and Outer Mongolia. Subjugating, then, the Mongol and Turkic groups to the north and the Tibetan tribes on his flank, he was ready to pounce on China, or rather, on the armies of the Chin Dynasty (Jurchen) which then held China's northern lands and borders. The old Sung Dynasty still survived in the south through all the upheavals in the north of Khitan and Jurchen rule.

His confidence was well founded in planning and strategy. The Mongol troops were organized in units of ten, one-hundred, one-thousand, and ten-thousand men—the *tumen* of Hsiung-nu times—and finally into wings on the left and right. They were officered by men in hereditary command who received their orders in relays from the leading generals. And since most could not read the Turkic Uigur script adapted to Mongol use, orders were transmitted in rememberable rhymes. The khan's own guard—a *tumen* in itself—was composed of the best soldiers, each one capable of replacing any officer in any of the other units.

The ordinary soldier was equipped, so Marco Polo tells us, with armor of buffalo hide. (Some had shingle-scale coats of mail as well). He carried two bows at least, a complement of arrows, and a large curved saber. An iron pot, a leather bag for kumiss, one for water, and a packet of milk curd under his saddle completed the inventory of dietary equipment. Perfectly sturdy and enduring, each man was able to ride for two days without sleep or rest. But he was not prepared to abuse his horse in this fashion. No horse was ridden oftener than one day in six, and each man had a large string of extras from which to choose. The Mongol horseman was absolutely obedient and neither killed nor plundered without permission. Each man obeyed battlefield signals and became master of the steppe tactic of feigned retreat and attack from ambush.

Within twenty years, the armies of Genghis Khan had taken Manchuria in the East and, in the West, much of Persia and southern Russia. In 1227, the Great Khan died. Twenty thousand people, it is said, were sacrificed along the route of his funeral train, and to this day no one knows his place of burial. The conquest of the world he left to his sons and great generals. They nearly succeeded in the task. Each carved out a part of the empire and ruled according to the Yassa, the book of laws of Genghis Khan. Each in time, recognizing that the old belief could not serve as a unifying force, turned to the world religions for support. Some embraced Islam as their subjects had done before them. Some became Buddhists. A few espoused Nestorian Christianity, long popular on the steppes. (There remains in the Ordos to this day the small Erkut tribe, still Christian, still ruled by priests.)

Each of the sons tried to continue in the use of the Uigur script and the Mongol language. Kublai Khan, grandson to the Great Khan, succeeded so well in China that Marco Polo found he could manage well enough with a command of Mongol and Turkic languages and never learned Chinese at all—even while he served for three years as governor of Yangchow.

It was Kublai's army which conquered the remains of the Sung Dynasty. The Mongol armies had less success in the steamy jungles of Southeast Asia and in the Japanese islands where storms and typhoons, as well as sturdy defending warriors, barred the way.

Kublai's reign as actual Emperor of China, founder of the Yuan Dynasty and nominal Great Khan of the empire established by Genghis, was perhaps the high point of Mongol dominion. After his death, it began to decay. In each of the separate Mongol realms, native unrest gathered, coalescing eventually into armed conflict which drove the Mongols out.

The descendants of Genghis Khan fled as refugees to Mongolia and began to nurse back something of their former strength. There followed many attempts to recapture what had been lost—lost land, lost rule, lost unity. The Mongol tribes were on their own, jockeying once again for primacy, abetted in their discontent by the efforts of the Ming Dynasty, which had in 1368 succeeded the Mongols in China.

For a time the four tribes of the Oirat Mongols gained ascendancy in Mongolia and Taklamakan, then were themselves driven west. Settling for some centuries along the Volga, they were at first allies, then subjects of the Russian czars.

Some returned to what had become Chinese Turkestan or, by its other name, Sinkiang—those lands drained by the Tarim River and closed by the Dzungarian Gates. Those who remained behind were the Kalmucks, whose Turkic-given name means just that: "those who remained behind."

In Mongolia, the intertribal struggles went on, with forays into Tibet and the reestablishment of influence there. And then, in 1644, the Manchus came to power. They had done so with the help of Mongol tribes, more apprehensive of Genghis Khan's descendants than of Tungus dominion.

The Manchus wanted to maintain the Mongols as they had found them: tribal, warlike, nomadic, raw material for Manchu armies. Chinese farmers were, therefore, forbidden to settle lands beyond the Wall. Mongol princes, laden with honors, were forbidden to participate in Chinese political life. And as a further ploy for control, Manchu officialdom encouraged the establishment of Buddhism in its Tibetan form. There were already many converts among Mongols, and the religion melded well with traditional beliefs. Soon, monasteries were everywhere, and a large percentage of the male population were monks or lamas (teachers), celibate and lost to the herding life, to the life of warriors. But not to political life. For the government of Mongolia came to be a sort of theocratic bureaucracy, the responsibility of literate lamas who did obeisance to the living reincarnations of divinity, the third most important of whom resided in Mongolia.

Theocracy among Mongols is no more, reduced to a few small monasteries in the People's Republic of Mongolia. The Mongols themselves are divided among the modern national giants or contested by them. The Buryat Mongols live in Russia. The Kalmuck, deported and scattered, have ceased to be an ethnic unit. In China live the tribes of Inner Mongolia and the Ordos, those of Manchuria, and the Monguor of Kansu. In between is the People's Republic of Mongolia, independent since 1911, but in terms of sympathy and ideology, allied to the Soviet Union. Thus it is that Genghis Khan, the culture hero of all the Mongols, has been downgraded in Mongolia as he has been among the Buryat in Russian lands. And there was, at one time, at least, a reason.

In the 1930s the Japanese invaded Manchuria and sought to win Mongols to their cause by promising a unification of all Mongols in the remembered glory of the great hero. A shrine was promised at Karakorum, the old city built around the main capital of Genghis Khan. In all else, however, the Japanese were as unfortunate in their attempt to win Mongol allegiance as others had been before them.

The Japanese are gone from the mainland, but the fear of the myth remains—the fear of Genghis Khan as a unifying ideal for all Mongols, as a lure to other ways and other allegiances. Not so in China's Ordos region where the Great Khan's shrine—very nearly in its promised Japanese dimensions—has been built. To it Mongols of many persuasions journey in pilgrimage and are warmly welcomed. There the Mongol language is written in a variant of the old Uigur script, long since abandoned or forbidden among the Buryat. For China means to regain her old sphere of influence with the age-old tactics of containment and defeat, division and rule, persuasion and reward. At long last, the Chinese can be glad of Genghis Khan or, at least, of the useful myth he left behind.

8

THE KIRGHIZ
Transformable Turks

OF all the tribes of the eastern steppes, there were none more adaptable, more apt to transformation than those of the Turkic-speaking peoples. In looks, in religion, in rule, in half a dozen other areas of human life, the Turkic tribes bent with change. Beaked noses and curly hair were, at various times and in various conquered lands, added to or subtracted from a basically Mongolic cast of features. At various times and under the press of various pervasive influences, Turks honored home-grown and home-trained shamans or Islamic mullahs; Nestorian Christian priests or Mazdaist priests from Persia; Buddhist monks or Lamaist monks. Turkic warriors traveled far and stayed where they landed: as far west as modern Turkey and Bulgaria; as far north as Yakutia in what is now Siberia. Whatever the transformation, whatever the distance, one thing remained constant, changeless, intact: the heritage of

Turkic words. Under every condition of change, it was the Turks who persuaded others to their words, not the other way round. Even though, in time, the Turkic mother tongue split into dialects, then into daughter languages, those languages remained mutually intelligible. The speakers of one could and can still understand the words of another, though often with some difficulty.

In Turkic words, so we are told by E. D. Phillips, lie the keys to power in the steppes. They are the signets of order, organization, and conquest. *Khan,* the tribal leader; *tengri,* "Lord of Heaven," are Turkic words. So, too, are *darkhan,* "free man, minor chief"; *toyon,* "nobility"; *ordu,* the khan's great camp or court (whence comes our own word, "horde"); *ulus,* a lineage group. The great army and tribal divisions of right and left along with the "wise kings" to lead them, patterns later used by the Mongols, were invented by the Turkic-speaking Hsiung-nu. So, too, the ordering of army units into multiples of ten, the royal guard as a nursery of officers, the tactic of feigned retreat. Concepts and words found partial acceptance among the Tungus and outright appropriation by the Mongols. *Tengiz,* the Turkic word for "ocean" provided part of Timuchin's later title, Genghis Khan, the All-Encompassing Lord. When, much later, the Mongols were dominant in Tibet, they revived the idea in a theological context, creating thereby the title of Tibet's chief prelate, the dalai lama. But this time they took care to use their own word for ocean, *dalai.*

The words remain because the Turkic peoples were first, first to learn tactics and techniques of the western nomads (Yueh-chih, Wu-sun, Ting-ling, Tocharians, whoever they were), and they used those techniques to conquer their teachers. The chief of the Hsiung-nu had a Turkic name, Tumen, the word for "ten thousand"—perhaps indicating the number of cavalry troops at his disposal. His son was the unfavored but successful Modun—in Chinese transliteration, something closer to Mao-tun; in Turkic, perhaps renderable, suggests Owen Lattimore, into Moduk or Makdur.

The Hsiung-nu put together a motley confederation. Clans and tribes of nascent Mongols, Tungus from the northern forests, remnants of Yueh-chih, the touchy Wu-sun. There is a frozen burial in Noin Ula near Lake Baikal, datable to times later than the tombs of Pazyryk. It is associated with Hsiung-nu chieftains and provides us with a catalogue of faces to be seen among steppe warriors of that time: some Western, some Eastern in type, with all kinds of mixtures in between.

Sometime friends and partners, sometime furious enemies of the Hsiung-nu were the Ting-ling who ranged the high Altai with their own allies and dependents, the Kirghiz. During a rare period of cooperation (around 99 B.C., that would have been), they received from their overlords a Chinese prisoner of high rank, Li Ling by name. He was, as well, a commander of valor and genius. So, too, had been his grandfather, Li Kuang, a general whose prowess with the nomad bow and whose popularity with the Chinese soldiery were both unsurpassed.

Li Ling had been sent into the field against the Hsiung-nu cavalry with a mere five thousand foot soldiers under his command. He had been promised instant support from his superiors once he had drawn out the Hsiung-nu. And draw them out he did, over 80,000 of them, but the Chinese support did not materialize. Nevertheless he fought, deploying with such skill his crossbowmen and his spearmen that the Hsiung-nu cavalry suffered very heavy losses. For several days Li Ling fought, retreating the while. Then, betrayed by one of his captains who told the Hsiung-nu that no Chinese troops would be forthcoming, fearful of the lives of his few remaining men, he surrendered.

The Shan-yu himself did honor to Li Ling, offering his own daughter for the hero's wife. But the Chinese emperor, Wu Ti, hearing of the defeat, was enraged by Li Ling's failure to commit suicide and condemned him to death in absentia.

Later, realizing that the error had been his own, realizing that he had neglected to order the promised support, Wu Ti offered amnesty. Li Ling refused, and the emperor, in retaliation, had the hero's wife, mother, and children slain.

One man dared to defend Li Ling, dared to remind the emperor of the commander's past services and valor. That man was the Grand Historian of the Han Dynasty, Ssu-ma Ch'ien. In the emperor's eyes, his courage was criminal. He was declared guilty of "deceiving the emperor" and was confined in the cold recesses of the royal palace, in the so-called "silkworm chamber," there to suffer castration.

Each of the sufferers, Ssu-ma Ch'ien and Li Ling, wrote later to a friend each apologizing for his failure to commit suicide, each explaining his reasons. Wrote Ssu-ma Ch'ien:

> *The brave man does not necessarily die for honor, while even the coward may fulfill his duty. . . . Though I might be weak and cowardly and seek shamelessly to prolong my life, yet I know full well the difference between what ought to be followed and what rejected. . . . If even the lowest slave and scullion maid can bear to commit suicide, why should not one like myself be able to do what has to be done? But the reason I have not refused to bear these ills [the castration] and have continued to live, dwelling in vileness and disgrace without taking my leave, is that I grieve that I have things in my heart that I have not been able to express fully, and I am shamed to think that after I am gone my writings will not be known to posterity.*

Li Ling, for his part, wrote:

> *I would die joyfully even now, but the stain of my prince's ingratitude can never be wiped away. Indeed, if the brave man is not allowed to achieve a name but to lie like a dog in a barbarian land, who will be found to crook the back and bend the knee before an Imperial Throne, where the bitter pens of courtiers tell their lying tales?*

And then, he added:

O my friend, look for me no more. . . . A thousand leagues lie between us. . . . I shall live out my life as if it were in another sphere; my spirit will find its home among a strange people . . . barbarian children will carry on the line of my forefathers.

They did. In the fourth and fifth centuries A.D., Li Ling's barbarian descendants had settled in the Tunhuang area. The census records and legal documents for centuries sealed in caves there have told us so. Another Li line, descended from Li Kuang and enriched as was that of Li Ling by barbarian marriages, eventually established the T'ang Dynasty (618–907) which was to mark the Chinese national character as indelibly as had the dynasty of Han.

There is yet more to the story of Li Ling. His final home was among a Turkic-speaking people, allies or subordinates of the Ting-ling and called in the Chinese chronicles of later T'ang times *Kien-kuen,* or *Kiet-kwat,* the closest possible rendering of the Turkic Kirghiz. It is a name which continues to this day among a people who live no longer close to the high Altai or the upper reaches of the Yenesei, their original home, but among the lofty valleys of Tien Shan and the Pamirs.

In the T'ang annals, the Kirghiz are described as tall, red of face and of hair, green of eye. Black hair, adds the chronicler, was considered an evil omen among them, but people with brown eyes were honored as descendants of Li Ling. The Kirghiz had begun to point to him with pride, acknowledging Li Ling as founding father of their ruling clan, if not the tribe entire—a compliment not to be lost on the Chinese. Thanks to Li Ling, though not to him alone, surely, Kirghiz looks were to lose the effects of long association with the Europoid Ting-ling and to become, in several hundred years, quite thoroughly Mongolized.

To put the Kirghiz into a historical frame, a bit of backtracking is now in order. Between the third century and the seventh—after the fall of the Han Dynasty and before the emergence of the T'ang—steppe tribes struggled for dominion. The Hsiung-nu fell, and their western contingents rolled toward Europe. The Mongol-speaking Juan-Juan rose to power, basing their armament on the work of Turkic tribes and Turkic refugees from China. These were called by the Juan-Juan "smith slaves"—indicating at once both value and scorn, for, in the steppe scheme of things, smiths were ordinarily close to shamans in esteem and always free men.

The smith slaves bided their time, collected arms and armies, and eventually drove the Juan-Juan out of the eastern steppes and on toward Western Europe, barely a hundred years after those lands had begun to recover from the Hunnish intrusion. The Turkic "smith slaves" followed their erstwhile oppressors, pushing, overturning, upsetting many other tribal groups and alliances in their wake until at last they reached the Caucasus. There the death of their khan halted their headlong pursuit of the Juan-Juan. In the Caucasus they remained to found the Khazar Khanate which would flourish for two centuries.

In the Altai and Yenesei homeland, the Uigur Turks had risen to dominance. Some of them, at least, had at a still earlier time spread into the oases of Taklamakan. Far less nomadic than their peers, with the enclosed urban outlook which invites elaboration of ideas and of art, the Uigur had received from the Soghdians, a Persian-speaking tribe, one form of the Aramaic alphabet. This they began to adapt to Turkic words so that, within a century, records of Turkic exploits began to appear in sources other than those written by the Chinese.

The Kirghiz of the Altai were vassals and also students of the Uigur and, by A.D. 800, had replaced them in sovereignty. Now was the time of Turkic flowering on the steppe, a time of expansiveness and—if we can trust the evidence of the writings—of joy. Always skilled at the forge, Kirghiz smiths produced works which were much desired abroad. Their jugglers and acrobats were popular in China. One has visions of troops of Kirghiz artists on foreign tour. Certainly Kirghiz enjoyed trade relations with many distant people. Historians of the T'ang Dynasty write:

> *The Kirghiz were always on friendly terms with the Dashi [Ta-Shih, or Arabs of Central Asia], the Turfan [Tibetans had, at this point, expanded into Dzungaria]; and Gelolo [the Karluk]. . . . Not more than twenty camels used to come from the Dashi with patterned silk fabrics. But when it was impossible to pack everything, the material was distributed among twenty-four camels. Such caravans were sent once every three years.*

Relations with China were equally good, so good, in fact, that Kyul-Tegin, the Great Khan of the Kirghiz, admonished his people in these words:

> *Chinese people who give without any constraint so much gold, silver, grain, and silk, always had sweet words and "soft" gifts. . . . By letting them tempt you with their words and luxurious gifts, you Turkish people have perished in great numbers.—This was your downfall. There [on the border] the "educated" people enticed you, saying, "Who lives far gives poor gifts." . . . Thus, O Turkish people, when you go to that land, you put yourselves in great danger. . . . Send only the caravans for gifts and remain in Utuken wilderness where there are no riches but also no oppression. You can live and support your eternal tribal union.*

It is the age-old plaint of the nomad leader, fearful lest his people lean too eagerly toward soft, attractive, civilized ways and lose themselves thereby.

Kirghiz writing appears as inscriptions on tombs, on commemorative stones, and in decorative patterns on the clothing of the dead. Stones, tombs, and all are to be found along the upper Yenesei and in rather more abundance along the Orkhon and Selenga rivers to which the Kirghiz removed on their accession to power.

An additional record of Kirghiz life and times appears in pictures incised on rocky cliffs of the Turkic homeland. There are mounted warriors, singly and in troops, splendid in full gallop, fighting, hunting great stags, herding cattle, bearing banners. For the banner was then and for a very long time to come the symbol of a warrior clan and of the man who held by hereditary right its leadership. Such figures, as Okladnikov tells us, are characteristic of Turkic peoples generally and are to be found as far west as Bulgaria where the Huns eventually settled down to agriculture and Christianity.

Epic tales of the Bogatyr, the warrior hero who pits his strength against monstrous forces of evil, are also characteristic of Turkic-speaking peoples and are preserved today among the tribes of the Altai region. Herewith a sample:

When the hero, Kogutai, races on his bull, heaven and earth shudder at the sound of his war cry. Mountains tremble, and the blue sea of a hundred bays is disturbed.

Living heroes of the Kirghiz were rewarded and their deeds extolled. On the Orkhon inscription stones we learn that Kyul-Tegin, he who admonished his people for their luxurious tastes, bestowed on one Bassbeg, in honor of his martial deeds, the hand of the royal princess, sister to the khan.

The form of Kirghiz burial itself speaks of ancient steppe connections, east and west, and of the warrior's pride of place. Even the graves of ordinary men contained the bones of a sacrificed horse, horse gear, war gear, and food offerings. Graves of the mighty were additionally furnished with art objects of gold and silver. Crypt and furnishings were then surmounted by a great stone slab and a high earthen mound.

Stones, pictures, tombs, clothing speak, for the most part, of heroic deeds, of triumph and of greatness. Now and then, however, we hear of the ordinary things of life, of birth and marriage and inheritance. For example, this passing comment:

> *Marriage with kin through the mother is most to be preferred. The sister's son may marry the brother's daughter.*

In other words, since one inherits property through the father's side of the family, one reserves affection for the mother's family. Indeed, one chooses a wife among the maternal relatives. It is the same sort of cross-cousin marriage preferred among both Mongols and Tungus.

For a more complete picture of life on the Orkhon, however, we must depend again on the watchful historians of China who seemed to hear everything and to be interested in everything they heard. According to them, the Kirghiz of T'ang times, at least, revered felt images of their god, images which they enclosed in skin bags and anointed with fragrant ointments. Sometimes the image bags were hung from poles in their encampments.

Kirghiz economy was said to be highly diversified. In addition to the ever present herds of camel, cows, sheep, and horses, there were revenues to be gained from the forge. Metal smiths were besieged with orders constantly. There were also among the Kirghiz some few farmers who planted millet, barley, wheat, but no fruits or vegetables.

The Great Khan of the Kirghiz, titled *Azho,* moved his capital southward to the Selenga, and this was duly noted in China. The *Azho,* it was further noted, could be recognized by the sable hat he wore in winter and by the headdress of white felt, fantastically shaped and rimmed with gold, which he reserved for summer wear.

Great ladies of the Kirghiz dressed in wool or silk, while the ordinary folk had to content themselves with sheepskin clothing and forgo the luxury of hats. Whatever one's station in life, shelter was much the same for all: the hut covered with tree bark or the felt-covered yurt. Whatever one's station, one drank fermented mare's milk and praised the spirits for it.

In the way of all steppe tribes, the Kirghiz lost their grip. The clans, tribes, hordes of their confederation constantly reformed, realigned. A battle was lost here, another there, and when the dust settled, the Kirghiz did obeisance to Khitan overlords. This occurred in the tenth century. It could not have been a graceful defeat. Years later, when the Mongol star was in the ascendant, Kirghiz aristocrats brought the tribe voluntarily to Genghis Khan and swore allegiance to his son Juchi, giving the young prince white geldings and ermine skins in token of submission.

The upheavals and redistribution of peoples, characteristic of Mongol rule, did not leave the Kirghiz unaffected. Nevertheless, they still maintained representatives on the Yenesei when the Russians arrived in the seventeenth century. Kirghiz are described in early Russian reports as being aristocratic, feudal, nomadizing. By then the old Kirghiz script had been lost. The language had undergone change. Soon the Kirghiz themselves would be gone—gone from the Altai region, but not gone for good and all. Gone simply to Tien Shan.

It was a long migration, accelerated from time to time by the incessant power struggles on the steppes. In the fifth century A.D., already the Kirghiz were on the move, led, as Bernshtam says, by "good princes." In the Tien Shan there were already remnants of Hsiung-nu, Wu-sun, and Ting-ling, well known from the Altai and Yenesei regions. The Kirghiz added their own contributions to the art forms and life ways of the mountains. The burials found there tell us so. They added more in the tenth century when Khitan victories sent more Kirghiz flying south—south to their distant and changing kin.

With each change in rule, the Tien Shan population grew increasingly Kirghiz in character. Another kind of identity was growing. While the Kirghiz of the Yenesei courted the Mongols, the Kirghiz of Tien Shan stood them off and successfully, too. Kirghiz began to fight for their identity so fiercely that they came in time to be known as "the wild lions of Mogulistan." But the pressures from foreign powers were intense, their own mechanisms of rule few, and the struggle for true statehood was doomed forever to failure.

There remained, at least, the language and the integrity of the life way developed in Tien Shan and the Pamirs, and it remains to this day. It is a mountain way, conformable to high, moist meadows, to cold summers, colder winters, and long, long snows. Much of the old craft skill was lost in transit, forgotten the dependence on farming. Here in the lost mountain valleys little could be raised, though that little counted heavily. Some wheat, some barley and millet, and as much fodder as possible were grown, usually by a family or clan group chosen to stay behind in the winter camp while their relatives followed the retreating snows of spring in search of richer graze. The love of the herds remained and dependence on them, as well, for meat, milk, clothing, kumiss, and all that made life possible. Sheep and goats retained their ancient importance in the herds, but only the sturdiest of steppe horses survived. Camels found the heights difficult to endure and, in many camps, were replaced by the yak, that long-haired, long-horned creature something like an American bison, something like a wild cow, but with its own unique qualities. Some of these qualities earned the yak respect, if not outright veneration, among people of the steppes. In one of the tombs of Noin Ula was found a representation of the yak bestriding great hills. And the standard of Genghis Khan was ever hung with white yak tails.

Yak cows give rich milk with a high butter-fat content. They will carry heavy loads for long distances. They forage well for themselves and will eat snow for moisture. They can also be ridden, and the Kirghiz do just that, settling their saddles along the yak's shoulders much after the fashion of the reindeer rider further north. One may see today, if one has the stamina for mountain travel, pack trains of yak carrying supplies to Kirghiz camped in high passes or on caravans of trade into Afghanistan or Kashmir.

Sixty years or so ago, the Kirghiz, known to the Russians as Black Kirghiz, were awesome raiders. Even neighbors and close kinsmen, the Kazakh of the lower steppes, for instance, were not exempt from their depredations. The Kirghiz were then still divided into the two great tribal wings hallowed in steppe antiquity, the *on,* or right wing, and the *sol,* or left. These never joined in concerted action or in residence. The left wing included then seven clans, but the right wing, always the larger, comprised six clan confederations. These were further subdivided—clans into lineages, lineages into *auls* (doubtless from the original *ulus*), and the ever-narrowing units were led by hereditary chiefs. Yet, the Kirghiz acknowledged no hereditary aristocracy. Clans were not ranked as among the Kazakh or among the Mongols: fame and honor followed personal achievement and certain qualities of character. The man of extensive and industrious kin, of many herds and a personality at once forceful and spiritual, of good counsel and common sense—such a man was sure to enjoy lasting reputation and influence among his peers.

Spirituality might or might not include fervent devotion to Allah and to Mohammed, his Prophet. For the Kirghiz, unlike the Uigur and other Turkic tribes of the oases, were and are lukewarm adherents of Islam. Onset of illness in a Kirghiz house is attributed to evil spirits, called (with deference to the sensibilities of the local mullah or other divine) jinns. Jinns, in the Kirghiz and Kazakh sense, are both good and evil. They are, moreover, subject to control by a *bagsha,* or shaman, who in trance wrestles with the evil ones, sends out his good familiars to determine the origin of illness, and later also forecasts the future in the time-old steppe manner. Mullahs, too, function now and then as healers, following the shaman's lead in technique but crediting Allah with the cures.

Rituals traceable to the Orkhon heyday and before are still cherished and performed. Clan souls are honored and invoked in a family setting and by the family elders. Mountain spirits, favored by the medieval Mongols, are honored and invoked. And yet, religious views are judiciously mixed. To the old traditions there has been added a devotion to the tombs of local Islamic sages and to the rituals associated therewith. The popularity of the out-of-the-way shrines increased greatly when Soviet authorities banned mosque attendance. After the ban was lifted, even the backsliding Kirghiz and Kazakh filled the mosques to overflowing.

So we are told by Professor Elizabeth E. Bacon who visited Central Asia in 1965. By that year, said she, old ways and new had come to a shaky accommodation all through the area. The Soviet push toward collectivization had been eased. Herders had returned to their nomadizing for at least part of the year. Yet, for this way of life, no modern shelter had then been found superior to the yurt, that portable felt home. European clothing, disdained by Central Asians, has been supplanted by ready-made robes and coats of traditional cut. Russian-educated Kirghiz persist in writing of old ways and themes when they are meant to choose for their art modern topics and modern political conflicts.

Family ties are still strong. Inheritance follows the old patterns. Marriages (at least among the highland Kirghiz) are still polygynous and still contracted on the giving of bridewealth. Indeed, says Professor Bacon, bridewealth for a Kirghiz or Kazakh girl is set so high that no outsider may claim her. Kirghiz men may occasionally take a Russian bride. The reverse is almost never true.

Even the seclusion and veiling of women, a custom never

followed by the Kirghiz and Kazakh (though common among the oasis folk), is now coming into general use. It is not considered a religious emblem or a female restriction, but instead a mark of wealth and prestige. Even girls educated in Russian schools have taken up as a fad the veil which, among women in other Moslem cultures, is bitterly resented and renounced at the first opportunity.

And yet change comes apace. Rapidly in Kazakhstan to which Ukrainians and other European Russians have migrated in numbers. Rapidly in the oases where men are tied to their fields and perpetually under the eye of officialdom. Slowly in the south among the Kirghiz. For the mountains that kept them for so long safe from the domination of foreign powers protect to this day their right to select what will be taken from the life way, what added, and what retained.

There are Kirghiz in China, in the mountains and oasis cities of Sinkiang Province. If Russian rule has been resented, then circumvented, then adapted into patterns already old, so, too, has been the rule of China. But Russian rule, in the long view, is new to the steppe folk; Chinese rule is old and familiar in all its nuances. For China is an ancient adversary. The long years of contact between steppe and sown lands, between nomad and townsman, the alternating conquests, the chain of adjustment and compromise have changed both ways of life and yet left each separate, distinct.

Perhaps the mutual exclusivity owes at least something to the difference in language. Those of the oriental steppe were and are still related, share a common origin, and describe what was once a shared way of life. The Chinese language differs utterly from those of the Ural-Altaic group. Its point of origin lies somewhere south of the Yellow River. And from the beginning it spoke of another way, another spirit, another destination.

Part IV

China, Heart and Hub

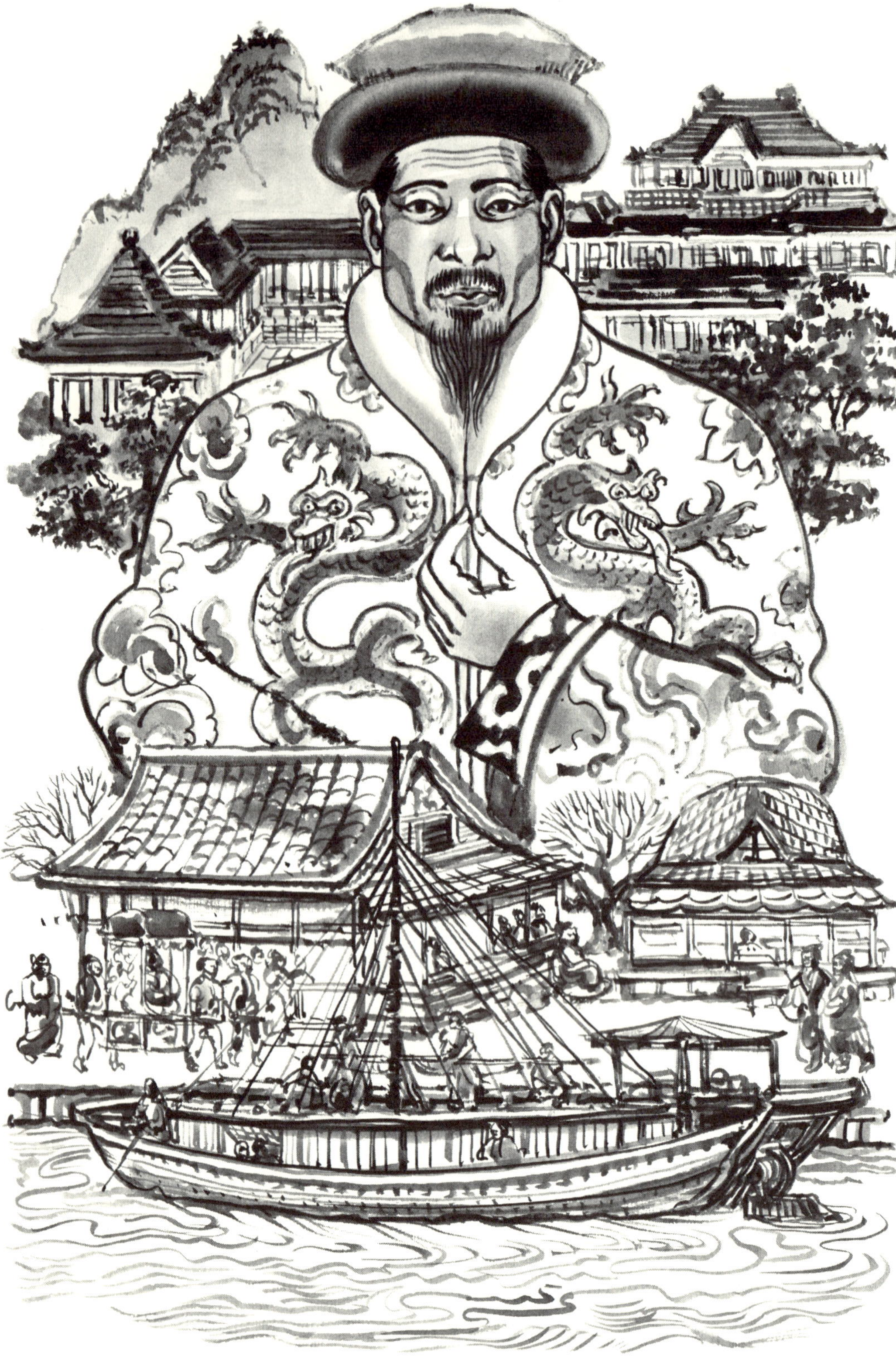

9

GREAT CHINA
A Dynastic Procession

IMAGINE the convenience of learning a language without gender or tense or mood. No bothersome conjugations. No puzzling out the vagaries of the perfect, present, future, or other tenses. Never a dither concerning the intimate "you." Imagine a language that translates, as anthropologist Ralph Linton once remarked, with all the economy and point of a telegram. That's Chinese. Similar sounds and word meanings, a similar structure (though not one equally spare) carry over into related languages spoken to the west and south of China. Altogether they belong in the Sino-Tibetan realm.

In terms of structure, Chinese and related languages are what the specialist calls "isolating." Sense and meaning elements (morpheme is the proper term for these) are conveyed in words of one syllable, each of which can stand alone. English, too, has come to be more and more isolating in structure

—unlike its Indo-European relatives. But many of its morphemes include two or more syllables (*major,* for example, or *wagon, establish, figure*), and not all meaning elements stand alone. Consider the word "friendly." The -ly must hang onto something else in order to convey its proper sense of "like"—in this case, meaning "like a friend."

Herbert Giles, a British professor in Chinese literature, gives us in his *Gems of Chinese Literature* an example of a Chinese poem, translated absolutely word for word:

Good man hold halberd bright
    glory inside
Know sir use mind like sun moon.
Serve husband swear intend together
    live die.
Return sir bright pearls pair
    tear drop
Hate not mutual meet not marry time.

Absent are the articles and modifiers that flesh out written English. Only the essential thoughts remain and those so spare as to be well-nigh unintelligible to us. Remember, too, that each of the quoted words consists in Chinese of one syllable. And conventions of Chinese poetry permit the one-word-to-a-line poem. Such an effort in English might be represented by this bit of doggerel by Dr. Giles:

Boy
    Jam.
Joy
    Cram.
Ill
    Bed.
Pill
    Dead.

For all the superficial simplicity of Chinese, however, learning the language does involve difficulty, particularly for the speaker of American, as opposed to the King's English. It has been said that American actors use a much more limited range of intonation than do their British colleagues. Countless cowboy heroes and cinematic private eyes have established as an American convention the level voice as well as the level head. And the average American businessman or student speaks, according to his British opposite number, in what is virtually a monotone. Such level voices speaking Chinese are apt to produce total confusion. Whatever the phonetic care exercised by the speaker, he might just instruct a youngster to "kiss your horse goodnight," when he really had mother in mind. "Horse," "mother," and also "scold," "hemp," "agate," and "insect" are all pronounced *ma*. It is the tone in which the sounds are uttered that changes meaning. For Chinese and related languages are tonal. The voice must rise, fall, remain level, or wiggle on every word—no mean trick for the American trained to be tight-lipped in manner and straightforward in tone.

Written Chinese presents yet another learning problem for the Western student, for it is largely ideographic, not phonetic. Signs evolved from pictures as they did in the earliest writings of Egypt and in the Sumerian cities of Mesopotamia. First came simple thing-pictures. Then what had been pictures of things came also to be pictures of ideas. The sign for "star," say, came also to mean "god." Then at last the drawing of the signs themselves changed, became formal, stylized, so that the original picture was lost to view.

The ideographic content of Chinese writing does not altogether exclude a phonetic element. So we are told by the linguist William S. Y. Wang. The rebus principle is used from time to time. (In English, for example, we could use pictures of bee and leaf to represent "belief.") In Chinese writing, the sign for "horse" (*ma* spoken in a swooping tone) becomes "mother" (*ma* spoken in a level tone) with the addition of the sign for "woman." Other ancient writings devised sound-signs, too. Written Egyptian, indeed, came to include a welter of purely phonetic elements to be used right along with thing and idea signs. Ideographic Sumerian was replaced by the cuneiform syllabaries of Babylon and Assyria. But written Chinese retained its original character. True, signs changed form to some extent (spoken Chinese changed much more). Of the several thousand earliest signs, less than half can still be interpreted.

The earliest Chinese writing appeared on the shoulder blades of oxen, heat-cracked in the Tungus manner so as to reveal destiny. Signs indicated the question which the diviner had posed, his identity, his interpretation of the cracks, the date, and a later verification of predicted events. Guidance was sought at first in matters relating to planting and the weather, to impending catastrophe, to the proper offering of ancestral sacrifice (always a royal ancestor honored). Later came questions relating to the health and well-being of the king. Carapaces of turtles eventually replaced shoulder blades in popularity. Their broader and smoother surface area offered more scope for the scribe. Scope was needed, for always there were more things to be put on record: lists of kings and events, accounts of rituals performed, inventories of animals bagged in grand hunts. Similar information may also have been painted on silk and on strips of wood and bamboo, as suggested by a very few fragments, luckily preserved. Eventually the records were also inscribed on jade and cast into bronze ritual vessels, permanent as well as beautiful documents.

The inscriptions on bones and turtle shells, the records of bamboo and jade, together with ancient oral traditions, were many times copied and recopied, compiled by generations of scribes into an ever growing body of historical data. By 842 B.C. chronology had become exact and was to remain so. The study and writing of history (on Chinese-invented paper before A.D.

200) emerged as the major intellectual exercise of Chinese scholars. And why not? There was available to them a body of materials and documents stretching back (we now know) to 1500 B.C. and preserved in a single written form. Chinese may not be the world's oldest writing, but it certainly takes the prize for continuity. No wonder the Chinese word *wen,* meant originally to represent "writing," came in time to mean "civilization" as well.

The use of thing-pictures seems to have emerged suddenly in the busy life of early Chinese cities, as suddenly as the horse-drawn chariot or the casting of bronze. And (as noted in Chapter 5) this suddenness has prompted many specialists to credit an outside source for its introduction. What is apparent, however, is not always real. The prototypes of Chinese writing may yet lie buried in the earth or repose on museum shelves, visible but unrecognized.

Writing began, held the Chinese scholars of early times, as people imitated the markings of nature: the paw print of foxes, the tracks of worm and snake, the sun's rays, the water's curl. And it is certainly true that pottery in oldest Chinese villages depicts with verve the look of nature: its forms and faces and creatures. On pottery of the period just preceding that of first cities, one can see, now and again, complex symbols, tantalizing symbols. Could they represent craft trademarks, the artisan's signature, perhaps, or something more? The matter of origins is an issue as yet unresolved but surely not burning. In the long run it matters little whether certain elements of culture were borrowed or invented on the spot. As Dr. K. C. Chang assures us, the essential, the unique character of Chinese civilization had been long in formation. New may have added to old an elaboration, a frill, a change in form but surely not in content.

The Chinese way had begun to take shape perhaps five thousand years before the first cities were built. Somewhere along the middle reaches of the Yellow River, just west of the point at which the river turns sharply into the Ordos, in this hub area for so much of Chinese beginnings and later history, the growing of grain was discovered and wandering hunting-fishing-gathering people began to settle down. The marks of transition, of what the specialist calls "intensive gathering," are few. The record of a changing life style, so clear in the Middle East and in Mexico, is, along the Yellow River, blurred and faint. It must be noted, however, that the cord-marked pottery found in first Chinese villages is somewhat reminiscent of earlier Jomon wares made by gathering-fishing folk in Japan. Even closer similarities can be found in the wares made by gathering-fishing folk who lived once along the small waterways of southern China and Southeast Asia. Some specialists believe it was in this southerly area among people who made corded-ware pottery that the domestication of root plants and of rice began, and in very early times, too. Whether the primary invention *was* made in this area (Dr. Chang has doubts about this) and traveled north or whether the Chinese nuclear area represents another home of invention, the idea of planting was there put to use with local grasses, especially with foxtail millet. The fossilized grains have been found along with the stone hoes used in cultivation.

The best known and most complete (but not the oldest) village sites in the Yellow River nuclear zone has been radiocarbon-dated to 4115 B.C. The forms and ways characteristic of this and other similar villages are known as the Yang-shao Culture. Yang-shao farmers tended barnyard animals as well as their fields. Bones of pig and dog have been found in early sites and, in later ones, bones of sheep, goats, and cattle which may or may not have been domesticated. Wild game was then still abundant. Remains of wild pig, wild horse, even rhinoceros and leopard appear in village refuse heaps. There are to be found, as well, the bones of wild deer—but not among the trash. These are gathered in burials, a custom which reminds us of the old hunting days up north and of the reverence for the deer felt there among hunters and herders. It was a reverence to continue down through the long years into the time of first cities when, now and again, some great noble secreted in the rammed-earth foundation of his house a cache of deer antlers, ceremonially arranged.

Fish were important to Yang-shao farmers, certainly in their diet, perhaps also in ritual. Fish forms, more than those of any other creature, appear as pottery designs. It is a fish which serves as headdress for the one human face known to have been painted on early village pottery. Modeled clay heads, fashioned to provide pot lids, appear in village sites at a somewhat later time, but never a face painted on a bowl's interior. Perhaps the one we know was meant to represent a village shaman who drew his powers from the water spirits.

Villages of early farm folk were, from the beginning, laid out according to plan. Always a central cluster of animal pens, storage pits, and houses—some round and semi-subterranean, their floors plastered with white clay, some square with level floors. Around this center, always a drainage ditch separated, on the east, the pottery kilns from the living quarters and, on the north, the living from the dead. The cemetery separation was only for adults. Infant dead were placed in pottery urns and buried in the space between huts, close to home and mother. In the cemeteries themselves the positioning of the occupants, the sorts of funeral offerings, and the occupants themselves help to reveal something of life in early village times. In one cemetery archaeologists uncovered ninety-nine skeletons. Their general look, say the Chinese specialists of our day, approaches a Polynesian rather than a Tungus model. The specialized, cold-adapted northern Mongolic face appears not yet to have characterized early Chinese farming folk.

As the years, then the centuries, then the millenniums

went by, farm villages ceased to provide each its own cemetery and began to bury the dead in land shared with neighbors. To Dr. Chang this change suggests a widening recognition of common family membership as numbers increased. Though farm lands might grow poor, though families might have to break up and move on to found other villages, the old ties were not forgotten, the pull of homeland remained strong. So it was that people wanted to return home at the end, wanted to lay their bones in native earth. This reverence for homeland as an extension, indeed a vital part, of family itself, can be noted in the earliest written documents and was to remain always a powerful, a persistent theme in the Chinese way.

The togetherness of kin, the apartness from nonkin, can be read, too, in the Yang-shao habit of clustering huts in the little villages and finally in their construction of large and imposing central buildings—perhaps intended for communal use, perhaps meant to house one leading family line and its extensions.

By 2000 B.C. or so, in larger, more elaborate villages built somewhat to the east of the Yang-shao sites, difference in rank became noticeable. Some families were clearly more important than others, and importance appears to have been confirmed by the possession of jade. Caches of it have been located, always in one or two village spots, never in even distribution. In much later times, in Chou Dynasty times (after 1100 B.C.), jade would carry heavenly connotations. Tablets of it were then used to cover the body openings of the dead—that is to say, of the dead whose family survivors could afford the cost. By 100 B.C. the very rich and the very important were wearing jade union suits to the grave. Just such suits, encasing the bodies of a prince and his wife, were discovered in 1968 by a unit of the People's Liberation Army detailed to archaeological excavation.

In 2000 B.C., during the second phase of northern China

village culture called by the specialists Lung-shan after the site in which the culture was first identified, when families had begun to draw away from one another and to emphasize differences in wealth and rank, whole villages were following the same trend. Each had begun to vaunt its individual identity, perhaps even its superiority over others. We can read this growing sense of village identity and the intensification of competition and conflict in the appearance of defensive walls built of rammed-earth. We can read it, too, in weapons of war —few in the Yang-shao sites, many in those of Lung-shan. In one site of the period a knot of skeletons has been uncovered, some decapitated, some with the contorted limbs of violent death. Clearly, villages had taken to war.

Life had changed for the Lung-shan people in other ways, more peaceful ways, as well. Farmers had begun to add to their basic crops rice, some legumes, and water chestnuts. In their pens were many cattle and sheep. Rarely were there horses, and the few remains found cannot be certified by the experts as domesticated. Skills in arts and crafts had flourished over the years. Pottery—some of it fashioned on wheels—was thin and fine with elegant pedestals or dainty tripod bases. Some pieces, surely too fine for everyday, may have been intended for ritual use. Celebrations and devotions were no doubt undergoing elaboration along with other areas of life. We do know that scapulimancy first came into vogue during Lung-shan times. How it began or from whence the idea came cannot yet be told. The shoulder blades are simply there, cracked but as yet uninscribed.

Writing appeared some centuries after 1850 B.C., after the transition had been made to city life, to the culture style called Shang after the dynasty which first ruled royal China. Shang cities were built, some of them, on the very ruins of their Lung-shan antecedents. In them the village plan, the pattern, the tendency to separate in space what in human life was distinct in function and condition, was brought to final expression.

In essence, each city was a network of interdependent suburbs, each one a seat of special activity or purpose. Always there was an administrative, later a palatial center with residences, the whole surrounded by walls of rammed-earth. There were also farming villages, their fields enriched perhaps (as in later times) by human waste carried out from the other centers. There were work-and-residence units for the potters, for the bronzesmiths (privilege and rank much in view here), for the workers in jade, for laborers in the bone factories where tools and implements were fashioned (mostly from human raw material). There were the various suburbs of the dead—the common dead (often sacrificial victims, decapitated and with hands and feet bound), the well-born, the royals. These last cemeteries would grow with time to monumental proportions as graves became veritable mansions, roomy enough to accommodate countless art treasures; dogs, horses, chariots; countless human victims all meant to accompany the ruler, to insure his immortality with the essences of their little lives.

Sacrifices of animals and men were made as well in the building of the city center, of its mounded altar of the soil, of its walls, and in the erection of its great pillars and the opening of its city gates. In later Chou times, though the numbers of victims had diminished, it was still thought necessary to provide a city with its spiritual guardians. Heads of soldiers conquered in war were buried beneath the walls. Dogs were thought to be particularly effective in combatting evil spirits and so were dug into the soil beneath the city gates. The living watchman installed at the gate was ever supposed to be a trusted vassal, so loyal, so devoted to his lord that he would willingly allow his feet to be amputated. Footless, he could never desert his charge.

In Shang cities, the greatest rituals were those offered by

the king to his ancestors who in turn communed with Shang Ti, the King of Heaven. Later the living king would be known as the Son of Heaven with more direct connections. We know the meaning of the beautiful bronze offering urns and wine vessels and of the dragons and monster masks which were their constant decorations. We know these things because, in the cities and the dynasty of Shang, history and prehistory meet.

The ancient *Book of Documents* traces Chinese history (the history of "the Middle Kingdom") back to the emperors Yao and Shun, presumed to have begun their reigns in 2356 and 2255 B.C., respectively. Ssu-ma Ch'ien, with access to written sources now lost, cites three additional figures believed to have preceded Yao and Shun. Together they completed the list of Five Rulers (the number five having mystical significance in Chinese thought). And, in the view of some scholars, even these five had their predecessors in the shadowy August Ones (three in number) who were believed to have begun their reigns sometime around 2852 B.C. after P'an-ku, "the dog of many colors" had helped to create the world or to deal with barbarians who appeared, it would seem, as a natural consequence of creation.

Centuries later, Ssu-ma Ch'ien was criticized by scholars for having given credence to old superstitions. Ssu-ma Ch'ien, himself a worldly and level-headed man, doubtless had his own questions about the mystical, magical Five Rulers and August Ones. Nevertheless, tradition sanctified through these images a system of social and political order extending back to the beginning of human time, and Ssu-ma Ch'ien must have appreciated the importance of such a concept. It established once and for all the primacy of moral order, ever to be expressed in the virtue of kings.

True Chinese history for Ssu-ma Ch'ien (and in the view of other scholars as well) begins with the Hsia Dynasty for which he listed a succession of kings. He listed also the particular virtues of its founding father and the errors of its final king. The archaeological record so far contains nothing to substantiate the existence of Hsia unless the memories and gathering traditions of the Lung-shan late farming phase persisted into historical times.

The Major Chinese Dynasties

Shang	c.1700–1100 B.C
Chou	1100–221 B.C.
Ch'in	221–206 B.C.
Han	206 B.C.–A.D. 220
Sui	A.D. 581–618
T'ang	618–907
Sung	960–1279
Yuan (Mongols)	1260–1368
Ming	1368–1644
Ch'ing (Manchu)	1644–1912

The last Hsia emperor, corrupt and therefore unworthy of rule, was thought to have been defeated by the conquering T'ang, scion of the ducal family of Shang. The chronicles peg this at 1766 B.C., a date which agrees well with those assigned by modern archaeologists to Shang city sites. T'ang was said to have established his capital in a city called P'o. Between the time of the founding of the dynasty and the move to the last capital at Yin (sometime around 1400), five other capitals were believed built and occupied by the royal court. Just which of the archaeological sites represents which named city is not yet finally determined. Yin, however, has been discovered near the modern city of An-yang, north of the Yellow River and considerably east of its great bend. One should say, rather, *rediscovered,* for it was never really lost. The people of Ssu-ma Ch'ien's own time referred to the site as "the ruins of Yin." Here records and remains converge, tombs can be identified, and correlations with king lists made. Here begin the inscriptions of oracle bones and the whole bureaucratic process of record keeping. Indeed, one pit was found to contain nothing but engraved tortoise shells and one human skeleton—the Keeper of the Archives, perhaps?

Record keeping was to continue unabated into the second historical dynasty, the Chou, whose founder, King Wen, defeated the last Shang ruler (as corrupt and unworthy as the last Hsia king) around 1100 B.C. There were the inevitable changes. The capital was moved west to Chou homelands in the ancient nuclear zone. More dogs were interred in royal Chou tombs and fewer human beings. More and fuller messages were inscribed on turtle carapaces and bronze ritual and commemorative vessels. Here is a typical message, dated to the tenth century B.C.

> *Third month, first quarter, day* ting hai, *King Mu, being in Hsia Yu, offered the sweet wine, and Ching Po the great Ritualist responded with the She rite: and King Mu offered the* mieh *rite to Chang Fu. Then [the king] came to Ching Po's place, and Ching Po was great in respect and failed in nothing. Chang Fu performed the* mieh li *rite and made bold to wish for the great prosperity of the Son of Heaven. To commemorate these occasions he had this sacral vessel made.*

Both inscriptions and traditional patterns preserved in the writings of later times suggest the condition of the family, surely the master institution of Chinese life. The line of the father was, in Chou times, more important than ever and more enclosed. Family lines and their many segments and offshoots had developed into clans claiming common ritual and ancestry but unable to trace exact descent. One now had to marry, not only out of one's lineage, but out of the clan as well. By Ssu-ma

Ch'ien's time it would be unlawful for a man and woman of the same clan name to marry—however distant their homelands and ancestral connections.

The new bride in any family was rather more a token of lineage and clan alliance than a figure of romance. Marcel Granet translates the early word for bride as "enemy." A young man married, after all, in clans where, in time of feud, he might very well fight. Doubtless the situation was eased all around when the family chose a bride who, enemy in name, was not necessarily so in claim, someone familiar, someone known—at least known to the future mother-in-law. For that lady had, after all, an emotional stake in the transaction at least equivalent to that of the young husband. A bride from mother's own lineage, her brother's daughter, could very well become a personal ally rather than a rival for her son's affection. Preference for the cross-cousin as marriage partner was made plain in modes of address. A child was instructed to call father's brothers "father." Their wives as well as mother's sisters were "mother." But mother's brother and father's sister were introduced from the beginning as father-in-law and mother-in-law.

In the royal house this custom of cross-cousin marriage would allow queens to control the marriages of their sons and sometimes more than that. Since the royal mother could reasonably expect her son to defer to her wishes (filial piety was ever the cornerstone of proper behavior), she could, if she tried hard, exercise control of the state as well. Any number of queens and concubines (ignored or ill-treated as young women) would acquire power in China through their sons. Of course it was first necessary to beguile, and to beguile thoroughly, the royal husband who might favor any number of ladies but who would recognize as heir only the son of his great wife. And so it was that intrigue, slander, threat, counter-threat, and outright murder were, from the beginning, commonplace in the royal and ducal harems as high-born ladies struggled each to give her son priority.

As suggested in Chapter 5, the Chou are believed by some historians to have had early connections with the northern barbarians. Ssu-ma Ch'ien tells us that the founder of the House of Chou, having quarreled with the then current Shang king, went "to live with the Western Jung, adopting their ways." Later this knowledge was to help Chou kings in their dealings with the Hsiung-nu. Whether skill in negotiations derived from fluency in what was or would become the Turkic mother tongue or whether it derived from outright descent must remain a matter of conjecture. But there are some intriguing questions about the Chou. *Shang-ti,* High Heaven God of the Shang, became known during Chou times as *Ti'en*—perhaps related to the Turkic *Tengri?* The Chinese often referred to themselves as the Black-Headed People, and so had the Sumerians half a world away on the other side of the Asiatic steppes. One wonders whether the title in both cases represents an effort to draw a contrast between own-group and neighboring folk. The Chou, it is interesting to note, called only their subjects the Black-Headed People.

Whatever Chou antecedents, whatever infusion of steppe influence, the old Chinese patterns of belief and behavior, of ritual and propriety continued and were enhanced. They continued after 770 B.C. when the Chou, hard-pressed by steppe nomads, moved their capital east of the Yellow River's great bend to Lo-yang. Continued as the Chou slowly lost power, lost authority, lost all but the right to perform for the general good the ancient rites which linked heaven and earth.

The Chou king's loss was the nobility's gain. Feudal lords great and small took unto themselves both the right to ritual and the right to make war. Houses struggled and contended, and, in a century or so, several large ducal states had emerged. On the northern marches, Yen (in which Peking would eventually be founded), Chin (divided later into Chao, Wei, and Han), and Ch'in in what had once been the lands of the Chou. In the middle tier were the dukedoms of Ch'i, Lu, and Sung. On the southern marches were Ch'u, Wu, and Yueh—the populations of all three composed of foreign peoples, speaking non-Chinese languages and holding to a greater or lesser degree customs incompatible with the ceremonious Chinese way. "We are barbarians," once growled a duke of Ch'u with rather more pride than the discomfiture proper to such an admission.

The states vied among themselves for leadership, their alliances and their enmities shifting as the years went by. Great lords undertook to build walls against the northern barbarians. They gathered to themselves vassals and retainers, scholars, historians, archivists. Ducal court protocol itself grew ever more formal and elaborate, and so did courtly art and courtly dress. Large-scale human sacrifice was reinstituted to enhance the glory and insure the immortality of great lords. The knowledge of iron smelting became known, and iron began to be used ceremonially in the tombs of the mighty, sometimes as collars around the necks of sacrificed slaves. A few great lords began to call themselves *wang,* or king, a title still at that time reserved for the Chou dynasts. And some even had the temerity to perform for their own people the royal rites. War ceased to be a chivalrous event and became an enterprise of conquest. Ambush and assassination and massacre were the order of the day. Over several hundred years the struggles raged, becoming truly epic during the years from 450–221 B.C., the so-called period of warring states. It was a time of fear and danger, a time when the old order had passed away and no verity remained.

Some scholars, sickened by the chaos around them, retreated to the countryside, there to contemplate the beauty of nature and to find what serenity they could. Just such a one was Lao-tze, a former treasury official of one of the contending states. The time of his retirement is usually set around 550 B.C.

though no one is entirely certain of this. What is certain is that Lao-tze did not remain alone in his hermitage. Disciples came, sat at his feet, and lived to perpetuate his philosophy. It was a philosophy devoted rather to the liberation of feeling than to the discipline of proper behavior, rather to the examination of the inward climate than to the perceptions of the outer senses. It sought the merging of the individual and his reality, indeed of every reality, in the Absolute, the Way, the Tao. Said Lao-tze:

*The heaven and earth join,
And the sweet rain falls
Beyond the command of men,
Yet evenly upon all.*

*Then human civilizations arose and there were names,
Since names there were,
It were well one knew where to stop for repose.
He who knows where to stop for repose
May from danger be exempt.
Tao in the world
May be compared
To rivers that run into the sea.*

Years later, Chuang Tsu, a follower of the Way, would write:

What, then, is Tao? There is the Tao of God and there is the Tao of man. Honor through inaction comes from the Tao of God; entanglement through action comes from the Tao of man. The Tao of God is fundamental; the Tao of man is accidental.

Taoism was in time to incorporate many of the ancient spirit beings of nature still loved and honored by country folk. It was to give credence to the spiritual charlatans who gained a powerful influence over Wu Ti, the soldier-king of the Han Dynasty. Its followers would, over the years, variously emphasize the call to contemplation and the call to emotional release; would make of it alternately a religion or a philosophy; would see in it a means of personal immortality, not in another world, but in this one. When Buddhism entered China, sometime around 200 A.D., it was confused for a time with Taoism and then, after a separation, both suffered persecution, resurgence, and at last an uneasy coexistence.

However many scholars dropped out of ducal bureaucracy, many more remained. For all the dangers and uncertainties, the period of warring states was a time of creative ferment. Ideas waxed and waned, attracted adherents, organized into schools. And schools of thought contended as energetically as did the armies of great lords on the field. There were the Taoists with their growing influence. There were the Legalists who advised their masters to devise ever more exacting laws and stronger armies, to punish and subjugate their people and in so doing to centralize power. There were the Mohists who decried war and preached universal goodness and universal love. There were the Namers who thought that by proper designation and classification all things could be comprehended. And then there was Confucius.

Born 551 B.C. in the ducal state of Lu, Confucius (K'ung Fu-tse) was trained in the ethics of rule, trained to do good service for a prince. Unfortunately, no one would hire him though he applied to seventy different rulers, great and small. "If someone would employ me," Ssu-ma Ch'ien, quoting *Analects,* has him say, "I would accomplish something worthwhile in no more than a year." Alas, his talents were, perforce, confined to his school and to the training of his seventy disciples: his "little children, ambitious and too hasty . . . who must be shown how to restrict and shape themselves." It was, perhaps, the best thing that could have happened, for he produced, instead of advice for one prince, advice which was to instruct and inform thinkers of the East in his own time and in our own.

His teachings were based on the *Ching,* the Classics, ancient writings some of which he merely collected, others of which were edited by him (so holds the persistent tradition). His own writings and those of some of his disciples would later be added to the essential body of literature. A knowledge of the Classics became in time the basic intellectual equipment of scholars, the subject of learned examination and commentary. Intellectual adventurers were not encouraged. "I am a transmitter," said Confucius, and so did his followers, thus shutting the door firmly against innovation. But why not? In the Confucian view, one received one's guidance from the past. Against its teachings one measured present behavior and built thence to a better, more virtuous future. Perhaps this is why technological achievements, such as printing, gun powder, the compass, attained so much earlier in China than in the West, caused in their home of invention so little stir.

The past and its Classics included:

The Book of Documents. Ritual and historical statements, edicts, exhortations, king lists, presumably from earliest times to about 670 B.C.

The Book of Odes. Poetry of rites and of love and sorrow; the songs of court and those of the countryside.

The Book of Changes. A manual of divination and healing.

The Spring and Autumn Annals. A spare account of events which took place following the sharp decline of Chou power, all seen from the standpoint of a scholar (scholars) of the state of Lu. To this book were later added three commentaries, at least one of which was a kind of popular history in its own right.

The Book of Rites. A manual of ritual and ceremony dating back to the times of the early Chou. Rites were important to

Confucius and his fellow scholars, not so much because of their relationship to the supernatural ("We don't know yet how to serve men," said he in the *Analects*. "How can we know about serving spirits?"), but because of their relationship to order. Whether rooted in the spirit world or not, ritual does reflect and express what is sacred to a people. Ritual shows men what to feel and how to feel. It purifies emotion and inculcates discipline. It upholds ideals of behavior and thus confirms the harmony of heaven and earth. This, in the Confucian sense, is fundamental to humanity.

To the Classics were later added *The Four Books:* the *Analects* (the conversations of Confucius as remembered by his disciples), along with the writings of three individual disciples. The whole has been much edited and augmented over the years.

Throughout the Classics and in other documents known to Ssu-ma Ch'ien certain themes are stressed. One concerns the Mandate of Heaven without which no aristocratic house might come to power. Celestial consent was believed to be manifested in signs and portents. Each of the great rulers and the founders of dynasties had been set apart by a miraculous birth. The mother of one was said to have conceived by stepping in the footprint of a giant; another by accidentally swallowing the egg of a strange bird; another thanks to a blue dragon which alighted on her breast; yet another through a dream of the sun, ruler of the sky. Reigns of heaven-sponsored kings were said to be marked by comets, eclipses, or by the appearance of dragons in the sky, always symbolic of beneficent moisture. Indeed the faces of such kings bore dragon-features (a beauty mark in Chinese terms). Even in later times Kao-tsu, founder of the Han Dynasty, was credited with a dragon face and a miraculous birth. Wherever he traveled, Ssu-ma Chi'en tells us, bright clouds followed his passage.

The Mandate rewarded only virtuous men, men of reverence, humility, and compassion. Said the conquering T'ang (founder of Shang) to his new subjects:

Do not [ye princes] follow lawless ways; make no approach to insolence and dissoluteness; let every one be careful to keep to his statutes that so we may receive the favor of Heaven. . . . The good in you I will not dare to keep concealed; and the evil in me, I will not dare forgive myself. I will examine the things in harmony with the mind of God. When guilt is found anywhere in you who occupy the myriad regions, let it rest on me, the One Man. When guilt is found in me, the One Man, it shall not attach to you.

In the *Analects,* Confucius held:

He who exercises government by means of his virtue may be compared to the north polar star, which keeps its place and all the other stars turn toward it.

And of the factors of government, he also said:

People must have sufficient to eat; there must be a sufficient army; and there must be confidence of the people in the ruler.

When asked which of these essentials might be expendable, he said, first the army, then sufficient food.

Virtue never seemed to reside permanently in a royal house. When it declined, the Mandate of Heaven was withdrawn. Thus the lines of Hsia and Shang ended in corrupt kings, toppled by conquerors newly blessed with the Mandate. But virtue could be cultivated, even, in some instances, throughtfully reconstituted. For this, the ruler needed a sage.

It may be no accident that the importance of wise counsel is constantly reiterated throughout the Classics. The Five Rulers were said each to have chosen, as his successor, a wise minister rather than a less capable son. Only with Yu, first of the Hsia line, could a son begin to have expectations of the throne. The presentation to Heaven of a chosen sage was considered one of the prime duties of a sovereign. A young king of the Shang, he who moved his capital to Yin, implored his chosen sage,

> *Morning and evening present your instructions to aid my virtue. Suppose me a weapon of steel;—I will use you for a whetstone. Suppose me crossing a great stream;—I will use you for a boat with its oars. Suppose me in a year of great drought;—I will use you as copious rain. Open your mind and enrich my mind. Be you like medicine which must distress the patient in order to cure his sickness. Think of me as one walking barefoot, whose feet are sure to be wounded, if he do not see the ground.*

Wrote a disciple of Confucius in *The Great Learning* (part of *The Four Books*):

> *To see men of worth and not be able to raise them to office; to raise them to office but not to do so quickly:—this is disrespectful. To see bad men and not be able to remove them; to remove them, but not to do so at a distance:—this is weakness.*

Kao-tsu of Han, when asked how he had managed to best his enemies and win an empire, answered that he had been surrounded by men of extraordinary ability and had known how to make use of them. "It is difficult to be a king," Confucius had pointed out in earlier times, "but it is not easy to be a minister, either."

In writing of the cautious Wen, second of the Han emperors to wield power in his own right, Ssu-ma Ch'ien extolled his humility and his virtue, his simplicity in the matter of mortuary arrangements, his compassion in punishment, his willingness to accept criticism. It was his indirect way of instructing in virtue the emperor of his own time, the capricious and vengeful Wu Ti (141–87 B.C.). In a palace with its endless slanders and intrigues, great punishment was often decreed for what we would consider small offense. One such was the crime of "deceitful advice"—meaning advice the emperor did not wish to hear. Ssu-ma Ch'ien himself had suffered for such advice and hoped through his writing to temper Wu Ti's callous cruelty, of mitigating the royal wrath. No doubt all the parables and maxims of the Classics were written in a similar hope, in a similar effort of wise and learned men to counter, to restrict absolute royal power with an ideal of virtue which, in its own way, was also absolute.

The sages in their ardent pursuit of wisdom extolled the self-made intellectual and were fond of pointing out how little high birth meant in the attainment of honor. Emperor Wu Ti (who had his own reasons for wanting to weaken the old nobility) was easily persuaded to choose for high position men of intellectual attainment as demonstrated by their understanding of the Classics. He caused the following to be proclaimed through the land:

Exceptional work demands exceptional men. A bolting or kicking horse may eventually become a most valuable animal. A man who is the object of the world's detestation may live to accomplish great things. As with the untractable horse, so with the infatuated man;—it is simply a question of training.

We therefore command the various district officials to search for men of brilliant and exceptional talents, to be Our generals, Our ministers, and Our envoys to distant States.

And from that time on, rank in government service was supposed to derive from success in competitive examinations, not by way of family position.

The unknown compilers of the Classics increasingly seemed to emphasize the voiceless will of the people. In *The Book of Documents,* the conquering T'ang was thus quoted:

> *The Great God has conferred even on the inferior people a moral sense, compliance with which would show their nature invariably right.*

Later in the same book, the conquering founder of the House of Chou was made to say:

> *Heaven loves the people, and the sovereign should reverence the mind of Heaven. . . . Heaven compassionates the people. What the people desire, Heaven will be found to give effect to.*

Mencius, a follower of Confucius, was later to equate the will of the people with the Mandate of Heaven.

Writings and ideals all played their part in bringing to the empire in Han times a greater stability and unity than it had ever known and, if not a strictly classless society, then at least one in which talented individuals could rise on their own merits—and fall as rapidly through failure. It began in 221 B.C. with the rise to power of the House of Ch'in (from which, by the way, China got its name). The conquering duke, who took the name Ch'in Shih Huang-ti, subjugated the other warring states, completed the Great Wall, and ousted once and for all the shadow king of the Chou. Firmly in power, he moved to consolidate his gains and to assure the future of his line.

This meant, for one thing, a great calling in of all weapons of war and, for another, a great burning of the Confucian Classics. He recognized in them a danger to his plans greater than the danger of weapons hidden and held. Ssu-ma Ch'ien says that the king not only burned books but buried scholars —alive. Those scholars who remained hale scattered, preached dissent, and supported with fervor the general uprising that occurred during the reign of the second Ch'in emperor.

The uprising was kindled by a common man, a peasant, and ended (in 206 B.C.) by a petty official of some learning and (according to Ssu-ma Ch'ien) limitless virtue. Here again the

Mandate was presumed to be at work. Generals, local officials, and relatives of the new emperor preempted princely fiefs and managed them more or less well. Barbarians north and south made inroads. There were about as many dissidents and revolts as in earlier times, but somehow the empire of the Han Dynasty held for four hundred years. What is more, it expanded far beyond its original sphere of rule or influence. This must be credited, in large part, to Wu Ti who harbored dreams of glory in the great world and who longed to receive the homage of foreign rulers, near and far. Army after army he sent against the Hsiung-nu and against the tattooed people of the south, using so many horses in the process that horse sacrifices had to be curtailed and wooden images substituted for the real thing. He spent such fortunes on his glory road as to beggar the country and then, in order to keep the treasury afloat, had to slap monopolies on iron and salt. He sold offices to the highest bidders (all the while loudly proclaiming his admiration for merit). He had the courts levy high fines for trivial offenses and pocketed the profits. He decreed death and mutilation and then allowed the condemned to buy commutation if they could. And all to stretch his borders in four directions, if not five. He pacified Korea and, it is said, accepted submission from Japan. His troops pushed north into Hsiung-nu territory and west into the great wastes of what is now Sinkiang, all the way to the city of Fergana on the western edge of Taklamakan. Through Fergana and the western oases would enter China the goods of other lands and their ideas, too. From this direction came Buddhism, Manichaeism, Nestorian Christianity, and later Islam.

In the southwest, in what is now Yunnan Province, Han troops extracted submission of the Kingdom of Tien. (Archaeological excavations here have revealed a way of life and an art strikingly reminiscent both of Southeast Asia and of the northern steppes.) Into the forests of North Vietnam went the Han troops and into the mountains of Tibet, carving an empire and a national sense that caused Chinese of the north ever after to call themselves Men of Han. Boundaries established by Han were fated to expand and contract as central governments tightened or relaxed their hold, as old provinces and ethnic groups gained or lost autonomy. China was at its largest during Manchu times (1644–1912). With the recovery of Tibet, the modern Communist state has regained that dimension.

From the earliest foundation of empire, the Chinese were able to count within their borders or on the periphery over a hundred ethnic groups. The Han added more. Many of these peoples, named in the Classics or in the works of Ssu-ma Ch'ien, remain to this day separate entities, as yet un-sinicized and much as they always were. The Miao and Lolo, cited in *The Book of Documents,* still inhabit southern China. So do the Chuang, the Tibetans (once called Ch'iang), the Uigur, Mongols, Tungus. The Hsiung-nu have vanished—absorbed by what people we do not know.

The Chinese attitude toward non-Chinese was, in Ssu-ma Ch'ien's time at least, ambivalent. He held that both Hsiung-nu and the people of Tien were descended from the Hsia emperor Yu, thus conferring on them human status. In spite of honorable origins, however, barbarians were considered clearly inferior to Chinese, not necessarily in terms of looks or language, but in their general ignorance of civilized belief and civilized behavior. The more non-Chinese came to honor Chinese notions of propriety, the more acceptable they tended to become.

This ancient ambivalence of attitude seems to have continued into modern times, though notions of what constitutes appropriate rites and beliefs have changed very much indeed. And notions of how best to foster propriety appear to change from year to year. For a time assimilation was strongly pressed. Today different policies prevail. Reporters for *The New York*

Times, traveling recently in China, have noted both government concern for the identity of ethnic groups and government care that identity not develop into separateness. Local religious practice, therefore—Mongol and Tibetan Buddhism, Mohammedanism, or lesser known tribal belief—is artfully discouraged though traditional religious shrines are scrupulously preserved.

Ethnic groups on China's frontiers (except the Manchurian ones) appear to receive special attention, are allowed to retain their own languages, both for schooling and in work, and Chinese administrators in these areas must perforce learn the local language. Russian newspapers, on the other hand, accuse the Chinese of genocide among their ethnic groups, particularly in Tibet and Sinkiang. As Tibet has been taken by force not too long ago, death and destruction were certainly involved. Border nomads of the north, who receive no overlord with joy, have complained of their treatment in both China and Russia. Tactfully worded accounts in Chinese newspapers of 1964 and the content of poster art and placards hint of trouble with minority groups. There is simply no way of telling just how non-Chinese native folk of Great China perceive themselves in relation to the central government.

Whatever the attitude of minority and tribal groups, it has developed through long contact and interaction. The Men of Han are not a new force to be reckoned with. Neither is the new order in China itself completely free of its ancient context, its historic roots. From the beginning of Chinese writing, there can be discerned a fairly constant strain toward Utopia and another, a counterpull toward the practical, toward making do with what is. The virtue of the common folk has been a continuing theme since earliest times, honored more in the breach than in the observance during some periods. In Han times, even while the royal dead, wearing suits of jade, were buried in rock tombs cut with the labor of many toiling peasants, village elders were being chosen to counsel with high government officials. Or so we are told by Ssu-ma Ch'ien.

Today Mao Tse-tung decrees that the past must serve the present, meaning that archaeological excavation must be interpreted in the light of present need and present belief. But the Chinese Classics have always served the needs of the present, rendering as history the moral lessons meant to shape the future.

In the study of the Classics, more than forty generations of scholars were trained and perhaps stifled. No more. Confucius himself—as memory or as saint—has been banned and degraded. His philosophy, insist today's leaders, inhibits the change necessary if China is to counter the barbarous but efficient West. Perhaps there are other reasons as well. China has a new Classic today. It is The Little Red Book, *The Thoughts of Chairman Mao,* and it is studied with all the concentration and reverence formerly devoted to *The Book of Documents* and *The Book of Odes.* Once upon a time, aptitude for higher education and for public office was determined by proficiency in the Classics. Today acceptance at university and in the professions depends first on proficiency in The Little Red Book and on demonstrated devotion to Marxist ideals.

In many ways, the new order has realized the old Confucian dreams of order and stability, of a society constellated around ideals of virtue. Vanished is the Confucian notion of the gentleman-scholar, the superior man. But then, any suggestion of superiority, physical, moral, or intellectual, is anathema now. Competition itself has been abolished, even the competition of ideas.

There was a brief time when it seemed this particular stricture might be eased. "Letting a hundred flowers bloom, and a hundred schools of thought contend", said Mao Tse-tung in 1957, "is the policy for promoting the progress of the arts and sciences." He naturally assumed that, in any intellectual free-for-all, the truth of Marxist ideas and ideals could only be reinforced. The response was quite other than anticipated. There were not only quibbles and complaints; the system itself was challenged. Hurriedly, the "hundred flowers" were cut, the "contending schools" silenced, and an anti-rightist campaign mounted. Indeed, some of the more outspoken among intellectuals were sent to labor in the fields or to clean latrines in universities where once they had lectured. In such humble occupations they were to perceive the more readily the errors of negative thinking. But universities and university personnel were to suffer worse indignities in years to come.

Between 1958 and 1965, his economic policies having failed, Mao was in eclipse. His surge back to power was borne on a wave of youthful idealism which quickly turned to excess. This was the Cultural Revolution meant to purge the four "olds"—old ideas, old culture, old habits, old custom. Young students sought to restore purity of Marxist thought by violent demonstrations and enforced self-criticism, by show trials and book burnings. Out with the old, the corrupt, the impure. Long live the new!

But book burnings are not new in China. The writings of the Sage, repeatedly and by a succession of rulers, have been found dangerously subversive. Self-criticism and thought reform, the constant re-education in orthodoxy, this is not new. Neither are show trials and wholesale disruption ending finally in the familiar political mix of autocracy and benevolence. Sudden shifts in the political cast of characters, reorbitings around the center of power, these have been familiar since Han times. So, too, has been the spectacular political rise and the just as spectacular fall. In Wu Ti's view, a minister might as well be punished for saying nothing at all as for saying that which the emperor did not wish to hear. "Disapproval at heart" was the name of the particular crime, and many a minister died because of it, because of insufficient enthusiasm, because of an inadvertent frown, a pursed lip, a wag of the head. Silent dissent is, even today, likely to cost a public official his job though certainly not his life.

Perhaps never since the bad old days of the warring states has the Chinese climate favored for any extended period the wrangling of intellectuals or the full expression of dissent. Perhaps it never will. Not in the cities where factory workers and apartment-block residents are organized into study groups —and sometimes "struggle" groups—designed to achieve uniformity of thought and correctness of behavior. Not in villages where the commune binds soul to soil and future to past, as once the family spread its subtle net. To the commune now come the oft resentful city children, sent landward by governmental decree to learn and revere the village way, ancient before ever the first cities were built in Great China.

10

VILLAGE CHINA
The Earth, The Grain, The Forefathers

They saw their various kinds of grain, each seed containing in it a germ of life. In unbroken lines rises the blade and, well nourished, the stalk grows long. Luxuriant looks the young grain. . . . Then come the reapers in crowds. And the grain is piled up in the fields. . . . It is not here only that there is this [abundance]; it is not now only that there is such a time; from of old it has been thus.

FROM earliest Chou times this ancient song was chanted by the Black-Headed People and by the king himself as he plowed the first spring furrow and prayed at the Altar of Earth and Grain. Men on their own farms would repeat the joyous thanksgiving:

With my vessel full of bright millet
And my pure victim-rams
We sacrificed to [the spirits of] the Land and to the Four Quarters.

Long before the dynasty was founded, the people of Chou built for their duke a great city and there

*reared the great altar to the Spirits of the Land
From which all great movement should proceed.*

In 1921, the anthropologist Sidney D. Gamble found Altars of Earth and Grain in Ting Hsien, a village complex near Peking.

In the early 1940s, sociologist Martin C. Yang found in the Shantung village of Taitou a shrine of the God of Earth and Grain, the guardian of village life, to whom sons reported a parent's death, to whom the new bride did homage on her wedding day.

In the 1940s as well, in Nanching, near Canton, the sociologist C. K. Yang found the God of Earth and Grain the focus of village concern and village honor.

In the 1960s, long after the old gods were giving way to the New China, the God of Earth and Grain was alive and well and living in British southern China, in the "New Territories" of Hong Kong. Anthropologist Hugh Baker found there the Earth God's shrines—small ones in each of the eight hamlets comprising Sheung Shui Village, and a large one near the oldest of the hamlets, earth-walled and moated for protection against pirates, bandits, other lineages, and an imperial army long since forgotten. It was to the Earth God that deaths in Sheung Shui were announced, and at the shrine appeared the hopeful bridegroom (as well as the bride) on the morning of their wedding day. It was to the Earth God that women prayed for fertility. It was from the Earth God that farmers begged abundant crops and protection against insect pests.

Surely the needs of the farmer are many. Let him build his tiny fields with ever loving care; let him collect with diligence the household wastes that feed the earth; let his women and children plant and water with utmost reverence: there yet comes the storm which strikes, the water which drowns, the drought which burns. And so he prays as his forebears prayed that the dikes and dams will not break, the storm not bend, and that the good grain will grow strong and tall.

In the North that good grain is millet (once thought to be a god itself) in all its many varieties: "Black millet and double-kernelled," sings a poet of *The Book of Odes,* "the tall red and the white." There is also kaoliang, the dependable sorghum, which can be grown in poor soil, and barley and soybean. From the flour of these is made the nourishing gruel, referred to in *The Book of Odes* as "the soup of sacrifice." In the North there is also wheat, the food of the wealthy—white wheat to make noodles and rolls for the wedding feast, white wheat to send in cakes to the bride's family. The successful man in northern China, says Martin Yang, is often compared to wheat. "Why should he not have a smooth face?" people say. "He eats wheat flour every day."

There are other foods. In the South there is the indispensable, the ever present rice, grown usually in wet paddy fields. There are vegetables in small gardens. And everywhere, in all parts of the land, there are sweet potatoes. In the North, says Dr. Yang, potatoes are considered food for the poor who do not admit to the dependence lest they be called, insultingly, "potato eaters."

However the fields differ in richness of crop and numbers of laborers, they and their community of farmer-owners must be protected from dangers without and dangers within. It was the God of Earth and Grain who personified this common concern, this communal need. From it had emerged the village watch, manned in turn by a member of each household. From it, too, derived the village council, formal or informal, which had to settle disputes and deal with capricious officialdom in the world outside the village.

In each house in Village China there burned a fire, and presiding over each hearth there was in the old days (and perhaps still is in Hong Kong) the Kitchen God and sometimes the Kitchen Goddess as well. They are the arbiters of domestic affairs and can, if properly attended, grant success in matters great and small. They also watch, and what is seen must be reported to the Heavenly Judges. Prudently, therefore, the housewife yearly daubs the god's mouth with sweets before he is "sent home." Let his report be honey sweet and no punishment befall the home! Kitchen gods in the Yangtze Valley village visited by Dr. Fei Hsiao-tung cannot report at all. Their mouths are sealed shut with sticky rice cake. And when the Divine Emperor asks, "Has your family been wasteful or shown disrespect for rice; have its members defiled the kitchen or thrown rubbish on the fire?" the Kitchen God can only shake his head.

In the market towns to which villagers of 1945 brought their grain, there were still many temples, some of them ancient but well kept, others crumbling and deserted. Some were large, others merely shrines accommodating each the single man or woman whose dedication had brought it into being. Some were bright and new. There were others whose original celestial tenants had been pushed aside for more popular deities. In the market town for Taitou and nineteen other villages there was, says Dr. Yang, a temple and priests for Kuan-Kung, sworn brother of the Emperor Shu of the Three Kingdoms, and for Tseng-sun, one of the seventy-two disciples of Confucius. There was a popular Buddhist temple and two Christian churches. There were also two shrines, one for the King of Cattle and one, unspecified as to deity, visited mainly by women. All except the Christian churches were supported by rentals from temple-owned land.

In the very large market town for the Ting Hsien complex, Dr. Gamble tells us, the temples were mostly Taoist and Buddhist. A scattering of Confucian temples, Christian churches,

Islamic mosques, and vision shrines completed the roster. In P'englai, an ancient walled city of Shantung Peninsula, there were also mosques and many important persons of Islamic faith, so Ida Pruitt was told by her informant, a working woman whose memory of the city stretched back to the 1860s.

Southward in Yunnan Province lies the little city called by anthropologist Francis L. K. Hsu simply West Town. There the visitor could find as late as 1945 the same variety of temples and faiths as in other Chinese cities. The rituals of several were built on scripture received by the pious in a dream. Each scripture contained elements of belief and form (old and new) then current, so that Taoist, Buddhist, Confucian, and Christian values and their celestial personages jostled happily in neighboring heavens. There were in West Town temple associations of great popularity and small shrines built to honor deified local folk. As far back as Han times celebrations of great men had been included in state rituals. And so it was that the deification of Confucius had come about. The practice stretched to include newer heroes as they appeared, and eventually prominent home-town souls.

Everywhere in China there seems to have been room for one more deity. Every individual interest, every nuance of belief could find a spiritual home. Through the long years, state persecutions of various organized religions had occurred, but infrequently and seldom as a matter of state policy. The concepts of orthodoxy and heresy (as these terms apply to religion, at least) are both alien to the traditional Chinese Way. Competing and cooperative gods are part of the natural order, as is a change of spiritual attachment. Perhaps tolerance is possible because, for the Chinese, early and late, the roots of life lie, not in the temple, but in the land; not in the transcendent bliss of the world to be, but in the world that is, a world that can be traced, solid link by solid link, family member to family member, from father to son forever and ever, time without end. Indeed, land and family are not so much two roots of a tree as they are the tree itself. Land and family are one. When land is gone, sold away, lost, then family is lost as well and forgotten.

On family land dwell the living. In family land lie the honored dead. Dead, and yet not dead, not extinguished as candle's flame is extinguished. For deceased forebears are merely transmuted to another realm, another dimension from which they may aid and prosper their descendants. The manner of their funeral predisposes them to benevolence, and sons exhaust themselves in expressing utmost grief and respect. The parental bodies are kept in the house for many days before interment; the longer the delay, the greater the respect. Coarse white cloth is worn in mourning. But the dead, mouths stuffed sometimes with sugar, hands filled with silver so as to placate the celestial dogs at Dog Mountain, are wrapped in garments of red, the color of life. In the South, in West Town, says Dr. Hsu, a small bowl of living, swimming fishes is interred beneath the corpse. Again the hope of life renewed, returned.

The funeral ritual is lavish. Hired mourners keen and wail, brass bands play, and paper effigies of horse and carriage, motor cars, houses, clothes, money are burned to comfort the loved one on his journey. Interment takes place in the family cemetery, the spot chosen and purchased for its favorable location. Not the kind of location that would necessarily seem favorable to us, not necessarily a spot with a picturesque view or good drainage or protection from gales. No. It must be land which in form, in configuration recalls the form of dragon or tiger. Such land, say the geomancers ("masters of wind and water" without whose advice no village or house or wall, let alone grave, can be properly sited), such land sends down roots to the very heart of life itself and confers upon living descendants life and fertility. *The Book of Odes* describes how a duke of Chou himself acted as geomancer in choosing the site for his city:

There the duke began with consulting,
There he singed the tortoise shell,
And the responses were:—there to stay and then.

As it was yesterday, so it is today (or was not so very long ago). To these favorable sites, to these homes of the ancestors yearly come their descendants. Picnic meals are brought and cooked and ceremonially fed to those gone on. Yearly, during the time of the winter solstice, the dead are invited home again to share a feast, to hear news of the harvest and of family doings. A poet presumably of Shang times sings in the *The Book of Odes,*

Ah! Ah! Our meritorious ancestor!
Permanent are the blessings coming from him. . . .
The clear spirits are in our vessels,
And there is granted to us the realization of our thoughts.
There are also the well-tempered soups,
Prepared beforehand, the ingredients rightly proportioned.
By these offerings we invite his presence . . .

In West Town, while Dr. Hsu was a visitor, surviving relatives took steps to contact the loved ones gone on in a tangible way, tried to learn their wishes and how they might be comforted. Dr. Hsu describes such a scene in the temple association. Here the ancestors were believed able to contact their relatives through mediums, able to write through living hands messages in sand. A scribe was always available to record the message on paper as well so that the relative might have something permanent to take home with him. Sometimes a god spoke in the soul's stead, providing such messages as this one, conveyed to a deceased man's sister:

This man is specially favored by superior deities; he suffered from no restrictions or punishments at all; scripture reading since death has raised him to guest house; he is waiting for opportunities to enter the world above.

In West Town, too, in each large, rich house, there was invariably set aside a room for the honoring of the ancestors. Tablets inscribed with their names were hung therein. Sometimes small figures of Confucius, Juan Jung, the Goddess of Mercy, Buddha, or other deities accompanied the tablets. Daily the mistress of the house decked the room with flowers and offered sweet incense. On feast days, meals were offered, too, and the general plenty was shared. Mingling with the wreaths of incense in the air was the smoke of paper money, burned in hopeful anticipation.

Direct ancestors of the house extended only so far as memory extended, and so it was that in West Town the ancestors common to many houses and so distant as to represent a kind of mystic et cetera were honored in special clan temples to the construction and upkeep of which all houses contributed, competing fiercely the while. Of course, all the houses of a clan united in making *their* clan temple bigger and better than those of other local clans. Typically, the temples resembled ordinary houses, and sometimes very ordinary activities took place there. True, festal meals took precedence. In the preparation of these meals men (not women) assisted; this fact alone would attest to the sacred nature of the occasion. But after the service, relatives often indulged in a bit of gambling, drinking, and general horseplay. It was the family, after all, and would the forebears begrudge to succeeding generations a bit of fun in their own house? Never!

Clans in rural villages might not always possess sufficient wealth for the building of temples. Even when the inhabitants of a village bore all one name, traced common ancestry, and counted common kin, they might not be able to express family pride in proper fashion. Sheung Shui in 1965 was not in such straitened circumstances. For thirty generations, says Dr. Hugh Baker, who carefully scanned the books of genealogy, the Liao lineage had resided in its collection of hamlets. Often segmented, expanded by adoptive children and distant refugee groups bearing the family name, it yet remained a maximal lineage, could not be called a clan because, holds Dr. Baker, descent could be traced accurately to the founder, a wandering blacksmith of the Hakka people—foreigners in the old view to the men of Han.

The Liao over the years had produced men of wealth and men of learning, and the family thus had prospered. Each kin segment, from smallest family unit to all-village unit, owned land and trusts, income properties devoted to the houses and rituals meant to honor the forebears. The all-village temple included three altars. The main one bore tablets commemorating the founders and senior descendants of the founders. The second displayed tablets honoring Liaos who had been merit scholars (up to and including recent university graduates) and therefore government officials. A third honored men whose wealth had built the temple or had contributed to its upkeep and renovation. The three altars mark the touchstones of rank in China: age, merit, wealth. These are emblems of success in every family, are starred and emblazoned in every genealogy, are inscribed on the portal tablets of rich homes. Age, merit, wealth. And the greatest of these is age.

We hanker after youth, stave off with creams, surgery, bone-wrenching exercises, and fevered vitality every sign of approaching senescence. Sweet sixteen for girls and the boy's magic one-and-twenty are for us the pinnacles of glorious youth. Not so for the Chinese. There it has long been the sixtieth birthday that looms as the anticipated milestone. After sixty a man takes his place among the nominal leaders of his lineage—nominal because in more recent times actual leadership has tended to fall to the better educated lineage members. After sixty, a man may personally offer tribute to the ancestors and receive the choicest food at feasts.

> *[Our ancestors] will bless us with the eyebrows of longevity,*
> *With the gray hair and wrinkled face in unlimited degree.*

So sang the poet of Shang times. With gray hair and wrinkles come respect and deference. Age truly is a sign of grace, and one is only a step away from ultimate glorification in ancestorhood.

It is a sin to die young, evidence of a personal flaw, a failing, a wrong. To a request for news of a young man dead at twenty-five, a god of the West Town temple association told his sister:

> *He bore stains of evil deeds committed in his last reincarnation;*
> *On top of that, he persisted in doing what he should not have done.*

Babies and children were not accorded a proper funeral. Wrapped in mats they were hastily interred on the edge of town. And so shallow were the graves that their bodies become food for dogs and other scavengers. When told that a child has reached age ten successfully, the invariable response, says Dr. Yang, was, "Good. He is out of reach of the dogs." Even the young man, wifeless and therefore sonless, was buried without ceremony. He had failed in his sacred duty to carry on the line.

Sings the poet in *The Book of Odes,* honoring the new palace of a duke of Chou:

> *Sons shall be born to him:—*
> *They will be put to sleep on couches;*
> *They will be clothed in robes;*

They will have sceptres to play with;
Their cry will be loud.
They will be [hereafter] resplendent with red knee-covers,
The [future] king, the princes of the land.

Daughters shall be born to him:—
They will be put to sleep on the ground;
They will be clothed with wrappers;
They will have tiles to play with.
It will be theirs neither to do wrong nor to do good.
Only about the spirits and the food will they have to think,
And to cause no sorrow to their parents.

Yet it was through the female, voiceless and disregarded, that the line could continue. However humble her position as a bride in the house, there could be no immortality without her. And so the traditional Chinese family took pains immediately following the birth of a son to consider whence should come his bride. In the South it was once customary for a family to arrange for a bride "in anticipation"—get her in the house early so that she could, while waiting for her groom to grow up, function also as his nursemaid. Or, as Dr. Fei tells us, a family might rear a foster daughter from babyhood as future bride for their son. Such a custom insured tranquility in the household and reduced wedding expenses to a minimum. If the son died betimes, his parents might procure for the bride a substitute husband. Resulting offspring would then be credited to the dead man and bear his name. Elsewhere such a custom is called "ghost marriage," and often the duty of "raising up seed" to the dead man devolves on his brothers. "Ghost marriage" is mentioned in the Old Testament and is common in many other societies which, like that of traditional China, hold sacred above all the continuity of the family line.

It was a mother's duty to see to the daughter-in-law.

Since mother and son in the Chinese family were close, often a boy might confide to mother his dreams of a wife. The cross-cousin—mother's brother's daughter—was usually preferred, and the boy, having at least seen her and perhaps exchanged a word or two, might well have invested in her figure his romantic dreams. Mother might or might not oblige. She was bound by the rules of exogamy to look outside the clan, hopefully for a girl with another surname altogether. And village custom decreed marriage out even when there were several clans in residence. Local matchmakers did a thriving business. The more money a family had, the wider became the field of choice.

Mother was eager to find someone suitable—suitable as to family standing and horoscope, compliant as to disposition, and able to work hard. In southeastern China, a girl had to be adept in the care of silkworms. Mother's choice was rarely made on the basis of beauty and charm. In the old days, however, prettily bound feet might well compensate (in the groom's eyes) for a multitude of facial deficiencies. As Ida Pruitt's informant told her, "A plain face is given by heaven, but poorly bound feet are a sign of laziness." She meant, of course, laziness on the part of the girl's mother who, for one reason or another, had not adhered to the strict regimen of hot-water bandages drawn daily tighter round the foot. Perhaps she had weakly relented, unable to bear the child's suffering as the bones of the arch were bent backward toward the heel, as the toes turned under and became part of the sole.

In nearly every time and in every culture the small female foot has been accounted a beauty mark. (Think of Cinderella, saved by her size three's from a life of drudgery.) But only the Chinese have taken such pains to achieve by art what nature might deny. Foot binding is thought by Dr. Gamble to have originated in T'ang Dynasty times when men began to admire certain court dancers blessed with dainty feet. Every other lady thereabouts thought she might do better with just a little time and pain and effort, and so the custom spread. Later rulers forbade footbinding but were successful only in the confines of the court. The "lily foot" had, by Ming times, become a permanent sexual attraction, had acquired a glamour that faded only with the advent of our modern age. The best erotic poetry was devoted, not to a lady's almond eyes or raven hair, but to her tiny foot and to the limping, mincing gait it produced. Men looked first at a woman's feet and only later at the face above.

Not so the mother-in-law. Dr. Gamble quotes a fragment of local poetry, popular then in Ting Hsien:

Here is a lady with two big feet.
She walks with a big noise;
But having big feet
She will not suffer in her mother-in-law's house.

Meaning, of course, that she can work all the harder with big feet, and that, after all, is what pleases mother-in-law.

Big feet, little feet, pretty face or plain, the bride had to be chosen eventually, and with choice there came at last the wedding day. The bride, replaced in her parental home with money and many gifts of dainty food, was veiled and dressed in red. Red, too, was the sedan chair in which she was borne to her new home. There she was introduced to the ancestral altars, to the kitchen gods, and to the gods of heaven and earth. She was in her place, to be rooted there forever more. In death she was buried with her husband's people. Should he die before her, she would remain with his people. Remarriage was considered disgraceful, and it was better to hang herself than to contemplate divorce. Thus it was in 1945, we learn from Dr. C. K. Yang, and so it had always been. A bride of ancient Chou times sang:

*Forever separated from my brothers,
I call a stranger father.
I call a stranger father,
But he will not look at me.*

*Forever separated from my brothers,
I call a stranger mother.
I call a stranger mother,
But she will not recognize me.*

*Forever separated from my brothers,
I call a stranger elder-brother;
I call a stranger elder-brother,
But he will not listen to me.*

The bride's duty was to her new parents. She had to serve without question or complaint. Arising at dawn before everyone else, she was last to go to bed at night. Before the assembled family, she and the new bridegroom were expected to display polite distance and feigned indifference: easy if the two had not managed to hit it off in the occasional privacy of their bedroom; difficult if real fondness had blossomed. In this case, the wise girl took care not to make herself beautiful or to smile overmuch lest mother-in-law accuse her of taking unfair advantage, of luring her precious son from his filial duty. The wise young husband took similar care never to praise his wife in public, never to sit with her, eat with her, talk with her. Never would he touch her hand or cast a tender glance in her direction, not in the house, certainly not in public. How often the young farmer, home from the fields, pled the necessity of washing up. Only with the basin as excuse might he snatch a few moments alone with his bride.

The young wife had to please either husband or mother-in-law. Preferably both, but certainly one. She had to prove to be virginal. And as soon as possible, she had to produce a son.

Otherwise she could be replaced in her husband's affections by a concubine and in her social position by a parallel wife.

This is how things were for a woman as recently as thirty years ago and in isolated places may be so still. Even then, however, a woman's lot was not without hope. On the farm, however stringent the rules of filial piety and preference, there was yet work to be done, and man and wife had to pull together. For the girl of a high-ranking family, educated abroad and confident of her superior skills and attributes, the rules could be broken or at least bent. But even the bride newly brought to a traditional home, a home of means and pretensions, could look forward to something. For the years would pass and one day she herself would be old, with sons of her own to defer to her, sons whose wives *she* would choose, direct, perhaps even punish as she herself had been punished. Ah, yes, her turn would come with age. Meanwhile she vented her feelings whenever and however possible. In the household, husband's younger sisters (as possessive of him as mother herself) could be properly tongue-lashed owing to the bride's rank in age. In the market place squabbles among women were common, reports Dr. Hsu of West Town. It was one of the few places females could let off steam.

A woman bore always the taint of uncleanness—the uncleanness of blood and birth, and so it might be that, in certain circumstances, her very presence could inflict bad luck. Should she produce a fit of hysterics in a home other than her own, that home could suffer misfortune. Certainly she would never be welcome there again, nor any member of her family. The cunning woman desperate to reform a husband addicted to gambling or opium or both might well use this weapon in gambling house or opium den. She would be beaten later, that is certain, but her husband could never return to the sources of temptation. Should she lose him once and for all and find herself alone in the world, the resolute woman could set herself up in the business of healing and purifying. It was an occupation that required spiritual powers, natural or cultivated, and few entered it by choice. But it was fairly respectable, at least, if precarious.

In her husband's home, the wise woman allied herself with her sisters-in-law. They were, after all, in the same boat, working under the same matriarchal direction. And their own sons would for long bear the same general term of address, differing only by the numbered sequence of arrival: Son No. 1, Son No. 2, Son No. 3, etc.

> *Brothers may quarrel inside the walls,*
> *But they will oppose insult from without,*
> *When friends, however good they may be,*
> *Will not afford help. . . .*
>
> *Loving union with wife and children*
> *Is like the music of lutes;*
> *But it is the accord of brothers*
> *Which makes the harmony and happiness lasting.*

How well the ancient poet captures the eternal conflict of actual and ideal, of proper behavior and personal inclination. The cautionary tales were legion. They were repeated by storytellers at festivals, incorporated in folk operas, starred on every page of a great family's genealogy. "Brothers, stick together!" "Honor thy father and mother!" "Family first, last, and always!" Self must ever be submerged in the bosom of kin.

For all the sacredness of sweet unity, there was, nevertheless, a constant undercurrent of competition. Clans in village and town competed openly in their displays of wealth and achievement. Less open but no less real was the competition for pride of place among the lineages of a single clan. And among the segments of a lineage. And within the extended family, brothers, too, vied with one another and eventually with father as well. In theory his power was absolute, and certain dynasties had strengthened this customary rule with legal sanction, so that a son could be punished by the state for a breach of filial piety, for disobedience of his father.

In actuality, as father grew old, sons gradually usurped his right of decision in the disposition of family holdings and the use of family farms. Eventually, family assets were divided among the brothers. In the house itself, this break was signified by a division of kitchens and living quarters. The ancestral shrines remained intact. On the surface all was unity. The family stayed together and certainly prayed together. It merely relinquished its common table and ceased to pool its assets. This sort of subdivision was possible in towns, among families of some substance. This, says Dr. Hsu, was why houses were built with plenty of empty rooms and space for additions.

The ideal of family and family unity colored every aspect of Chinese life so that business, club activity, education, even government all came to be expressed in family terms and were nourished on family connections. Small craft shops, as described by Dr. Hsu, included the master, his wife and children, one or more journeymen advanced in the craft, and one or more apprentices just learning the skills and functioning meanwhile as servants to the rest. Junior relatives would probably better describe the positions of journeymen and apprentices. The master might even formalize the arrangement by making of his helpers "dry sons" or "sworn sons," equal in his affection to his own sons though certainly unequal in inheritance.

Customers who patronized the shops, small or large, came as much for pleasant visits as to strike good bargains. A proprietor welcomed his clients as much for themselves as for the profits they represented. Wealth was not scorned, that is certain, but profit as motivation for trade seems, in most instances, to have taken a back seat to other satisfactions: the continuity of old friendships, the joy of craftsmanship, the means of establishing family land. The selling of land itself was rather more reminiscent of the wedding than of a business transaction.

Village people and town people had long ago learned to cross-cut family ties with clubs, cooperatives, and associations. There were insurance clubs, clubs for cultural uplift, clubs for athletic events, clubs for opera productions, and clubs built around money pools. In these every member contributed a small sum at regular intervals and in good time collected the pot. Even the clubs, however, took on a family connotation so that the membership was fraternal (or was expected to be) in attitude and interaction and regarded the club founder as yet another kind of ancestor. So says Dr. C. K. Yang.

From the authority of the father to that of the emperor-father had represented simply another step in the hierarchy of respect and obligation inherent in the family. The success of an emperor, indeed of a dynasty, was measured always (says Dr. Hsu) not in economic terms, but in familial, in human terms. How loyal were one's subjects, how cheerfully obedient, how happy in the royal presence? Until the overthrow of the Manchus, Chinese bureaucrats had always depended on families—on lineages and clans—to maintain order in countryside, village, and town. After 1911, the old rules, the old values began slowly to change. With the inauguration of Communist rule, the change was complete. Family and family organization were seen as major obstacles to the new order. Family authority was replaced by political authority, family sanctity by the sanctity of the state.

In every town and village, Dr. C. K. Yang tells us, the local temples and private shrines were ignored by officialdom. Even the earth god was left untouched. It was instead the houses of family worship that everywhere were closed, their rites forbidden, their membership abolished, their plaques of honor burned. Schools managed by clan or lineage were assigned new teachers who knew the Classics no more. Family councils—even those with a distinctly communal orientation and a leadership of youngish, capable men—even these were abolished. The community watch, armed agent of the clan council, fell into disrepute. Its weapons were confiscated, its members were punished, sometimes imprisoned on the suspicion of hiding weapons.

New codes now protect the rights of women and the young—those on whom the old system had borne most heavily. Filial piety has given way to conjugal harmony. Mother-in-law no longer has the right to forbid romance. Behavior between the sexes yet remains circumspect. There are to be seen in modern China no public demonstrations of conjugal affection. No longer does mother-in-law forbid the bride's primping. Even so brides do not primp. No one does. Men and women alike wear trousers and tunics of identical color and cut. Hair is plainly dressed and with an eye to practicality of upkeep. Not a single face blushes with rouge; not an eye is lined with kohl. Such a face would betray the vanity of its owner. And vanity betrays individualism. And individualism is the ultimate sin. It threatens, not the sacredness of filial piety, but the sacredness of citizen-piety, of one's duty to the state which is the ultimate parent of all.

The sanctification of a higher loyalty has brought to the Chinese people many gains, says biologist Arthur Galston, who has traveled recently in the East. No one starves. No one lacks medical care. Everyone has at least an elementary education. There is no venereal disease, no gambling, no drugs, no crime. Surely a great accomplishment! There is also no family, at least not in its larger sense, not in the sense of lineage, lineage segment, clan. There are instead the farm brigade, the factory association, the revolutionary committee. And notions of belief, virtue, and propriety are transmitted, not by the elders nor yet by the gentry versed in Confucian Classics, but by local leaders who receive their instruction from on high. These leaders will be replaced and replaced again, an endless stream of men and women dedicated to the state as Family and the people as One. Yet, when they are gone, who will remember? What plaque in what high-rise apartment or on what factory portal will tell of their devotion and recount their honors? Cut off from those who have gone before, from those patient toilers in the earth and grain, cut off personally from those yet to come, their identities stand incomplete and alone, to be lost one day in the anonymous et cetera of those who founded the state and lost the many in the one.

Part V

Between China and India

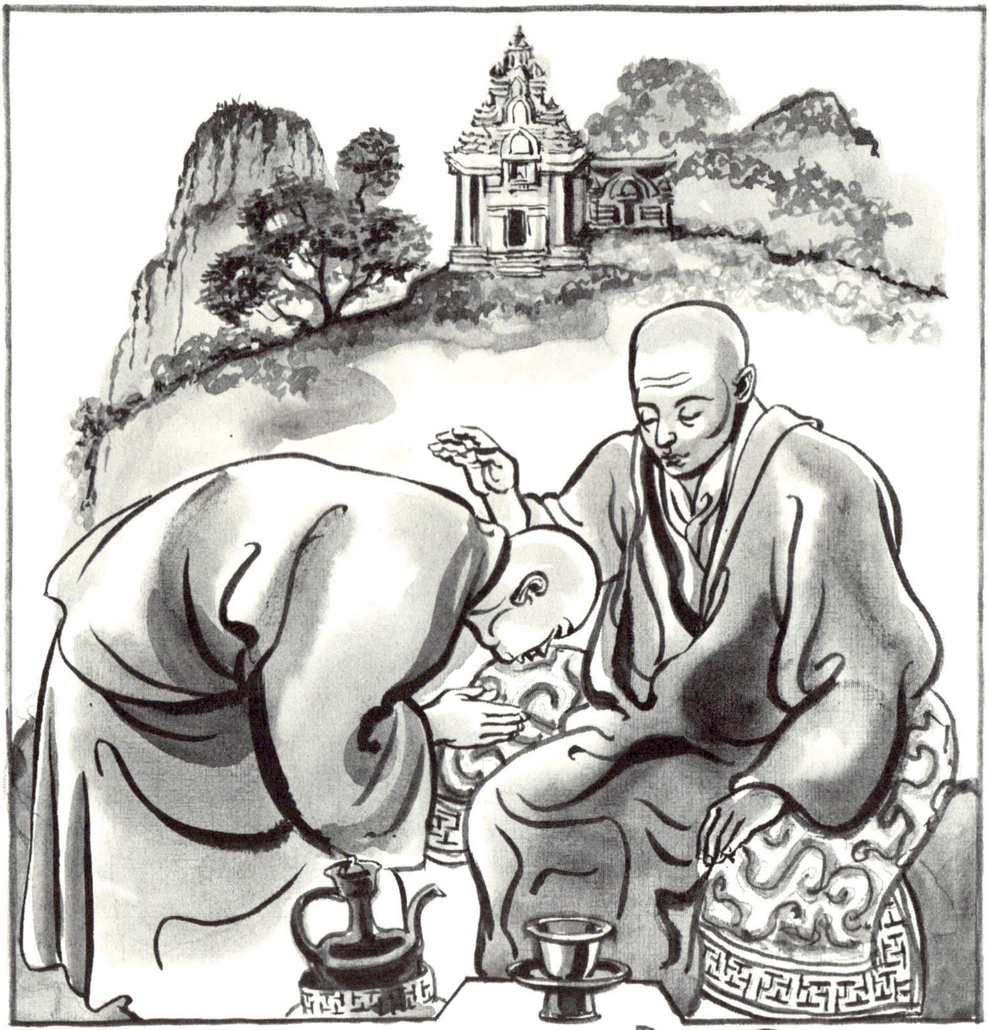

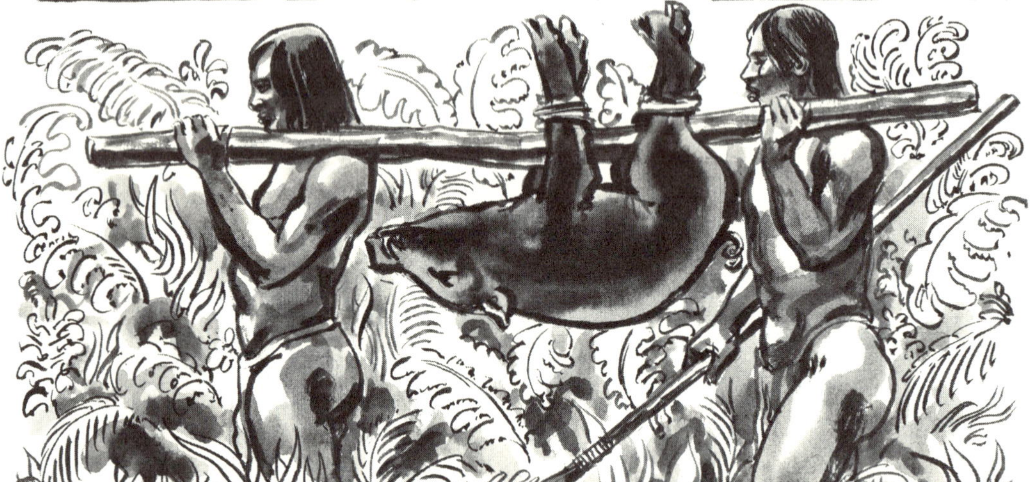

11

TIBET
The Pillar of Heaven

BERINGED by barbarians, men of Shang times defended the Middle Kingdom with a moving wall of chariots. Behind this wall they were, for a time at least, invincible. Theirs for easy taking were the captives needed for sacrifice. On oracle bones and shells (we are told by the Sinologist H. G. Creel) these captives were listed simply as so-and-so many "men," anonymous victims unidentified even by tribal name. There was one exception. Victims from the west were singled out in an ideograph made with the sign for "sheep" joined to the sign for "man." They were shepherds, these particular people, and they were called Ch'iang.

In time, as the barbarians of the North learned horse and chariot warfare, the Chinese built there other walls, walls of earth and brick. In the west the mountain walls were considered guard enough. But no. These were to be as easily and as often breached as the man-made walls of the north and, like them, breached by the one-time victims of Shang.

By Han times the Ch'iang, shepherds and mountaineers of Bod, the Land of Snows (to us, Tibet), were spilling down from their high plateau, ravaging the Middle Kingdom at will. On their tough, shaggy little ponies they poured through the gorges where the Yellow River begins and, joining with their relatives in the Nan Shan Mountains, invaded the lands around Lake Koko Nor.

Over and over Han officials wrestled with the problem. What to do with the Ch'iang? Send troops in force and the barbarians would simply vanish into the heights where lowlanders gasped for breath and fell and died. Left to themselves, the intruders might make contact with the Hsiung-nu. Were they not, after all, hand in glove with the steppe folk? Had they not given refuge to the Lesser Yueh-chih after Modun had expelled the great horde? Had they not allied with the Southern Yueh (about 112 B.C. that would be) to stretch a line of cavalry from the mountains to P'an-yu (Canton)? And all to bar the way to Han manifest destiny in the southlands! Surely they seemed willing to make common cause with anyone willing to fight Chinese. What to do? Ignore the Ch'iang?

The historians of *The Book of Documents* had done so. Both as sacrifice and as predator the Ch'iang were frequently unnoticed. They were simply lumped with "wild tribes" of the four quarters, all of whom (at least in the early sections of the book) were pictured as suppliants, drawn irresistibly to the potent virtues of the mighty and mythical Yu, first of the Hsia Dynasty. Humbly they came to submit (or so it is claimed), and with them were the wild tribes of the west bearing hair clothes and the skins of beasts to offer in tribute. It is a pretty tale, a literary expression of belief that wishing will make it so.

There is surely wishful thinking in the report of a Han ambassador who, in A.D. 5, tried to persuade the mountain folk to give over the contested land around Koko Nor and submit to Chinese dominion. Cheerily he informed his emperor that

> *leaders of Ch'iang tribes, whose numbers might be 12,000 persons, wish to be received as your subjects. They offer the Hsien-shui Sea, the Yun Gorge, and the Salt Lake. The level land with fine grass is all given to the Chinese people, and the [Ch'iang] will themselves dwell in the narrow and difficult places and act as guards at the frontier.*

Two years later the mountain warriors were back in their old haunts and had even spread across the Nan Shan Mountains to threaten Tunhuang at the end of the Wall. Indeed, some tribes in the area were giving themselves dynastic airs.

And yet their peculiar ideograph remained unchanged. To the Han, the Ch'iang continued to be shepherds pictorially with all the rustic, peaceable ways the name connotes. Neither wishing nor tradition made it so, for the Ch'iang were far from peaceable folk. They were warriors and in their dim beginnings hunters. Much of these original habits and turns of thought linger still among Tibetan nomads—the High Pasture Ones, wanderers, herders, the freest, perhaps, of all the mountain people.

The meat of wild game is not really essential for the survival of today's High Pasture Ones, but it gives renown. The old gods of the mountains look down with approval as men stalk the wild yak, wild sheep and gazelle, wolf and bear and snow leopard. And of these gods the hunter demands success, promising in return a taste of blood. The old rituals of division still prevail, so we are told by Robert Ekvall who, brought up in China, has spent many years of his life traveling with the High Pasture Nomads of Tibet. Of the spoil, says Robert Ekvall, every soul in the home camp shares, but the hunter keeps skin and head for himself—unless, of course, he has borrowed the successful weapon. In this case, the trophies are claimed by the weapon's owner.

If the mountain gods like a taste of blood, they do not like the smell of broiling, roasting, or frying meat, and so the nomad, perforce, must eat his meat dry or raw or boiled in everlasting stews. He must take care, too, in building the hearth on which stews are cooked. The Earth Lord is offended by undue disturbance, and so a man cuts the sod ever so gently, offering prayers the while. Fear of the Earth Lord makes the nomad wary of mining for gold though he will do so if really hard pressed for cash. Tradable salt and borax he cheerfully collects from the crusts and pans of old lake beds. These are, after all, surface deposits, and their removal can be considered a thoughtful grooming operation. Among the old gods of Ch'iang times there must also be counted the Fire God who watches and guards. When the families of a camp move on, each throws into the hearth left behind a final offering of *tsampa,* the ground barley which, mixed with tea, butter, and cheese, provides the daily staple of the nomad's diet. Fires in these high altitudes do not last long without constant tending, without frequent use of the bellows. So, when travelers reach the first ridge, they turn back to see whether the fires are smoking still. Smoke promises happiness in the next camp site.

It is with these old gods of the highlands that the yak belongs. Sheep are, to be sure, important to the nomad. So are cattle and yak-cattle hybrids which are grown, used, harvested (in Ekvall's term) without sentiment. Used, too, are the few sturdy horses, prized mounts in raid and feud. The name for horse (like the name for Tibet itself) seems to have been borrowed from the steppe folk. Unlike them, however, the High Pasture Ones do not milk their horses or eat them or do them special honor. This sort of attention is reserved for the yak.

It is the yak which both marks and makes possible the high pasture nomadism of Tibet. Only here does the yak run wild. And surely it is here that the animal was originally domesticated. From the yak comes milk for cheese, yoghurt, and the indispensable butter to be used in cosmetics, in religious offerings, in lamps, as gifts, as currency, and in every teacup. Low Tibetan tents are made from the black belly hair of a yak steer, always pulled out hair by hair, never shorn. From yak shoulders and neck, blood can be drawn and cooked to provide protein during seasons when no butchering may be done. The yak can be ridden or packed with gear whenever the camp moves on. Yak dung, collected and dried, makes bricklike windbreaks or the fire which keeps the black tents warm and the Fire God fed.

The nomads cross ordinary cattle with yak and use the tractable, strong hybrid which results. But they kill the offspring of a hybrid cow lest the old gods object, and they believe the hybrid bull to be quite sterile. Their own yak cows they like to mate with wild yaks when this is possible and admire the resulting calf. Once a year tent groups set free a "god yak" to wander as he will, hoping always his choice will be to follow the camp. It is, thinks Robert Ekvall, a final atonement for the original binding and taming of an animal which belonged to the old gods and to the old wild ways.

They are old wild ways that linger still. For the herder, with his wealth on the hoof and in the open, stands to lose all in a single raid and must be quick to take and quicker still to defend. Even in temperatures considerably below zero Fahrenheit, none but the very old sleep inside the black tent. Most men, wrapped tightly in their thirty-pound sheepskin coats and covered with felt, sleep at the edges of the tent circle. Their great, fierce mastiffs wander restlessly around and over the swathed forms, and no one enjoys a whole night's sleep until the moon is full, and raiders, fearing detection, keep well away. Always prepared, hardy, well fed, the High Pasture One, whatever the size of his herd, feels himself the superior of any valley farmer. He moves as he likes and depends only on himself and on the members of his tent family.

True, tent group families are usually related in some way or another. Lineages are recognized but are, as Ekvall says, in constant process of division. The tent circle permanent enough to elect a headman is rare. Named tribes have, of old, wandered their separate regions and have come and may still come together in times of military need. The tight kin organization of the steppe nomads, however, the clan leaders and revered chiefs seem to be missing here or have, at least, lapsed in importance. Parties to a serious quarrel depend on the careful mediation of friends to end the dispute and, failing that, elect to go it alone, confident of their ability to surmount all difficulties and come up smiling. The highest compliment one man pays another is to call him "son untamed," which means, roughly, "you unsubdued one."

Indeed, one so salutes the good tent wife who serves white tea and fresh butter to the guest. In most ways she, like her husband, is unsubdued. The Tibetan woman—even the aristocratic lady of the valleys and towns—is and has always been as unlike her Chinese sister as it is possible for a woman to be: unlike in rank, unlike in rights, unlike in recognized abilities. Town women, so Giuseppe Tucci tells us, are often sent to substitute for their ailing husbands in administrative offices and are expected to perform with as much competence as the officeholder of record. Though town woman and nomad girl alike are supposed to accede to parental wishes when it is time for marriage, in fact, each makes her own choice and makes it stick, and no one thinks less of the bride who comes pregnant to the ceremony or with child in hand. Sometimes the Tibetan woman might marry two or more brothers at once, a custom called polyandry and formally recognized in only a few places—most of them in Tibet and immediate environs.

In a polyandrous marriage, the eldest, or perhaps the most

important male is recognized as father to all children produced, the others being addressed as "uncle." Sexual jealousy is considered in bad taste. Even so, exquisite care is taken to guard against wounded feelings and to insure equal attention to all. The problem is ordinarily solved by the nature of the Tibetan economy which constantly hies men off with the herds or to the fields or in the company of foreigners in need of guides and protectors. Polyandry, so the standard reasoning runs, keeps herds and arable fields (always at a minimum) intact and unfragmented and limits the population to what the land can comfortably bear. It can also be argued, however, (and often has) that life at high altitudes tends to limit fertility in any case. Marriage in Tibet is not exclusively polyandrous. It tends to be, more often than not, monogamous with a bit of polygyny turning up now and again. Monogamous and polygynous marriages carry somewhat more prestige than the polyandrous sort, and there would seem to be more involved here than a simple adjustment to ecological demands. Like any other human custom, polyandry seems to be a product of some need and lots of habit. And like any other custom (particularly those customs meant to regulate marriage), it sometimes works effectively and sometimes does not.

If marriage (of whatever variety) does not work, the tent wife receives on demand all the goods and animals that made up her dowry, plus the increase earned by her own efforts. When children grow up and request that holdings be divided, each of the children, boy and girl alike, receives one share of the family estate. The wife, like her husband, receives two shares of the estate. And she has earned them.

As tent wife she works hard. Babies are early weaned so that she can meet her economic responsibilities. Her duties and those of her husband often overlap. Both collect animal hair and spin it into yarn, but only she weaves. Both help pack the animals. He handles the religious furniture and she the kitchen goods. Unlike most other pastoral nomads, High Pasture Ones believe a woman is especially handy with animals, with the yak, six feet at the shoulders and armed with spreading horns; with the huge, fierce mastiff which she must hold as the approaching visitor waves scarves of greeting. Certainly she is absolute mistress of female animals, attending their deliveries, treating their illnesses, collecting their milk. It is she alone who sells milk products and, in the interest of greater yield, feels perfectly free to dispute her husband's decisions in the management of the herds. At her belt she wears (as Ekvall tells us) the silver hook of her calling, the hook used in milking. She wears it with pride.

On her husband's belt is the knife, and he wears it with guilt and with a sense of shame, for with it he kills, butchers, harvests the herd. Even in hunting, even while exulting in the chase, he cannot but tremble. In the high pastures, among his animals, known and loved, he suffers deeply. For all his cleaving to the old ways, he is yet a Buddhist, and to the Buddhist all sentient life is sacred and must be preserved. It is easy for townsmen to wink at the law, relishing the meat so long as someone else plays the butcher. In the high pastures there is no one else, no despised caste of butchers for the fearsome task. The herdsman himself must kill, must harvest his animals as the farmer must harvest a field, so that human life can be sustained.

Killing is accomplished amid a torrent of prayer. Prayer wheels spin in the tents and prayer banners fly from its corners. There are ritual gestures to accompany spoken prayers, solemn trudgings around sacred objects, and longer trudgings on pilgrimage. And there are, above all, offerings to be made to the monks and lamas of the local monastery, for their words can bring blessing, can help to dissipate the dreadful feeling of guilt.

It was not by way of China that Buddhism came to Tibet, even though monasteries and shrines to the Buddha had been well established in China since the second century A.D. No one is quite certain exactly how early it was introduced to the Middle Kingdom. The historical Buddha had lived in India in the sixth century B.C. and, realizing that to live was to suffer and to suffer was to desire, found a way to end both suffering and desire. The simplicity of his rule and of the eightfold path to enlightenment was elaborated in time by his disciples and by *their* disciples into a church, transcendent, triumphant, and in two branches. One placed its emphasis on the individual soul and its progress through life after life to eventual peace, to blessed nothingness in the bosom of eternity. This was known as Hinayana (or Therevada) Buddhism, and it was to dominate Southeast Asia. The other branch, Mahayana, or Greater Vehicle, emphasized salvation for all mankind through the work of countless saviors—Bodhisattvas—incarnations of the Buddha who, having found personal enlightenment, renounced that glory in order to carry forward the world's work. The Greater Vehicle was a form which sought conversions and found them in kings and common folk through northern India and into Kushan, the land won by the Yueh-chih in their flight from Modun. Pushing then into the Tarim Basin, oasis by oasis, Buddhism made its way into China. There it found quick initial acceptance, especially by the Taoists whose penchant for meditation and whose view of life as illusion seemed akin to the new religion. The similarities proved to be essentially superficial, and though each group strongly influenced the other, the two eventually diverged. Buddhism was viewed by men in political power as a means for change, for alteration of some of the old ways. Never did Buddhism enjoy so great a popularity as during T'ang Dynasty times and in the Toba Wei and Sui Dynasties that preceded it. Never after those times was there to be again in Great China such a proliferation of Buddhist schools and sects, monasteries and organized priesthood.

At the end of T'ang, Buddhism suffered persecution and

later made little headway against the old, the prevailing religious forms. It was, somehow, a bit too metaphysical for Chinese tastes, too antifamily, too otherworldly. Buddhism was certainly to flavor the Chinese religious brew, was to add bright notions of an afterlife and give place to those who found themselves outside the family system, outside the frame of family values, outside class pretensions.

Buddhism, when it came to Tibet, came by way of India and Nepal, and it came to stay. In the end it would convert warriors into priests and make of Tibet a land ruled by religion, its people bound to a single quest: enlightenment and release.

Perhaps it was the nature of the land itself that made Buddhism congenial to its people—the barren, dizzying peaks and lost, jewelled lakes—the sense of immensity, dwarfing the plans and schemes of men. Perhaps it was simply the right time for something new. Or perhaps it was the nature of the original religion which could be made to meld—not at once, not without a struggle, but meld all the same—with the new. This old religion was called Bon, and it was simply the way of the shaman, much codified and enlarged. In traditional Tibetan belief, every mountain had its special being allied of old with kings and great clans. Near every dangerous pass and hanging bridgeway could be found a pile of stones, offered by travelers in hopes of a safe crossing. So were mountain men half a world away in the South American Andes wont to offer to their guardians of passes a stone and an eyelash in payment for protection.

In the old religion, fire was itself a spirit which must daily be honored with offerings and purified by priests whenever its flames were sullied by dirt or by a stew that had overboiled its pot. There was then, as among the nomads still, the Earth Lord to be honored with first reapings of the grain. Tree, lake, winds —all had resident spirits. Every rushing river was a spirit snake to be given bodies of the dead, perhaps in hope that, as the snake sheds its skin and is thus immortal, the river snake would lend to the dead one life anew.

There were more: clan spirits, family spirits, and spirits of the underworld; evil spirits of sickness and death. And it was these last the Bon adepts sought to control. They used magic: burning juniper boughs and blood sacrifices and spirit traps into which evil ones could be lured. They ate trance-inducing berries and, sitting on their shaman drums, invited the spirits to possess them entire, to try spirit strength against shaman strength and chanced life and sanity in the struggle. Thubten Figme Norbu, himself a High Lama, speaks with characteristic understanding of such beliefs, acknowledging the good intentions which motivated those contests with dark powers, acknowledging the importance of our remaining ever open to new (or old) truths. But, he adds, dealing with dark powers is serious business, even selfish business. The true teacher, the lama, must direct his efforts toward the common concerns of humankind, not to the esoteric or the personal.

When Buddhism arrived in Tibet it was already much changed from its original form. Many of the old Hindu gods, in aspects both horrifying and benign, had crept back into the fold bearing new Buddhistic names. Now, the linking of old with new to the greater glory of both is a familiar staple of religious practice. Christianity in its early years, beset by the competition of other, perhaps stronger faiths, was not above transforming tutelary deities into Christian saints and arranging the calendar so that Christian holy days should fall where holy days had always been.

Some of the Buddhistic gods were seen as reincarnations of the Great One, returned once and to return many times to come in the service of mankind, and there were ever new reincarnations being born or newly recognized. Tibet was blessed with many such. Especially revered was Chenresig, the God of Compassion, Patron of the Land of Snows. And, said the monks and sages, why not many gods and blessed forms and demons themselves, for that matter? Surely there are many realities, and we must meet our people at whatever level of reality, of comprehension they happen to be. If they believe in gods, then to those gods we must relate. If they fear demons, then let us be about the business of exorcism though what we drive out is, to us, merely illusion—as men are illusions, as gods are illusions, as pain and fear themselves are illusions, the greatest illusions of all.

However the Buddhist pantheon was enriched, however many schools arose, each interpreting differently the words of Great Buddha, all were pointed to the same end: salvation through rebirth in beautiful incarnations or final enlightenment and release. The emphasis was on striving through those incarnations to gain merit, to atone for past misdeeds. But there were some schools, the Tantric schools, which sought shortcuts to enlightenment. Their followers believed that by total devotion to a teacher, himself an enlightened one, a student could attain release in this life. They were willing to use the great powers inherent in meditation, in bodily control, in discipline and deprivation, in the sexual act. The followers of these schools merged in Tibet with some forms of Bon and became nearly indistinguishable from them.

It is said that a golden begging bowl dropped from Heaven at the feet of a Tibetan king, signifying the blessings soon to come. One of his descendants, Songtsen-gampo, invited to his court Buddhist teachers from India and Nepal. Sometime after 625 A.D. he sent ministers south to learn more and to bring back and devise for Tibet a form of writing in which the sacred scriptures could be preserved. They returned with a form of the Indian Gupta alphabet, and there then appeared in Tibet inscriptions on stone, records of all kinds, and holy writ. Many of these early writings were preserved in dry, sealed caves in Tunhuang which was, at one time, under

Tibetan rule. Songtsen-gampo did more. He had built the first temple and collected therein the first monks. He also brought change through marriage with foreign princesses, one from Nepal and one from China, each a Buddhist and a champion of the new religion.

Very soon the Bon priests, recognizing a coming thing when they saw it, modeled their own sacred writ on Buddhist originals until the king had to caution them about plagiarizing. There followed seesaw persecutions as the devotees of Bon and Buddhism struggled and in the struggle came to be more and more alike—pointing each toward the end of life and toward incarnation in the next.

Thus it was that the time of death and shortly thereafter came to be the most important moment of life, a time when the lingering soul could be turned toward a happy incarnation, if not full release. After forty-nine days, after the soul had flown, the mortal remains mattered little. Some were thrown into rivers. Others were exposed on mountain tops where their flesh fed the birds and, says Thubten Figme Norbu, offered in death a final gift to life. Great folk and holy men were cremated, their ashes to be collected, molded with water into figures, and stored with precious religious objects in a wayside shrine. Such shrines are called by the Tibetan *chorten,* by the Indian *stupa,* and in China and Southeast Asia *pagoda.* They were, and are, built in a form which recalled the universal elements and events of the Buddha's life.

Over the years Tibetans paid much gold to visiting teachers from India and Nepal. A great debate between these sages and the monks brought from China confirmed the primacy of the southern influence in Tibetan religion and, indeed, in Tibetan religious art. Soon, however, Tibetan artists outstripped their teachers in skill, and Tibetan scholars began to organize their own codifications of holy writ. They had to. By the thirteenth century A.D., Islam had come to India. Indian monasteries and universities were destroyed, and Tibet and her relatives and neighbors along the Himalayan fringe, suddenly deprived of their sources of inspiration, found themselves very much on their own.

In the great monasteries, schools of interpretation developed much as they had in India. In each of the centers could be found at least one reincarnation of a great savior or teacher, willing to forgo release in order to guide mankind. Sometimes a savior whispered in dying where next he could be found, in which child soon to be born. Always the searching monks would find in the child signs of recognition, the evidence of rebirth. Only to Thubten Figme Norbu, brother of the Dalai Lama and himself a declared incarnation of the great lama Tagtser, was recognition denied. Perhaps, he says, this is punishment for misdeeds in a former life. Even so while in his monastery he worked hard and with dedication for his order and his people. He speaks eloquently of monastic rule, of its vows of celibacy and asceticism inaugurated during Tibet's Middle Ages. He speaks of the decline of miracles and magic in favor of study. He describes the way in which the great monasteries became collections of colleges with complex curricula to the mastery of which one might well devote a lifetime. As monasteries became centers of study, they became as well centers of civil rule so that Tibet was, in effect, a theocracy.

It was not so in the beginning. Tibet's early kings were thought to be sacred, let down to earth near the Yarlung region. Their tomb mounds can be counted there—mounds into which went horses, retainers, and goods as well as king himself. These kings seem to have wielded little personal power. The heads of great clans, holed up each in his fortress stronghold, seem to have exercised what power there was. Their strength was guaranteed by the king's eternal youth. He had to die, so the old rule held, when his own eldest son reached the age of thirteen or was able to bestride a horse, whichever event came first.

Why ritual regicide at this time, in this way? Did the king's sacredness depend on youth? Or was the sacred essence distilled in each successive generation so that a man's son necessarily possessed more than father himself? The reasons are muddy, but the results very clear: a young king under perpetual domination of his maternal relatives and endless political strife.

This we learn through earliest Tibetan writings, preserved in sealed caves in Tunhuang on the far side of Taklamakan. We learn more of Tibetan kings in the writings of T'ang historians. For there came to the Tibetan throne sometime around A.D. 625 a man certain to attract attention in foreign courts. This was the great Songtsen-gampo. He championed Buddhism, possibly (suggests Giuseppe Tucci) as a means of ending ritual regicide, of breaking the old tradition of kingship and making of the office something entirely new. He also broke out of Tibet. His armies captured the lands around Koko Nor, invaded Nepal and northern India. After initial polite refusals, he was given princesses to wife, Chinese and Nepali princesses, each of whom was to bring from her country sacred objects of Buddhism.

We can imagine the dainty T'ang princess watching as her marriage bargain was sealed in the blood of dog sacrifice, anathema to practicing Buddhists. We can imagine her reaction at first sight of her future husband, dressed like a nomad in leather and felt, unwashed, uncombed, his face smeared with red ochre as was then the custom in Tibet. It was a custom she would soon change. She would also later influence—or serve as convenient excuse for—a change in royal residence. The king moved from the Yarlung region to Lhasa and on the site of an old fortress caused to be built the first massive walls of the Potala, later home of the Dalai Lama.

Treaties are seldom lasting documents, and neither were those made by Tibet's kings with the emperors of China. The two countries soon fell out and made war. Armies of Songtsen-gampo's successors moved out to occupy the oasis cities of the Tarim Basin, cutting off the trade route to China. For one heady moment in 763, Tibetan troops even occupied Ch'ang-an, the old Chinese capital. The last treaty with the weakening T'ang Dynasty was signed in A.D. 821 (and presumably sealed in marriage to yet another Chinese princess). Its terms are preserved in an inscription in Lhasa. And then both Tibetan unity and military might began to fade together.

After 860 the conquered territories were lost one by one in battles with the Uigur Turks, always sympathetic to the T'ang, and the vacant lands around Koko Nor were occupied by the Monguor, a people part Mongol, part Turkic, and part Tibetan. At home, the noble followers of Bon, resenting their own loss of power in the alliance of king and Buddhism, rebelled and placed one of their own on the throne. The new king promptly disestablished all the state-supported Buddhist monasteries and turned the monks out to pasture. He was promptly assassinated by a Buddhist monk under orders from on high. But it was too late. The kingdom was in wreckage, and for long no one cared to reclaim it.

In the tenth century a revival of Buddhism began along the border of present-day Kashmir, the area known as Ladakh, but power was never again reconstituted in the figure of a national king. It coalesced instead around several of the great monasteries so that in 1207, when the Mongols appeared at the mountain gates, the red-hatted Grand Lama of Sakya Monastery was sent to treat with them. He submitted graciously to Mongol rule and in so doing forged the first link in a chain which was to bind the Mongols to Tibet, not the other way around.

The Sakya abbot visited the court of Genghis Khan and later that of his son, where he is said to have helped mold Uigur script to Mongol spoken language. All in all, he managed so to charm and awe the court that he was designated Mongol viceroy to Tibet. His descendant (celibacy was not required for abbots in the Sakya monastery) quite as thoroughly charmed Kublai Khan to whom he became teacher, mentor, spiritual guide. The two entered into the relationship of patron and priest, a pattern which, with various struggles and adjustments, was to prevail between Tibet and China for some time. And Sakya dominion in Tibet was secure.

It became less secure as the Mongol Yuan Dynasty faded and was superseded by that of the Ming whose rulers allowed the relationship of patron-priest to lapse. They were a bit scornful of Tibet and its lamas, but they were also busy elsewhere, busy with the Mongols who were distressingly unsubmissive in defeat. Problem overrode hauteur, and in 1408 the third Ming emperor called to his court the High Lama of the Gelupka or Yellow Hat sect. For the Gelupka order, founded by Tsong Khapa in the mid-1300s, was on its way to preeminence in Tibet. The Gelupka represented a movement of reform, stressing a rule of celibacy and study modeled after the blameless life of the founder himself. Tsong Khapa sent a representative to the Ming court and would not go himself. In spite of the snub, the emperor was persuaded to encourage meetings of Mongols and monks. And so it was that a later incarnation of the Gelupka abbot met the chief of the Tumed tribe and revived their old religious connections with Tibet. Under the High Lama's influence, Altan Khan was moved to outlaw blood sacrifice among the Mongols and make Buddhism the state religion. It was he who conferred on the abbot the Mongol title, Dalai Lama. (In Tibet, the proper title is Gyalwa Rinpoche.) When the third High Lama of the Gelupka died, his incarnation was discovered, happily, in a great grandson of Altan Khan.

So the Mongols were subdued at last. Not so the temporal problems of Tibet. There were the last secular pretenders to the throne to be quelled (and not without singularly un-Buddhist battle). There was the civil administration to be put in order and lay leaders to be drawn into the government. These were the achievements of the fifth Dalai Lama.

When the Manchu emperors came to power in China, the relation of patron and priest had to be reestablished. The Manchus were rather more rulers than patrons and disliked uncertainties of any sort on their western flanks. From time to time, Chinese troops were sent in to do garrison duty and were heartily resented the while by Tibetans whose resources were too slender to accommodate a sudden influx of hungry mouths.

In 1911 the Manchu Dynasty was expelled by the Revolution, and the Tibetans considered themselves free. The new government did not. The old relationship was to continue with the government playing, not only the patron's role, but dabbling in the priestly one as well. The choice of lama incarnations was manipulated for political ends. The Communists, when they came to power in 1949, went still further. They invaded Tibet, and the old roles of patron and priest were dissolved completely. Monks and lamas were evicted from their monasteries, and soldiers were quartered there instead. After trying vainly to come to terms with the new "patron," the Dalai Lama fled to India there to establish a government in exile and to plan for changes long overdue in isolated Tibet, changes he might never hope to realize.

Others fled, too—farmers and herdsmen and religious folk. Some were airlifted to Switzerland where every effort was made to keep the old forms intact and the old beliefs alive. Residence groups were organized, each around its own lama, and religious schools were built. There was change all the same. Butter was first to go. Too dear to be purchased in the new land, it was replaced by margarine. Herdsmen in the new land, separated from their familiar animals, abandoned herding altogether for work in factories and with machines.

Related Tibetan peoples on the Himalayan fringe—the Ladakhi of Kashmir, the people of Mustang and Sikkim and Bhutan, the Sherpas of Nepal—these also received the refugees. Change came in their wake. All these lands and peoples must now let the world come in, bending to its demands. But they *can* bend, adjusting slowly, holding their religion intact if not their political autonomy. On the other side of the border, Tibetans have not this choice.

By 1963, Robert Ekvall tells us, the farms of Tibet, located most of them along the fertile Tsangpo (Brahmaputra) Valley, had been collectivized. Only the High Pasture Ones were then still free to roam. The harvest of their herds was and is needed among the Chinese, ever protein shy. And so the herdsmen, the Unsubdued Ones, were neither pressured nor pushed by their new masters, who instead attempted to lure them to the valleys with the promise of winter fodder for their beasts, with the promise of permanent homes for themselves and schools for their children. Whether they have by now taken the bait and descended from the heights, whether they have become, like the yak, subdued at last is not known. Qualified observers, indeed outsiders of any sort, are not encouraged to visit Tibet. And Tibetans who flee their homes, Tibetans able to report current conditions there, have not yet done so. At least, not for publication.

12

EAST BY SOUTH
Crossroads or Source?

In northern Chinese cities of early T'ang Dynasty times, a traveler could visit wine shop after wine shop and see there the empire's bright young officials, gathered in two's and three's to say goodbye.

"It must not be true," one would say to his friend. "You cannot be posted south! It is no place for a civilized human being. Who could endure the heat, the mists, the poisons? Who could live among the serpent-folk?"

"Nevertheless I must go," would come the inevitable reply. "Here is the letter appointing me secretary to the governor of Chiao-chou [near Hanoi]." And then, after a long pause, "Take care, my friend, to offend no one in power lest you be sent south to join me."

Doleful conversations of this sort were not uncommon during early T'ang times (A.D. 618–907). For the rulers of that dynasty were determined to win back lands taken earlier by the Han and later lost or lapsed from Chinese dominion. The northern borders had been secured through friendship with the Uigur Turks, really almost partners by T'ang reckoning. It was the South that wanted retaking, and no cost was accounted too great. If officials viewed service in the southlands as political exile, well, let them. Could they not, did they not, after all, line their pockets handsomely while in that exile? If convicts had to be sent under military guard to settle and consolidate new-won territory, then so be it. If peasant families had to be uprooted and sent to live among barbarians called the Man, then so be it. Never mind their fears of the tree ghosts and the rock ghosts, of the goblins summoned by the Man as they beat their booming bronze drums. Never mind the complaints of soldiers, perishing in the heat and unceasing rebellion of the serpent-folk whose warriors were led at times by women. Women! One could well understand the soldier's shame and his fear, too, for these women soldiers could fight with magic. From many insects they distilled the *ku* poison and released it with the shake of a lovely, pointing finger. And that was the worst of it. They *were* lovely, these women of the South, loose in their movements, strong among their menfolk as Chinese girls were never strong, and all the more seductive for it. But never mind *that,* said the lords of T'ang.

Never mind anything so long as the South could be won and its benighted people made somehow to approximate civilized human beings. They were not, after all, like the northern barbarians who had begun to be really quite acceptable in terms of deportment. (In any case, the Chinese had too much need for Turkic horses to quibble about Turkic manners.) The southern folk were yet to be tamed, yet to be won to a world which should be by rights Chinese in polity and in culture.

It was a familiar vision. Emperor Wu Ti of the Han had expressed it best and gone furthest in its achievement. Ch'in

Shih Huang-ti, however, had preceded him in the conquest of the southland. In Ch'in times and before, everything south of the Yangtze was unknown territory peopled by the Yueh, non-Chinese-speaking barbarians. (Yueh is, in fact, simply one of the Chinese terms for barbarian. It is from Yueh, so Edward Shafer believes, that the name Vietnam eventually emerged. Nam means "south." Added to Yueh—with later changes in pronunciation—it became Nam Viet, the southern barbarians.) As the T'ang consolidated the gains of their predecessors, the frontier was pushed south. The land which now encompasses the Chinese provinces of Kwangtung and Kwangsi came to be known as Lingnam, Land Below the Southern Passes, with P'an-yu (modern Canton) its administrative center. Below that was Annam, the Peaceful South (again the penchant for wishful naming) with Chiao-chou (modern Hanoi) its administrative center.

The southlands were known early in Shang and Chou times both as a place of banishment for hardened criminals and as the home of wild tribes variously called Miao or Man (later the terms would have more specific application). These were expected to make short work of the banishees. It would seem they did not. Many Chinese outcasts or culprits in flight were made entirely welcome among the barbarians. The records tell of several such individuals who, to save their skins, had them completely tattooed and lived with the natives happily ever after.

By the time of the warring states (450–221 B.C.) the Yueh south of the Yangtze had become organized into the southernmost of the Chinese dukedoms. "Yueh of the hundred tribes," so Ssu-ma Ch'ien describes it. That these hundred tribes could pursue concerted policy both in alliance with and opposition to other ducal states argues for leadership in tune with the times, leadership Chinese-trained, if not Chinese. The most important of the southern ducal domains was that of Ch'u whose rulers vaunted their foreign heritage and whose tombs support the claim. Themes in art, clothing styles, bronzes, while Chinese in general conformation, have yet something of a southern air. Forms of writing revealed in Ch'u tomb excavations are similar but not quite the same as those of northern China. Indeed, that writing is often thought to represent a language altogether non-Chinese (Thai, perhaps; we cannot be sure).

The dukes of Ch'u were as ambitious as their colleagues of the North and regularly sent their armies out to conquer neighboring domains. The state of Wu was quickly gobbled up, and the states of Pa and Shu in the west were next on the Ch'u list. A general of noble birth was duly dispatched and duly carried out his charge. On his way home, however, he found the way blocked by invading Ch'in troops and prudently retreated to Lake Tien where ruling Mi-mo clans (so Ssu-ma Ch'ien calls them) had organized a state. The general was received with great courtesy and reciprocated by fathering a line of Tien kings who (again in Ssu-ma Ch'ien's description) lived in settlements, watched their people farm, and wore their hair "mallet-fashion"—knotted, perhaps, in the manner favored by some hill and island folk even today. To the north and west of Tien lived other folk, relatives of the Mi-mo but not farmers. They were, rather, pastoral nomads, driving their herds and flocks from place to place, without chiefs to guide them.

The testimony of the spade has revealed in the Tien site this mingling of influences. Archaeologists have found, cast in bronze, musicians and dancing figures that recall scenes of a Chinese court. They have also found much of the South: serpent figures, birds, and tiger motifs; representations of pile-built houses and boats meant perhaps for the afterworld journey dear to southern hearts. Women seem to have enjoyed a certain importance in the Tien scheme of things, for female figures are shown in litters borne by many attendants. There are scenes of human sacrifice and mushroom-shaped bronze drums, ranging from tiny to enormous in size.

But along with the strains of East and South are those that speak of steppe influences. Bronze horse warriors in battle would look at home in a Pazyryk tomb. So would the bull figures, so many as to indicate the special esteem in which their living prototypes were held. Human faces in all the art are cleverly, individually modeled, and their features do not appear strikingly Chinese. There was, it would seem, a corridor which stretched through western Szechwan and into the steppes. Down this corridor traveled horsemen and their goods, stopping now and again at way stations and trading posts. Sites uncovered in this corridor area suggest as much.

In the turmoil that followed the Ch'in rise to power, its fall, and its replacement by the Han Dynasty, Tien was all but forgotten. Then Emperor Wu Ti happened to send an envoy questing for routes of access to the west safer than those across the desert. The envoy probed here and probed there without success. In western Szechwan, Ch'iang tribesmen barred the way. All down through Yunnan there were others, barbarians and bandits ready to slit a traveler's throat for the handkerchief in his sleeve. At last the envoy stumbled into the kingdom of Tien and was made welcome by its ruler, a kindly soul who offered to send explorers of his own to find safe passage through the mountains. It is not recorded whether such a route was discovered, but so ample was the king's hospitality meanwhile that the envoy, on his return to the Han court, could talk of nothing else. Such hospitality, such riches, thought Wu Ti, would be an adornment to his empire. Tien was very promptly annexed, and the line of Ch'u kings there came to an abrupt end.

There were Ch'u lines elsewhere, however. Earlier, during the Ch'in invasions, a Ch'u general named Chao T'o conquered Southern Yueh (that dukedom of the hundred tribes) and held it, too. All the way to the Red River Delta, he went, to the very heart of Yueh country. There, near modern Hanoi, archaeologists have uncovered the remains of a culture remarkably similar to that of Tien. No writing has turned up, but there is evidence, as in Tien, of class structure, of specialized occupations, of organization, and of rule. The bronzes in both centers tell of a way of life complex and widespread, stretching at least from Lake Tien to the sea. The Hanoi branch has been called Dong-son, and it appears to have terminated in fire, in the ruin of a great conflagration. Perhaps the troops of Chao T'o were to blame.

When the Ch'in Dynasty fell, Chao T'o set himself up as King Wu of the Southern Yueh with a respectably large and impressive domain. The Han Emperor Kao-tsu was perfectly willing for him to remain so, provided he acknowledged the sovereignty of Han. An envoy was dispatched to convey the news. This proper and stately personage found Chao T'o tattooed, barefoot, sprawled on a mat, distastefully at ease. Sternly reprimanded by the envoy for his breach of propriety, Chao T'o apologized and promised to mend his ways. But Chinese court dress was never designed for tropical wear, and Chao T'o lapsed again. Worse yet, he began to give himself imperial airs. This time it was the Empress Lu who took offense and dispatched an army to administer punishment. Her men died in the heat and damp south of the Yangtze, and Chao T'o was reprieved again. When Emperor Wen succeeded to the Chinese throne, he chose to be tolerant, and so Chao T'o managed to live to a ripe old age. His descendants were not so lucky. They committed one diplomatic blunder after another, eventually giving Han rulers an excuse for annexation. Perhaps it was then that Southern Yueh began to sound like Nam Viet.

No sooner had the Han men arrived at the southernmost limit of their new territory than they came into contact with the outpost of another kingdom, that of the Cham people. The outpost was called Lin-i or Lin-yi, and it was described with further notes and comments after the Champa Kingdom (to which it belonged) sent envoys in A.D. 220 to the governor in Lingnam. Champa was believed to have been founded in A.D. 192. Perhaps that event somehow involved the wave of invaders who, some sixty years earlier, had attacked Chinese settlements on the coast. The invaders were from the west, so the annals held. More likely they were from the Indonesian islands, for the Chams spoke then as now a Malayo-Polynesian language. The fact would be made clear a few centuries later in one of their beautiful inscriptions, written in the vernacular.

The Chams were described as having black skins, deep-set eyes, turned-up noses, and frizzy hair which they wore rolled up in tight knots at the back of the head. The Chinese approved of their cleanly ways and frequent applications of musk. They neither approved nor understood the Cham habit of reckoning descent through the female line and sniffed at the Cham fondness for a female goddess addressed as the Lady of the Kingdom. Even though the right to rule, unlike commoner descent, was supposed to be inherited from father to son, there were altogether too many powerful princesses, too frequent accession of maternal nephews to suit the Chinese sense of propriety.

Perhaps it was through the Chams, perhaps by way of even earlier rumor that the Chinese heard of yet another kingdom called Funan, really a small empire, farther south. They did not remain long in suspense. The king of this mysterious realm sent envoys to China in 225, and the Chinese (although then in a state of some dynastic disarray) returned the compliment in 268. Their ambassadors had this to say about Funan and Funan's people:

> *The men are all ugly and black, their hair frizzy; they go about naked and barefoot. Their nature is simple and they are not at all inclined toward thievery. They devote themselves to agriculture. They sow one*

year and harvest for three. . . . Many of their eating utensils are silver. Taxes are paid in gold, silver, pearls, perfumes. There are books and depositories of archives and other things. Their characters for writing resemble those of the Hu [a people of Central Asia using a script of Indian origin].

The visit to Funan must have occasioned considerable culture shock. Naked bodies at work in state archives! What incongruity!

The name Funan, it seems, comes from the Chinese mispronunciation of *Bnam,* a Mon-Khmer word which, in modern Cambodian, is *phnom,* or "mountain." Funan, then, was the realm of the King of the Mountain, and about his origins there were various explanations. The most popular story (one to be enshrined in later court ritual of Cambodia) held that their ruler, the Snake King, had given his daughter in marriage to an Indian Brahman, thus establishing the royal line. Such a story, needless to say, did nothing to weaken the Chinese view that all southerners harbored suspicious serpentine connections.

But Funan was, after all, far away. Champa was next door, just over the frontier. It was a frontier frequently crossed by raiders traveling in both directions. In the late 500s when Sui emperors briefly occupied the Chinese throne, Lin-i was attacked and looted and its prince beheaded. For a time Champa was subdued. The incoming T'ang were somewhat more circumspect, but the Chams took no chances. In 623 and 630 they sent tribute trains to the Chinese capital, hoping to forestall further attacks, hoping also to encourage trade. And what trains they were with their orchestras and dancing girls, their porters bearing caskets of jewels, white elephants trained to crush a convicted criminal on order, brilliant parakeets that could talk, and monkeys said to understand human speech.

If the T'ang officials did little to provoke Champa they certainly ruled Nam Viet with a heavy and extortionate hand.

Each administrative area was made to pay and pay handsomely. Each tribe, each village had something special to supply. Even the mountain savages were forced into service (when they could be caught) as slaves if nothing else. Female slaves "with buttery skins" (in Edward Schafer's words) were much in demand, and traffic in them bustled. Pearls, jewels, gold were desired as well, along with perfumes and spices and cinnabar (the marvelous, magical red substance that could be refined to silvery mercury). The Fukien area specialized in providing boys to be made eunuchs for the royal court. Castration had, by T'ang times, ceased to be a political punishment and had become instead a qualification for certain palace offices.

The people of Nam Viet, enraged by their exploitation, rebelled again and again. Finally they invited the Kingdom of Nan Chao to intervene. Almost certainly descended in some way from old Tien, long ago subjugated by Han armies, Nan Chao had consolidated near Lake Tali. Nan Chao had grown powerful enough to best one Chinese army after another and, though eventually driven out of Nam Viet, was instrumental in setting that country free of China in A.D. 939. Nam Viet, or Dai Viet, as it was then called, remained free, save for a brief Ming intrusion, until the nineteenth century.

By 939, however, lowland Vietnamese of the rice-paddy villages and of the crowded towns had become so thoroughly Chinese in outlook and culture that they sent to the imperial capital a written apology for their victory. They would do so again in later years after they had repulsed Mongol invaders. It was, after all, the proper, the Confucian thing to do. And the people of Vietnam (or Nam Viet) by now honored the Sage in all things: in their sense of family order, in their demeanor and address, and in their approach to life. This thorough-going conversion was sanctified in Confucian shrines that are to this day called Temples of Literature.

As native Viet dynasties formed and ruled, the ritual proprieties learned from China continued to be observed. Every three years the ruler at his capital in Hue performed the ancient sacrifice to Heaven and Earth and to the royal ancestors. The Vietnamese ritual included all the pomp, the solemnity, all the trappings known to imperial China. One could see (assuming one happened to be male and a court official) the selfsame altars; the selfsame robes, dragon-embroidered in yellow and blue; the selfsame jade tablets inscribed in gold. There were only a few necessary differences. Sacrificial animals were buffalo, pig, and she-goat rather than cow, sheep, and horse. And they were cremated in monster urns of bronze. The Sacrifice to Heaven and Earth was last observed by a westerner in 1927 when it was performed by a prime minister for the Emperor Bao Dai, then absent in Paris.

Even with the disappointing loss of Vietnam, the Chinese sense of duty was fulfilled. Civilization had indeed been carried southward. And a great deal more besides, many specialists would add. Most aspects of culture in the Far East are (or were recently) viewed as radiations from a Chinese center. The domestication of plants, some think, traveled south and perhaps pottery as well. If not those two, then certainly that style of village life known in northern China as Lungshanoid. Later followed a knowledge of metals which stimulated creation of the great bronze drums of Dong-son.

It is a tidy sequence; too tidy, perhaps, to stand up under close scrutiny. The formation of human life ways, the give and take of influences among them, these are necessarily untidy and complex, matters of process rather than event. It is, however, the nature of *our* life way to seek and construct a sequence of events, an orderly understanding of the way things really *were* at any given moment in the human past. And in writing this book, I am a true child of my culture, trying to sort things out for myself. But please be warned. Form and order are illusory. They constitute only a very hazy map, much like those produced by medieval cartographers who filled blank spots with the quaint admonition: "Here there be tygers!"

It is safe to say that maps of cultural beginnings in Southeast Asia are going to be hazier before they grow clearer. For one thing, archaeological activity has become intense only in recent years. It is true, of course, that temple cities have been cleared and restored, and deity figures are continually refurbished and gilded by the faithful. Much religious merit accrues to such activity. Interest in really ancient times, however, was stirred only in the 1920s when, not too far from Hanoi, some curious caves came to light. They contained, all of them, stone choppers and grinding implements and much used flakes. In upper levels were stone tools of a somewhat different sort, cord-marked pottery, and quantities of shell. The culture was termed Hoabinhian after a neighboring village. Over the years many similar sites have been discovered throughout the lands south of the Yangtze River and on Taiwan. Some near water courses include the shell mounds and stone net sinkers that give evidence of fishing activity. Hoabinhian might rather be called (as archaelogist Chester Gorman suggests) a technocomplex rather than a culture, for its characteristic utensils and tools have surely been used by many peoples speaking different languages, holding varying beliefs. One has only to think of the automobile, think of its many sorts of drivers, all equally concerned with changing tires, finding gas, observing stop signs, to understand what is meant by a technocomplex.

Some botanists have long speculated that plant domestication might well have been first accomplished in Southeast Asia. Not in northern China, not in the Middle East, here—and perhaps in a Hoabinhian context. Finds and dates have done little to substantiate the proposition. Then, in the late 1960s excavations were begun at Spirit Cave by Chester Gorman, at that time a student of William G. Solheim, archaeologist at the

University of Hawaii. The cave overlooks a tributary of the Salween River in northern Thailand. For five thousand years it had sheltered generations of residents. After their final departure it became the repository of local dead in their boat-shaped coffins. Thus the name: Spirit Cave. Radiocarbon analysis of charcoal from hearths at various levels indicates a first occupation of the cave sometime about 10,000 B.C. and abandonment after 5600 B.C.

Throughout the cave Gorman found the familiar Hoabinhian complex, though around 6800 B.C. newer ideas in the form of edge-ground tools and rather sophisticated, cord-marked pottery arrived. These newer things were used but never fully replaced the older implements. There was more. The food of millennial dinners revealed itself to Gorman's painstaking siftings and sortings of soil. The people of Spirit Cave had consumed many sorts of small animals. Gorman found their bones cut into pieces, all untouched by fire. This suggests to him a cooking process used today by the Semang, a hunting and gathering folk of southern Thailand and central Malaysia. The Semang stuff with bits of meat a long joint of green bamboo and hang it or prop it slantwise over the fire. The bamboo may char but never burns quite through. Before this happens the meat inside is more or less cooked. It is interesting to note that the charcoal from Spirit Cave derives almost entirely from bamboo.

Meat was not the sole item of diet in the cave, however. Since the beginning, residents had consumed nuts of various kinds—almonds and butternuts among others—and had chewed still another—the betel, ever popular in the southlands as a mild stimulant. They had also been fond of beans and bottle gourds and cucumbers. Had these been cultivated in fields below the caves? It is as yet impossible to say for certain, though Dr. Gorman and his colleagues think this highly likely. Beans usually turn up in a gardening context wherever in the world they are found and at whatever time period. The relative permanence of occupation indicated in Spirit Cave might also argue for some sort of plant arrangement and plant care else the occupants would have had to forage far afield, moving daily in their quest as the Semang must move today, although even they have learned to tend patches of wild yams, an activity which shortens the forest circuit. They have also learned to camp near thick groves of wild fruit trees, groves which they themselves inadvertently maintain. The Semang eat fruit, seeds and all, and when these are eliminated, already in a prefertilized condition, they are bound to take root. Perhaps the people of Spirit Cave followed just such habits, were learning the ways of plant care if not planting itself.

An early development of true gardening in the southland would not be too surprising, however. Dr. K. C. Chang has found on one group of Taiwan sites the cord-marked pottery and ground-edge implements similar to those which appeared in Spirit Cave around 6800 B.C. Some of the Taiwan stone implements seem to be especially adapted for garden work, being hoelike in form. A recently obtained date for one of the sites has been pegged at 3695 B.C. It should be noted, however, that this date is associated with a collection of cord-marked pottery which is late in type. Other of the corded ware sites are certain to be much older. Studies of pollen-bearing soil cores have yielded interesting, even tantalizing information. It seems that some time around 9000 B.C. there occurred on Taiwan many fires, a general burning of the ancient, the original vegetation. Some specialists very tentatively relate this event to the farming habits of Southeast Asian hill folk today who "plough with the torch and plant with the spear," burning over the trees and brush and planting in the ashes.

It is safe to say that, whenever gardening appeared in the South, grain crops were not first to be put in the ground. The sequence might well have followed the one which has been reconstructed for the Senoi, slash-and-burn gardeners and neighbors of the Semang. First with them came bananas and the root crops, taro and yam. Then came "the mother of foxtail millet" and later millet itself. At some point thereafter maize and manioc were brought to Southeast Asia from the New World and trickled down eventually to the Senoi. Last came rice, appearing among some groups no earlier than fifty years ago. So says Dr. Robert Dentan who has lived with the Senoi. We should not be surprised, therefore, to find in the archaeological record as in the record of living men evidence that sophisticated farming communities were neighbors both in space and time to simple gardening folk whose remains scarcely attest to their skills.

As for southern archaeological sites clearly agricultural in nature, William G. Solheim and his colleagues have been digging in one since 1965. It lies south of Spirit Cave along the Mekong River in an area where Thai dam building threatens the record of the past. The site is called Non Nok Tha, and it appears to be older than 3500 B.C. In human burials at the lowest levels of the site have been found the bones of sacrificed pigs, dogs, and bovine animals. A close comparison of the bovine bones with those of various living relatives has convinced some specialists that they belonged once to domesticated animals. If so then they represent the earliest known domestication of cattle in the area. If not, then it is at least likely that the inhabitants of Non Nok Tha knew how to keep herds of wild cattle close at hand.

At Non Nok Tha there appeared what may be the oldest metal in the region. It is in the form of a socketed ax of copper, possibly hammered cold into shape, and it was found on the skeletal chest of a man buried long ago. How long? The mechanics of dating are unfortunately contradictory on this point, the date of the bones, the thermoluminescence date of an associated pot, and dates obtained from identical burials vary widely. Donn Bayard, the discoverer of the ax, is settling for the moment on 2400 B.C. as a likely time of manufacture. It is a date which correlates well with the pottery datings in nearby graves.

In the ordinary sequence of events, copper tools precede the discovery of metal alloys which yield the harder and more usable bronze. And Bayard has turned up a number of bronze axes in the Non Nok Tha site as well as the two-part pottery molds in which they, or similar examples, were cast. These are all reliably datable over a period extending from 2300 B.C. to 900 B.C. This would appear to be the earliest use of bronze now known in the Far East and, says its discoverer, the style, the process owe nothing to outside influences. He is supported in the claim by the recent appearance of similar bronze work at a site in South Vietnam dated to 1950 B.C. Excavations in North Vietnam have uncovered bronzes definitely older than those of Dong-son and of a style quite different in nature.

There is yet more. In a pot recovered from the lower levels of Non Nok Tha one can see very clearly the imprint of a rice husk. Not surprising. All sorts of vegetal materials are used as binders in ceramics. The rice husk, however, is of the domesticated species *Oryza sativa* commonly used today. How old is it? Hard to say. No datable materials have been found in conjunction with the pot. There are, however, radiocarbon dates available for materials in layers overlying the rice-husk pot. These suggest to Dr. Solheim that the pot is at least 5500 years old (3500 B.C.).

This in itself would not seem especially startling news. New radiocarbon dates for sites near Shanghai tell us that domesticated rice was in that area and under cultivation certainly in and probably before that. Another Shanghai site with related pottery styles but without direct evidence of rice has recently yielded a date of 3835 B.C. Rice was known to the city folk along the Indus River (in what is now Pakistan) by 3000

B.C. Clearly rice was at least by 3500 B.C. an old familiar staple throughout the southlands. Exactly how old, how familiar we cannot know and may never know unless some lucky and determined digger uncovers a site containing evidence of the wild grain from which today's rice was domesticated. And that may never happen.

It is not just the presence of early domesticated rice which gives the Non Nok Tha its significance. It is the combination: rice and the bones of possibly domesticated bovines and metals (these last two in their earliest appearance anywhere in the East). The very existence of this combination here in Thailand must change the image of Asia south of the Yangtze from that of receiver of ideas to that of creator of ideas. It is not likely that southern China and Southeast Asia provided models for farming in the North. It must be said, however, that their peoples were contemporaries in this new enterprise.

But some things begun in the South *do* seem to have had an impact up North. The Lungshanoid culture—that special style of village economy and belief given expression in exquisite, wheel-made pottery—may well have originated in the South. So suggests Dr. Chang. The dates of Lungshanoid, rice-bearing sites along the Yangtze are far older than those in the northern China nuclear area.

Linguist Paul Benedict claims that the Chinese words for plow, seed, kiln, pottery, ax, boat, and others are borrowed from languages of the southlands. Dear old P'an-ku, the dog of many colors, seems to have been introduced into China from the southland where (as P'an-hu) he has long been venerated and is honored still as founding father of the Miao and many other remote tribal folk. On the journey north, sometime after Han Dynasty times, P'an-hu became P'an-ku, hero of the barbarian wars but also mighty separator of earth and sky, first being and first cause. In this role he served to flesh out a cosmology a bit too spare to suit every questioning soul. In later years, as the writing of Chinese history became more literary and formal, P'an-ku lost his canine identity altogether and was described as a very small giant or a very large dwarf so benevolent as to give over his own body to the creation of the world.

In the southland P'an-ku for long remained in his original form, just as his devotees for very long kept to the good old ways. After an original burst of creativity, after innovations had been accomplished in domestication and the use of metals, there followed a long period without a sign of change. For generations, people seemed content with village life, their horizons stretching little farther than the village over the next hill. Not for them the feverish city building and state building and empire building that occupied the North. And then, bit by bit, the great world without began to make itself felt. The northerners pushed in forcibly, assimilating as they went, making Chinese whatever they could. But the empires that eventually rose in the southland, empires of whose marvels the Chinese first heard tantalizing rumors and then witnessed for themselves—these had been built on ideas from India, as Tibet's theocracy had been so built. To Southeast Asia the ideas traveled, not over mountains, but by boat, blown on the monsoon.

When Shang civilization was in formation, the great cities of the Indus River were already old. Sometime around 1500 B.C. they were overrun by Indo-European-speaking charioteers of the steppes, and a dark age in India began. When civilization blossomed anew it was far more complex than it had been before, its peoples more various, its beliefs more subtle, its cults manifold. Indian society had settled into layers, into castes initially formed on the basis of color, then on the basis of occupation, still later with reference to divine decree. Its religious life was composed of many themes old and new, refined, elaborated, and infinitely subdivisible.

One of the subdivisions begun in the sixth century B.C.

was Buddhism. Through the energy and resolve of King Asoka two centuries later it came to prominence in India. And then it reached others. Whether the diffusion of Buddhism can be credited to missionary fervor or to military unrest at home or simply to a revival of trade, the new religion did travel. It was carried to China, to Ceylon, to Tibet, and to Southeast Asia. In all its adoptive homes, Buddhism thrived while fading away in the motherland.

A revival of trade and travel seems to have been instrumental in bringing both Hinduism and Buddhism to Southeast Asia. Merchants may have come by caravan route into Burma. Certainly they came by sea. By the first century A.D. they were crossing the Indian Ocean to the narrow waist of the Malayan Peninsula, then overland to another boat and on to the Mekong delta, to the Land of Gold. It was by this name that the Burma coast had been known for a hundred years and more. The lands to the east were soon included.

Where the Indian merchants came ashore to haggle with the natives for gold and ivory and spice was built first a trading post and then a settlement. Whether the Indians encountered a native culture simple in form or one of more sophistication, Dong-sonian in cast, that we do not know. All we know is that there developed in this area the kingdom of Funan with which (as we saw earlier) the Chinese were glad to exchange envoys. Only one of its cities, Oc-eo, the coastal settlement, has yielded any appreciable remains—statues of Hindu gods, Indian rings and seals, coins from faraway Rome, and Chinese bronzes. No buildings have yet been located; the Funanese may have built in wood. Neither have inscriptions been unearthed though the Chinese ambassador of A.D. 268 spoke of writing and the keeping of state archives. Funan was, nevertheless, powerful and strong. Over the years her influence spread north to what is now Thailand, west to Dvaravati, Thaton, and Pegu, the growing kingdoms of the strait-laced and religious Mon people on the Menam, Salween, and Irrawaddy deltas. The Mon languages are closely related to Khmer, thought to have been spoken by the people of Funan. Funanese influence may even have extended as far north and west as the middle Irrawaddy where the Tibeto-Burmese-speaking Pyu people were building Srikshetra.

East and north of Funan was Champa, a kingdom which vied with Funan in the matter of influence as in all else. In its heyday, Champa stretched in a narrow coastal arc from somewhere north of Hue to a point near the Mekong Delta, later wrested from them by Funan. The Chams were a sea people, a pirate people, so the records hold, and it may be that the drubbings they received at Chinese hands were not altogether undeserved. Champa was, over a thousand years, to lose ground bit by bit to the encroaching Vietnamese determinedly moving south.

The Chams initially worshipped Indian gods, Vishnu and especially Siva. Many temples were built in their honor, statues were fashioned, inscriptions carved, first in Sanskrit, the old religious language of India, then in the native language. Even after Buddhism became popular among the common people and in later years Islam, the worship of Siva for long set the royal family apart.

Other kingdoms honored Siva, too. Chenla, which in the sixth century swallowed up Funan, built lavishly in this god's honor. So would its successor state, the greatest empire of the Khmer-speaking people. Centered on the great lake region of the Mekong, that empire grew rich on new methods of irrigation farming. At its height it included modern Cambodia and much of what is now Thailand, Burma, Vietnam, Laos. Often it is called the Empire of Angkor after the exquisite temple cities built by its kings. They were cities which in plan, in form, in their very existence reaffirmed the divinity of the king and his rightful place at the center of the world.

In Indian religious doctrine the world at its beginning was composed of seven oceans and seven continents. In the center of these encircling boundaries stood the sacred Mount Meru, home of the gods, around which the planets revolved. Indian cosmology received in Southeast Asian kingdoms architectural translation. World beginnings were made manifest in every capital with a temple which was holy Meru and a king who was the founder-god. In Champa and Cambodia the king was thought to be an incarnation of Siva, sometimes Vishnu. Later, with the rise of Buddhism (so Robert Heine-Geldern tells us) kings were thought to have been, in past incarnations, helpers of Buddha who had stored up such treasures of merit as to have earned the right to rule. And even though Hinayana Buddhism insisted that gods were as illusory as the men who prayed to them, the principle of cosmic centrality remained with the sacred city as its symbol. The main temple continued to be Meru around which were built the walls and gates that symbolized the boundary oceans, the heights, and the four directions. Sculpture, however, devoted its attention largely to the figure of the Buddha himself.

The source of Buddhist orthodoxy from about the seventh century on (so Dr. Bernard Groslier suggests) lay surely among the various Mon-speaking people. It may well have been they who popularized and spread the reformed faith which now dominates the region and is visible constantly in the persons of its yellow-robed monks. But it dominates with a light hand, it would seem. Even today Buddhism, Hinduism, and the earlier reverence for the old spirit essences of nature cheerfully coexist. Every Thai family has its little spirit house at the bottom of the garden. Every Burmese takes care not to offend the *nats* who, like Western goblins, lie in wait for the unwary or lend a helping hand. Shamans possessed by these beings are consulted in a variety of problem situations.

In the course of her history Burma produced a host of

reverent rulers and none more so than the kings of Pagan who rose to prominence in the ninth century. They rose because the Pyu kingdom fell, not to themselves but to Nan Chao, later the savior of Nam Viet. That was in A.D. 832. Altogether three thousand of the vanquished were taken back into what is now Yunnan Province to populate K'un-ming. Hill folk themselves, the people of Pagan eagerly, even assertively, sought religious tutelage of the very orthodox Mon at Thaton and, with all the new-found fervor of the convert, outdid their teachers. The kings of Pagan built shrines and temple cities as lavish and beautiful as those of Angkor and built with equal attention to cosmic significance. The central "mountain," however, was not the home of the god but the home of the king. However elevated the symbolism, politics were politics, and rule was rule. Indeed the very sacredness of the royal symbols and trappings in Southeast Asian kingdoms generally made usurpation all too easy. Just get the king out of his holy place, lay hands on the sword, the crown, the royal umbrella, and you, too, can become an instant king. This is what aspiring and unscrupulous princes learned along with their lessons in Sanskrit. Eventually rulers grew wary of leaving their temples or palaces for any reason whatever. One refused even to pace the perimeter of his temple precincts, the final and essential act of his coronation, the final binding of kingdom and self. Someone else, he thought, might seize the house while he tied the knot.

For peoples supposedly devoted to the religious ideal—the ideal of the middle way (neither too much anger nor too much joy and above all *no* desire), Southeast Asians made war with energy and delight. The Khmer fought the Chams and vice versa, one elephant cavalry against the other. The Chams fought the expanding Vietnamese and vice versa, until Mongol armies in the thirteenth century appeared on the horizon, and the one-time antagonists cooperated long enough to keep the invaders offshore.

Pagan and Nan Chao before her had a great deal more difficulty with the Mongols. Nan Chao fell, and in 1287 the elephants of Pagan simply made wonderful huge pincushions for Mongol bowmen. The Khan claimed a victory (corroborated by Marco Polo in his account of the battle). The Pagan king called it a draw. We may never be sure what happened or what might have happened afterward, for the Mongol leader died and his armies withdrew. The Pagan king, humiliated beyond endurance, went into a long decline and his kingdom along with him.

New folk filled the vacuum. Some specialists believe that the defeat of Nan Chao released a good many Thai-speaking warriors for action. What were they doing in Nan Chao, supposedly a Tibeto-Burman kingdom? It is hard to imagine. Functioning as the ruling elite, some specialists think. Whatever the case, it seems clear that, after the Mongol intrusion, Thai groups did begin to push south in great numbers. Several Shan princelings (Thai-speakers, all) preempted lands once ruled by Pagan. A number of Thai groups settled within the Khmer orbit, grew disaffected and strong and forced Angkor into retreat. This was the beginning of Siam, now modern Thailand. Between the Mekong and the mountain ranges of Vietnam, other Thai-speaking people called the Lao formed yet another kingdom, one which suffered as much from the rivalry of its own nobles as from the depredations of neighbors.

The Vietnam dynasties, little by little, managed to obliterate Champa and turned their strength against the Khmer. Angkor went under and was re-formed as the Kingdom of Kambuja (whence comes the name Cambodia). And then came the French and English. Invited in first as allies against local enemies, they remained to divide responsibility for Southeast Asia. Vietnam, Laos, and Cambodia became wards of the French. Burma, bordering as it did on India, entered the British sphere as did Malaya. Only Siam remained independent, no one is quite sure how. Mrs. Anna Leonowens, teacher to Siamese royal children about this time (the 1800s), thought independence must be credited to Siam's remarkable ruler, King Mongkut. Those of us who have seen this king portrayed in films by actors Rex Harrison and Yul Brynner probably think so, too.

Europe has now been evicted from Southeast Asia. American armies, called in to fill the gap, have left, and American influence is on the wane. The Southeast Asians face one another with all their old enmities intact. Cambodia fears both Thailand and Vietnam. The two Vietnams reflect a division of soul as well as of land, and who knows when or whether they can be rejoined. One part cleaves to the Chinese heritage (though not necessarily to China herself). The other part, anciently the kingdom of Champa, pulled now east, now west, may still be bent on that domination of the southland interrupted by colonial intervention.

But these are the ambitions, the enmities of the flatland folk, the delta folk, the rice-paddy farmers, the city workers, and the educated elites. Into the hills have washed the others, the refugees of earlier crises of statebuilding and of a thousand prior conflicts on the plains, migrants who want to remain what they have always been, to change only just enough to stay nearly the same. They do not farm as the lowlanders farm, with plows drawn by water buffalo. They plant their rice dry in fields cleared by fire, and when the land weakens they move on. Their languages are not always those of the city folk, the government officials nearest them. They pray to different gods and count kin in different ways and hold onto customs that the flatland farmers and city folk call "savage." In other times the Chams called their hill tribes *mlecchas*, "savages." Today other words are used, but they mean the same thing: *moi* in Vietnamese, *kha* among Laotians and Thais, *phong* in Cambodia, *taung thu* in Burmese.

And yet these countries, born in war and torn by war, can survive only by taking their *moi* into account. The loyalties of the hill people must be attracted, their dignity upheld, their rights secured. Hope lies always in linking yesterday to tomorrow. And yesterday in Southeast Asia stretches far beyond the lovely temples overgrown by vines. Yesterday is also the village in the hills midway on the ladder of change between the twentieth century and the time when farming was something new and one's own green hill world enough.

13

PEOPLE OF THE HILLS
Yesterday and Tomorrow

TODAY a "savage," tomorrow a member of the ruling class. It is a story old in history but new for every successive generation —never more so than for this one. But the scenario is not invariable. Current denizens of Southeast Asian hills may not have the chance to become tomorrow's ruling class, indeed may continue in the ways of their ancestors who were the "savages" of yesterday. Certainly the old Chinese annals are full of titles applied to "wild" tribes of the west and north and south, of the dry places and the jungle places, of high places and low. There were the Miao, the Man, the Min, the Yueh— strange and unfamiliar southern tribesmen. Do they have living descendants? Can we find in their life ways a reminder of things past? An examination of the ethnographic record is in order.

Ssu-ma Ch'ien speaks of a people called the Lolo, besought by Chao T'o, the erstwhile King Wu, to join his realm. The Lolo had their own king, so Chao T'o later informed the Han emperor, and were located to the west of his own lands.

T'ang armies of later times knew the Lolo, a people connected in some fashion with the Kingdom of Nan Chao. It was claimed that a Lolo clan, called by T'ang writers the Black Man, was said to have founded Nan Chao. A related tribe living to the east was called White Man, presumably because of the white smocks worn by their women. Black Man, too, were styled by the color of female dress.

In the high mountains of the Szechwan homeland and in outliers through Yunnan and into modern Laos there are Lolo still. And they are divided still, black and white, but not by garment color. They are divided by "bone." It was once Mongol habit, you will recall, to divide by bone. The aristocratic lineages of every clan were "white bone" lineages; commoners were "black bone." Among the Lolo, too, bone means rank, but the color significance is just reversed. It is black bone which, for them, marks the nobility, the horse-warriors and herders, those who disdain labor in the fields. This is work fit only for the White Lolo, their serfs and slaves. They may be humble, these White Lolo, but they are many. The silent pressure of their numbers can influence the choice of clan leader. And the clan is all, all there is of law and order. Rival clans fight or ally or exchange marriage partners according to the need of the moment. No central government imposes its dominion over the Lolo. Or so it was as recently as 1943 when the anthropologist Lin Yueh-lua visited them. At that time the Lolo were still trafficking in Chinese slaves, and Dr. Lin himself often had cause to wonder whether he would return in one piece, a free man.

There is much about the Black Lolo (or Nosu as they prefer to be known) which speaks of steppe connections, a stake in Nan Chao, perhaps even a claim to ancient Tien.

Noblewomen hold rank nearly equal with that of men and are privileged to act as peacemakers between feuding clans. There are hereditary priests who alone can decipher the ancient Lolo writings. And the future is divined by way of scapulimancy, a method rare in Southeast Asia. Westerners first in contact with Nosu at the turn of the century were impressed with their stature, their high-bridged noses and faintly Europoid look not to be seen among the White Lolo even then. Already these had begun to be Chinese and must today be nearly all the way there.

The Lolo speak a Tibeto-Burman language, one of the branches of the Sino-Tibetan language phylum. Other hill folk who belong in this group are the rice-farming, traveling Akha and the Lisu who grow poppies for a cash crop. These are to be found mostly in northern Burma, as are the Kachin who have been given their own ethnic state there.

The Karen, too, are found in two states of northern Burma devoted to their use, but they have spilled over into the Thai hills as well. Their languages are often thought to constitute a special branch of Sino-Tibetan, coequal with Tibeto-Burman, as are those of the Miao-Yao peoples.

Here are old names, older far than Lolo. The Yao tribesmen are still called Man, and the pronunciation of Miao in Southeast Asia as *meo* is said to stem from the Vietnamese word for them: *Man-Meo*. They call themselves Hmong, the Free Men, and would like to be so addressed by all, though, given the firm entrenchment of old titles, this would seem to be a vain hope.

Miao, once a generic title for barbarian, still carried some of that connotation even after Sung times when it came to be applied to a specific people, people whose homeland seems to have been somewhere along the middle Yangtze. The Yao were early located near that river's Red Basin. Both peoples were pushed southward by the steady pressure of the Chinese.

The Hill Tribes of Indochina

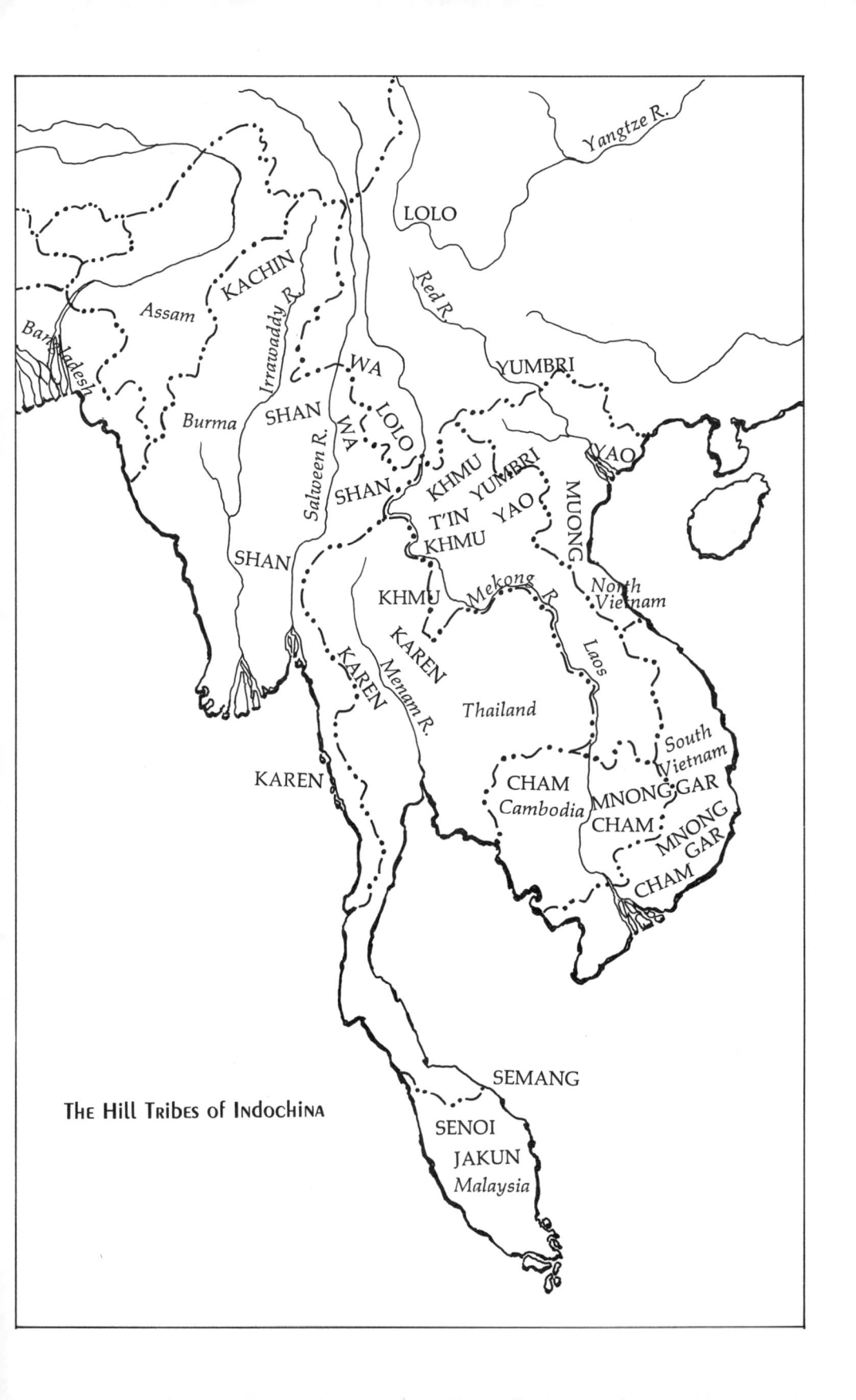

Surely they must at one time have been counted among the many tribes of Yueh. In the last two centuries, the Miao-Yao have migrated farther south, first into Vietnam, then into Laos, then Thailand. And the steady infiltration continues first because both Miao and Yao are aggressive and industrious, secondly because they choose the highest peaks and flanks of hills for their farms, land not overly attractive to other settlers. On these hilltop farms they grow the poppies from which opium is made. From the poppy comes silver with which, say the Yao, "a face may be washed" (or saved); silver "which makes things clean." It also makes the Miao-Yao relatively well to do. Even though they are harried from one country to another; even though they are exploited by lowland central governments, themselves ruled by the politics of opium; even though poppy growing is now encouraged, now forbidden according to the mysterious will of foreign folk, the Miao-Yao prosper. They are certainly more affluent than their dry-rice-growing neighbors who work for them in the poppy fields, hired sometimes on the mere promise of the opium to which they are addicted. The Miao themselves will not countenance addiction among their young, considering it the just reward of infirm old age.

Both Miao and Yao maintain their way of life with vigor. They rarely marry out of the language group, holding onto their unique social organization even in the refugee camps to which they must now and again repair when wars rage around their hill tops. And they are notably able in defense. They fought a long series of battles with the Chinese during the last centuries of the empire. Indeed, in the genealogy of Sheung Shui village, the founder records with pride his part in the Miao Wars. The Miao-Yao, nevertheless, do not support pan-tribal movements. They may in different nations sit or fight on opposite sides of a political fence, opposing the central government in one, favoring it in another. (Much depends on the disposition of the poppy crop.) In recent years they have begun to push their way into the seats of power, occupying now and again important government posts.

And yet, while admitting new things, the Miao-Yao preserve much of the old. It is their women who, the rumors say, know the way of *ku* poison. Bronze drums long played an important role in their rituals in southern China and still do in their Southeast Asian homes. They have been last to relinquish the sacrifices to P'an-ku, used in connection with healing ritual. *Ku* women, adepts in sorcery and magic, to this day fear the dog and cannot use their powers against this animal, though the pig is notably susceptible. High into the air they send their magic bamboo rods to attract the dragons that lurk there like lightning ready to strike. They can bring sickness and misfortune, these women, but they can also hold their husbands. No man married to a *ku* woman has ever been known to stray.

Altogether the Miao-Yao do not fit the common picture of hill folk, being neither poor nor isolated nor especially downtrodden. And in the mountains of South Vietnam, the Rhade and Jarai, too, vary somewhat from the stereotype although they were almost certainly, at one time or another, refugees from the wars between Champa and Cambodia, Champa and Vietnam. The Rhade and Jarai speak a Malayo-Polynesian language, as do their lowland relatives, the Chams, but, unlike those relatives, they have not embraced Islam, cleaving instead to beliefs that were old even before Indian influences penetrated these lands. Most hill folk are villagers, recognizing little in the way of wider loyalties. The Rhade and Jarai have some experience of village alliances, even tribal alliances forged through the leadership of powerful shamans, their *sadats* of Fire and Water, with whom even Cambodian and Laotian kings have been glad to treat.

North of the Rhade in Vietnam are other groups, once

surely among the hundred tribes of the Yueh. These are the Thai-speaking peoples. T'ang annals mention the Huang of southern China who fomented constant trouble in the area; mention, too, the Nung and the Mak, tribal names that still live and are attached to Thai-speaking people today, some of them in southern China. The Thai languages are, most of them, so similar as to argue very recent dispersal of their speakers. As to the connections of Thai with other groups, however, the picture is not so clear. Specialists who concentrate on the study of Southeast Asian languages often disagree with one another's classifications. In no area is the controversy more profound than in the matter of Thai. Does it relate distantly to Miao-Yao? Is it closer to Chinese? The controversy has hotted up considerably with Paul Benedict's designation of Thai as a single phylum which includes the archaic languages of the Li tribes of Hainan Island, resident there long before the beginning of Chinese history.

Thai speakers, whether or not linguistically related to the Chinese, must have had a long contact with them, long enough to add to their cultural repertory the forms and rules of state organization. Ssu-ma Ch'ien attributed the Yueh capacity for leadership to a distant descent from the sage Emperor Yu and said:

> *Although Yueh is a land of barbarians, its former rulers must have treated the people with great wisdom and virtue. Otherwise, how could their line have lasted so long? For generation after generation, they held the title of chieftain or king. . . .*

After the thirteenth century, Thai-speaking groups began to build in Southeast Asia, along the Middle Mekong and the Menam. Even in the highlands, however, in the small upland valleys occupied by the Thai in North Vietnam and Laos, the rice-growing folk are ranked in classes, high, priestly, and low, and each small valley is ruled by its prince, thought to have special connections with the earth spirit which enriches the valley.

In the northern Burmese highlands, there are the Shan principalities, larger and much more complex. Each prince long ago embraced Buddhism and recognized (but only nominally) the overlordship of the Burmese king with his domain along the Irrawaddy lowlands. Each Shan prince had his own liegemen among the tribal peoples of the hills—among the Kachin and the Karen clans. Whole villages of these tribes have tailored themselves to the Shan model. Some—especially the Karen—have joined with the Shan in opposing the Burmese central government today, a government which, to Shan minds, offers altogether too much threat to their own princely autonomy.

In addition to the Kachin and Karen, other tribal groups have found the Shan model attractive or, ignoring the model, have nevertheless found cooperation with Shan princelings to their advantage. Such a people were the mountain Wa, so called by their Shan overlords. The Wa collected heads in the old days (and are still rumored to do so today). The heads, they claimed, were necessary in providing guardian spirits for their earth-walled, moated villages. In the old days they were said to prefer Chinese heads, and Shan princes were quick to use this Wa predilection to their own ends. The Wa were apparently also bandits who exacted protection money from passing caravans and discreetly guided those of their own princes through enemy territory.

The Wa claimed to own the land, to be first there, and why not? They have, after all, a language of the Mon-Khmer family which, with other languages in the Austroasiatic phylum, is surely one of the oldest in the area. The Thai, the Miao, the Tibeto-Burmans, the Karen—all have come from somewhere else. The speakers of Mon-Khmer were always there, or were at least earliest to inhabit the flat lands and deltas where they built great kingdoms, first to lay claim to the hills and highlands, out of sight and out of reach. And they long ago traveled afar: into Indian Assam where the Khasi speak a Mon-Khmer language, into the Indian subcontinent itself where live the Munda whose language is a very distant relative.

In northern Thailand, not too far away from Chester Gorman's Spirit Cave, live the Lawa, another Mon-Khmer people who claim once to have been lords of the land, declining as the emergent Thai organized first into principalities and then into the Kingdom of Siam. The local prince of their district saw fit to protect the Lawa, to call them Older Brother, and to lecture them on best use of the land for their dry-rice farming. Karen and Meo (Miao), later immigrants to the area, recognized the Lawa priority of rights, paid them yearly tribute, ignored them otherwise.

Due east of Lawa country, in Thailand and Laos, are the Khmu, one of a variety of Mon-Khmer hill people the Lao call *Kha* or "slave." At one time at least they were just that, subject to forced labor at call. And yet the prior rights of the hill folk are recognized in ritual if in no other way. Yearly at the royal Lao court, the drama of Kha defeat at the hands of incoming Thai must be enacted with a real live Kha in the leading role.

It is a ritual which gives the Khmu and their fellows no joy and little pride. They are a submissive and dejected people, conscious of their poverty and lowly position in the grand scheme of things. Many of the hill folk, Khmu among them, have taken enthusiastically to Christianity. It is different, after all, from the Buddhism of their betters, and it carries more prestige (and a lesser financial burden) than their old religion. The Khmu Messiah is one who will bring feasting and plenty and a respite from labor. So we are told by Peter Kunstadter and Joel Halpern who have worked in the area. To Christian Meo, on the other hand, the Messiah represents a call to arms and a call to action. Down with Lao officialdom and up with the Meo!

There is only one people who can be snubbed with impunity by the Khmu. They are the T'in, yet another Mon-Khmer hill tribe. And the T'in, even lower on the social ladder, have only the vanishing Yumbri, a hunting-gathering people, on whom to vent their frustrations. The Yumbri they shoot on sight.

In North Vietnam the hill folk are mostly prosperous Meo, Yao, and Thai. But there, too, are the Muong, country cousins of the lowland Vietnamese, reminders of what they once were before Chinese influences took the upper hand. Viet-Muong as a language group is thought to belong with Mon-Khmer in the Austroasiatic phylum, though not everyone is entirely happy with such a classification.

Further south in the hills and forests of the central highlands are the Mnong Gar, an old Mon-Khmer-speaking group, neighbors to the Rhade. As late as the 1930s the Mnong Gar were known to kill French officials sent to parley with them. In later years they accommodated more readily to French direction. Somehow they never became acquainted with, much less connected to, the native officials of the lowlands. How the present Vietnamese government will eventually come to terms with the Mnong Gar is anybody's guess.

In means of livelihood, general belief system, and stance toward life, the Mnong Gar are like other hill tribes of the area. But just as no individual—even in the same family—is quite like any other, so no culture, or even community within a culture, is identical with any other. Each is in itself unique, as Georges Condominas, the French anthropologist tells us. From 1948 to 1950 he lived among the Mnong Gar in one of their villages carved out of the enveloping trees and bamboo thickets.

They are called by other mountain men the People of the

Forest, and it is by way of the forest that they reckon people's ages and events in time. "Let me see now," a father might say, looking at his growing son. "He was born during the time we ate the Forest of the Stone Spirit. And since then we have moved our village twice."

Every stretch of jungle in the territory of a defined group has its name and guardian spirit. And the people move from one to another, gathering the wild foods, fishing the streams, trapping game, and slashing and burning the trees and brush to make fields. There is a new one for each new year. The old is left to fallow for another ten to twenty. Every seven years —sooner if epidemic or bad luck strikes—the whole village picks up stakes and "eats" another named part of the jungle. There are wild animals in these wild jungles—tigers, elephants, wild buffalo, deer—no more than two hundred miles north of Saigon. But the Mnong have not been untouched by war. Their lands astride the Male River where Dr. Condominas lived in 1950 were, during the war years, used for the An Lac air strip and a special-forces camp which included American Green Berets.

The Mnong Gar, some of them, were drawn to the Americans who wished to arm all the Montagnards (as the various mountain folk were originally called by the French) and train them to fight for the South Vietnamese government. Others were loyal to the Viet Cong which promised autonomous zones for ethnic groups as the Vietnamese of the North had done. Still other Montagnards rejected both combatants. One fancies, however, a particular bitterness directed toward the South Vietnamese government which had disarmed them in spite of American support, fearing the Mnong Gar and other mountain tribes might constitute a threat as dangerous in its way as that of the Viet Cong. Some villagers bent whichever way the wind blew, allying themselves now with the Americans and South Vietnamese, now with the Viet Cong and

North Vietnamese. "Whatever happens," said one elderly man to the photographer Howard Sochurek who visited the war zone in 1968, "whatever happens, we must survive."

Survival means as much as possible a continuation of the old way which Dr. Condominas knew so well. By 1950 when he was among them some things had already begun to change. The Mnong Gar were even then less inclined to beautify themselves in the old way—by breaking the upper front teeth to the gum line, filing the lowers to points, and lacquering all a shiny black. For men short-cut hair had slowly begun to replace the traditional knotted bun decorated with tin-plated combs and pins. And pants were just beginning to find favor along with European overcoats and vests. Village chiefs, appointed by the French, still enjoyed little authority.

During Dr. Condominas's stay the village was largely kept in order by its various family heads. Each represented a long house perhaps forty yards in length, bamboo-framed and heavily thatched. In the house lived several related nuclear families, each with its own hearth, granary, and entrance. Descent among the Mnong Gar is traced through the mother. A child takes the name of his mother's clan and has special ties to her elder brother. But perhaps because of the force and influence exerted by a child's own clan, he is taught to honor the clan of his father by promoting father's sister's children a generation, addressing them by the same terms he uses for father's sister herself, depending on whether she is older or younger than father. A man goes to live where his wife lives, which, in the ordinary scheme of things, is with her mother. But no rule of residence ever works out perfectly, and a widower might just wind up in his maternal uncle's home (which is where uncle's wife is). The core occupants of a long house are not always related in the female line, and a house roster is often subject to change with village removal or with death or after angry words have been exchanged, even as our own patterns of residence alter and shift. So it is that every village includes representatives of several clans whose members gather from surrounding villages when there is need.

Some long houses are headed by *kuang,* a "potent man" married to the chief matron of the residence. Houses of *kuang* are marked by carved bamboo posts or by false kapok trees, also carved and adorned with tasseled bamboo. Here by these special trees are sacrificed the many buffalo whose souls enlarge the "buffalo soul" of a *kuang* and give him renown among his peers. Other animals are offered in sacrifice—pigs, chickens, ducks, dogs. But it is the buffalo that count, and buffalo are not easily come by. They are not used in Mnong Gar dry-rice farming, and, the danger of tigers being what it is, cannot be maintained in numbers. They must be bought from the lowlands for every ritual, every marriage, funeral, or healing. And that takes wealth.

One acquires wealth by acquiring metal gongs from the lowlanders or the elegant jars of bronze or clay meant to hold the rice beer essential to sacrifice. One goes down to the lowland folk with the beautifully woven cloths made by one's wife, cloths worn sarong-fashion, and one trades for jars. Or one goes to a neighboring village to trade. For this one requires the services of a go-between, that indispensable functionary in every transaction, be it business or social, secular or ritual, or somewhere in between. He mediates, bargains, smooths the way, and for this service receives many gifts. Every contract is consummated in sacrifice, in rice beer, and in the beating to death of a dog, the animal of exorcism. For trade goods come from strangers, carry (in Condominas's words) "a charge of hostility," and must be safely secured to their new home.

The greatest of the bronze jars have names and personalities and spirits, even as the buffalo do, and may be properly offered as return gifts. No sacrifice with its attendant distribution of meat can be accepted without return. Every gift must be reciprocated. And this is especially true when two *kuang* of different villages become "sworn friends." An instant sacrifice, tit for tat, takes place, first in one village, then in the other. Each man has gained much in the ritual: added spiritual potency and a powerful protector as well, one who will insure his safety on business ventures away from home. But such a connection carries with it heavy obligations. Should a man die before he can reciprocate goods given in swearing friendship or in any other ceremony, his family is forfeit. They are made slaves. Even in so simply organized a society as that of the Mnong Gar, the advantages and responsibilities of wealth and rank are serious matters, never to be taken lightly.

Others hold rank and influence not necessarily based on wealth. Each village has a shaman or two who officiate at various ceremonies and rituals and who heal the sick. (The shaman may, if sufficiently angered, bring on sickness as well, in which case he is functioning as a sorcerer. Among the Mnong Gar suspected sorcery constitutes ample grounds for clan war.) One pays a shaman, not in jars and gongs, but in rice for his services as go-between. For that is what he is, a mediator between the world of the spirits and the one here below. Charcoal, too, is thought of as a kind of go-between, a magic and mediating substance, the means by which spirits can be notified of need and of hopeful offerings.

In the old days village authority was vested in shamans, in the *kuang,* and especially in "the sacred men of the forest and village"—three or four especially revered souls elected in each village to see to the allocation of land and to the periodic village relocations. They were also responsible for the great rituals which honored the spirits of the earth and of the rice. Such rituals stretched over days and required the sacred men to paint their own houses and granaries with designs in rice flour paste and to make altars of bamboo wands shaved at the ends into tassels reminiscent of the Ainu prayer sticks. The sacred men also presided over the ritual consumption of rice beer. What with one ritual or another, everyone was assured a fairly frequent taste of meat and an almost continuous tipple.

Sacred men, according to tradition, could be harmed supernaturally by the forbidden and unnatural behavior of their village fellows. Unnatural social behavior was thought also to invite unnatural cosmic occurrences, to invite lightning and thunder and flooding rains. And the most unnatural, the most abhorred was and is still incest.

Everywhere and at all times in history society has forbidden marriage or sexual relations within the nuclear family (save for those royal exceptions which only serve to emphasize the general rule). The Mnong Gar forbid such relations in the clan, no matter how distant the common ancestor of the erring couple. Do they bear the same name? Then they are brother and sister, taboo to each other, and that is that.

While Dr. Condominas was among the Mnong Gar, he witnessed just such an unnatural event (and its cosmic consequences in the form of heavy rain). He also witnessed its expiation. The couple, condemned before the village (whose members were summoned by the culprits personally), had to purge the group of its taint of sin. Never mind that their common ancestor was distant genealogically in the past. The two were made to "eat" the collected wastes of human, dog, and pig; were made to cleanse themselves ritually in the river and in the blood of a sacrificed pig while the substances of purification were sent with charcoal downriver to the dragon spirit. They were then made to part forever.

The woman in the case, a widow of not very compelling attractions, appeared to enjoy the unwonted attention. It was the young man who suffered profoundly for his sin, suffered guilt and the destruction of his own self image; suffered, too, the loss of home and place in life. The villagers found him next day strangled by a knotted loincloth hung from a beam in his uncle's granary.

We inhabit a world of many faces and voices and human contacts. It is an impersonal world, difficult and vexatious, complicated often beyond our ability to control, much less to comprehend. The world of small horizons and few faces holds for us a special appeal. It seems, at first glance, simple, peaceful, slow, and above all manageable. But every life way gives with one hand while it takes with another. Every life way imposes its own rules and exacts for the breaking of those rules a heavy price. Every life way has its special joys but carries also its special pain focused always on family, spirit, ambition, on death and on love.

14

HUNTING AND GATHERING FOLK
A Vanishing Link With the Past

Hidden in the bamboo thicket, they huddle close to the small fire they have made there—six men, a woman, and a child. The eldest pushes the woman nearer to the heat and sprinkles ashes over her, for she has the open, running sores of yaws, and this is all the people know to do for her. They shiver in the cold of the mountain heights and pull about their bodies the cast-off rags given them in the Meo village they visited some moons ago. They look rather like Meo themselves though they are much smaller and thinner and somehow sadder, too. They do not laugh as they sit there by the fire. They do not smile or even speak more than a necessary word or two.

Perhaps it is because they lost, just yesterday, yet another of their women to marauding tigers. Her torn body lies now far back in the jungle under a coverlet of leaves. Before that they had lost a young man, the boldest among them, shot by a T'in villager before he could offer the honeycomb he had wanted to trade for a scrap of metal or a bit of tobacco. An older man, a wiser one would have stayed long under cover, would have waited until the villager's tribal gear could be plainly seen. Everyone knows the T'in shoot gathering folk on sight, fearing their ghostly presence will curse the village.

But where *is* everyone? Where are the others like themselves, wanderers of the high places, the thickets, the jungles? In flight, most likely, as they themselves must fly. The Meo have warned them of a village headman nearby who means to capture one of their band alive, to exhibit him in a cage and charge admission, to prove the forest wanderers are not ghosts after all.

Why can they not find their fellows? They have left sacrifices to the spirits at the bases of their special trees. Each man has fed the spirit of his long spear. And all the other spirits have been feasted on pig cooked in green bamboo and left overnight for the unseen ones to enjoy. And surely that is sacrifice indeed. Not every day is so large an animal bagged. More often the band goes hungry, managing to keep body and soul together only by means of roots and tubers which their little orange dogs smell out for them.

There is a distant crackling in the bamboo thicket. A footfall, perhaps? Arms freeze. Eyes dart to and fro. All listen, hushed and tense. The sounds draw nearer. Someone smothers the fire. The child is snatched into its mother's ruined arms, and the whole band melts into the forest. When the Lao hunter, ancient musket in hand, cuts his way through the bamboo, he will have to look hard to notice signs of human habitation. Of these there are but two: the embers of the tiny fire and a crude lean-to shelter thatched with the withering and discolored foliage that gives its builders a name. And the Lao hunter, when he returns home, will boast of having almost but not quite surprised the Phi Thong Luang, Spirits of the Yellow Leaves, who call themselves Yumbri.

In 1956, after a long search, the explorer Robert W. Weaver found just such a band of Yumbri in a remote part of northern Thailand. They were then sick and few, and after some days they left for the rock ledges and caves that were their protection during the rainy season. They promised to rejoin the Weaver party but they never did. He could not find them again, and no Westerner has seen them since. From time to time there are rumors of Yumbri bands living toward the south and some over Burma way. But whether these are tales of real people or ghosts, who is to say?

There are others like the Yumbri in Southeast Asia and its island chains, neither legendary nor ghostly but living people, people who hunt and gather for a living (or did so in the recent past). Small people, they are, with a Mongoloid cast of feature, people shy and in retreat from encroaching strangers, sometimes in downright flight. In Malaysia live the Senoi who speak languages distantly related to the Mon-Khmer tongue of the Yumbri. Of the Senoi only one group still lives exclusively on the forest's bounty. The others have adopted in addition a casual kind of upland farming: slash, burn, and move on after each crop is taken. Westward in the Nicobar Islands live the Shom Pen, hunters and gatherers speaking yet another of the Austroasiatic languages distantly related to Mon-Khmer. And northward along the island chain one of the Andamanese groups represents an outlier of this language phylum.

Hunters with Mongoloid features but speaking Malayo-Polynesian languages hide in the hills of Sumatra and Borneo. In the Philippines are the newly discovered Tasadays. The Jakun, neighbors of the Senoi and like them converts to farming, have been lumped with this Malayo-Polynesian-speaking group. They may well be just Senoi further along the road toward becoming like the Malays in speech as in other ways.

There are still other hunters and gatherers whose claim to the land may be still older than that of the Yumbri and Senoi and Jakun. These hunters and gatherers are unlike the Mongoloids in appearance, resembling nothing so much as Pygmies of the Congo Basin in Africa. They are even smaller than the Senoi, averaging four feet, seven inches in height. In some areas, they are slight and graceful of build. In others they are plump and with the swayed back that encourages an exuberant development of the buttocks. They are black to dark brown in color with hair tightly coiled and close to the head. Everywhere they are called Negritos—the Little Blacks.

How they traveled from Africa—if indeed they traveled at all—no one is prepared to say. True eastern Negritos closest to the African continent can be found in the Andaman Islands, north in the chain that stretches from Sumatra to the Irrawaddy Delta in Burma. Between the Andamans and Africa lie thousands of miles of water. The close resemblance may not represent common ancestry but rather what the specialist calls convergence—a case of similar environmental conditions having made possible in widely separated areas the success of similar physical types. Certainly Negritos seem to have been long in residence in Southeast Asia. Some of the skeletal remains found in association with Hoabinhian artifacts suggest Negrito stock (so we are told by Dr. Georges Coedes). When the Little Blacks of Southeast Asia traveled from their mainland home it seems to have been seaward. Negrito hunters and gatherers are found, as we noted, in the Andaman Islands. With the exception of one small Austroasiatic group, they speak languages unrelated to those of Southeast Asia and as yet unclassified. There are several Negrito groups in the Philippines. They dominate New Guinea and adjacent islands where they have doubtless added their genes to the kaleidoscopic variety of looks to be seen among Pacific people.

If we can believe the eyewitness reports of Chinese travelers, Negritos left their mark on both Chams and the Khmer people of Cambodia (often thought to be representative of the first Mongoloid folk in the southland); left a certain duskiness of skin and shortness of stature before being themselves absorbed or expelled. There is said to be a remnant group of Negrito hunters still living somewhere in the Cambodian area though this may be another of those persistent rumors. Legend insists that, in one of their many wars with the Chams, the Cambodian army was assisted by a contingent of Negrito bowmen.

Again behind the legend lies living fact. In southern Thailand and northern Malaysia are the Negrito Semang. They have been described over the years by a succession of visitors including, in the early 1900s, King Chulalongorn, successor of the great Mongkut; in the 1920s and 1930s Father Paul Schebesta; also in those years anthropologist Ivor H. N. Evans of Cambridge; and in the 1950s Major P. D. R. Williams-Hunt, Adviser on Aborigines, Federation of Malaya.

The Semang are divided into a number of territorial groups to be called tribes only in the sense of their sharing each a common dialect and set of beliefs. The wandering bands that make up each "tribe" manage their own affairs and contact others only often enough to add a little spice to life and make sure that single young people have a decent preview of eligible spouses. For long the Semang have lived close to the Senoi whom they regard as persons like themselves, not like the outsiders of every sort, fearsome and perhaps not quite human. Over the years the two peoples have intermarried so that some eastern Senoi look very like Semang.

They have exchanged ideas as well. Some Semang have taken to planting catch crops or perhaps simply tending stands of wild yams, activities which tend to inhibit their wandering ways. Within recent years they have dropped the bow and arrow which was their major weapon and taken to using the

Senoi blow gun instead. This is a double tube of bamboo or hard wood, seven feet or longer, through which poison-daubed darts are delivered on a stout puff of breath. It is likely the Semang had in earlier times poisoned their arrows, for they prefer for their darts a paste made from the ipoh tree while the Senoi use another sort of poison. Just where or when the Senoi added or developed the blow gun is not known.

Unknown, too, is the matter of language origin. The Semang tongue, very closely related to that of the Senoi, belongs in the same Austroasiatic phylum. Whether it is their original language, borrowed by the Senoi, or whether the positions of donor and recipient should be just reversed is anybody's guess. Most specialists are inclined to make Senoi the donors as they have been for flutes and dances, bamboo ornaments, and bark cloth. Both groups seem once to have favored, as an item of female dress, little aprons made of fringey moss.

Certainly Semang admire the Senoi to a degree. Evans claims they would like to be called Sakai by the Malay as the Senoi are addressed, instead of as Negrito or, in Thailand, Ngo (which means "frizzy"). The Senoi, for their part, cordially detest the name Sakai, for it connotes something like "dirty savage" and actually means "slave." And that is just what the townsmen, the Orang Kampong, have tried to make of Semang and Senoi, capturing them or their children with the help of "tame" decoys of both races. Perhaps as a result, both have become shy, hesitant, and suspicious, have learned to keep themselves hidden when they could, to dissemble when they could not hide.

It is the kind of game played to perfection by African Pygmies of the Ituri Forest who pretend to be slaves to their "masters," the tall village folk, and who run away to the forest once they have tricked those masters into giving presents of bananas and metals and pots. The Semang and Senoi have also learned to feign stupidity when it serves their purposes. But they seem to have learned as well a reluctant admiration for the Malays (celestial beings, for example, are sometimes described as looking like Malay chiefs). The Semang have learned more; they have learned to be ashamed of, to belittle, their black skins. Once, they say, everyone in the world looked like the Malays. And then there was a big fire, a huge fire, a conflagration from which all escaped unharmed—all but the Semang. They were so singed in the fire that their skins have been forever blackened and their hair forever crisped.

The Senoi like to be known as People of the Forests—or of the hills or valleys. This works out often to the term *Orang Utan,* by which name, of course, the largest ape of Southeast Asia is also known. Both Semang and Senoi live in the wooded hills and especially the little upland basins through which small streams wind. During the Communist uprisings of the 1950s, Dr. Robert Dentan tells us, those upland drainage systems were crucial to both Communist insurgents and defending troops, and the forest folk were caught in between, pulled first to one side and then to the other. They feared and distrusted both sets of soldiers and learned new ways to dissemble and to hide. Even in this precarious existence they did better than in the lowland refuge camps set up for them by the British, then still managing Malayan affairs. Semang and Senoi died rapidly in these camps and had to be moved to "jungle forts" where they recovered but still did not thrive. Only after the conflict, after they had returned to their homelands under the watchful (and, it is hoped, benevolent) eye of the Malaysian Department of Aborigines, set up along with the new independent government, did they begin again to be themselves.

To be themselves means to travel. The Senoi move yearly when the burned-over soil of their little fields weakens. Then they build another village of long houses laid on piles, partly in trees, and airy throughout. The Semang move much more often and use shelter rather reminiscent of the Yumbri lean-tos, perfectly suited to a warmish climate and wandering ways. Each lean-to is occupied by a nuclear family—father, mother, young children (growing boys make a shelter for themselves). Women build the windscreens and own them, and when divorce occurs, it is father who decamps. The windscreens of a camp face inward toward one another in an uneven circle. If two families are particularly close, the tops of their screens are made to touch, forming a sort of gabled roof. There may be six or so shelters in a camp for people who are all related by blood or marriage. A Semang can be a guest on any band's territory, can live wherever he can count kin. The composition of a band, therefore, is apt to change frequently—with quarrels or marriages or when the pickings are lean.

And the pickings? Small game, and that mostly monkey. Father Schebesta thinks the changeover from bow and arrow to blow gun may have occurred with a change of prey, a change of diet preference, a dearth of large game, or all three at once. The Semang tell stories of elephant hunts in long ago times. They never hunt elephant today though there is surely no lack of these great beasts. "Now," say the Semang, "we do not hunt elephant or bear because these animals were too recently human. We do not eat dog or cat because our ancestors did not know them." There is no suggestion of hunting tiger, an animal formidable in spirit power as well as in fang and claw. Wild animals raised as pets are not eaten either, for they have been nursed by one woman or another as if they were human children. Like children they have known only affection and praise. It is forbidden to tease and mock an animal, forbidden to torment an animal for pleasure. The breaking of this taboo brings fearful consequences. The Semang are not above describing with relish and verve the drama of the hunt: how the monkey was transfixed with fear, how it fled, how its mother mourned. But once taken, the animal must be killed quickly and without pain.

Game is owned, in the way of all hunting folk, by the man

whose dart pierced its hide. But he must give the meat away and becomes more than ever a man in the act of sharing. It is the prime commandment for all hunters everywhere. The Semang share their meat after it is cooked and share, not meat alone, but gathered vegetables as well—indeed, everything that has been steamed in bamboo over a family's hearth. Dinner time is the occasion for much rushing back and forth of child messengers bearing leaf-wrapped treats from one fire to the next. Each gift must be immediately returned, banana for banana, yam for yam. For the food nourishes relationships as well as bodies and binds together the membership of a band. The visiting stranger need not be fed, and no one feels constrained to offer hospitality.

Dinner includes fish more often than meat. No taboos apply to fish, no ceremony. Neither do fish figure in myth. Birds do. They are the messengers who bear away the souls of the dead and, like the obliging stork in our mythology, deliver the souls of the newly born. The Semang profess (like some other peoples of the world) to be ignorant of biological paternity, to be unaware of the father's role in conception. When pressed, however, they admit that, well, they guess sexual union *is* responsible for the baby's body, but what would the body be without a soul? And everyone knows the birds bring that!

Of all nonhuman things that help or harm, that may be eaten or must be shunned, it is plants which dominate Semang dinners and Semang imagination. Many kinds of tubers, leaves, berries, fruit, and fungi are known and eaten. Many kinds of trees supply products of use. A bamboo thicket, for example, is a veritable supermarket, furnishing tools, weapons, housing material, bedding, and food. But of all trees, two are very special. Two are individually owned as game is owned. Unlike game, however, these constitute permanent property to be transmitted to one's heirs. One is the ipoh tree from whose collected sap, warmed and condensed in bamboo, poison is made. The other is the durian.

No one may climb another man's durian tree, but fallen fruit is anybody's to claim. That fruit is large, round, and heavy, covered with a thick rind and sharp spines. A falling durian can be a formidable missile, particularly if it lands on one's head. It carries with it as further protection a formidable stench as well (something like rotting onions, one explorer noted), a stench that makes it virtually inedible in a closed room. But once opened and the smell ignored, the durian becomes the Queen of Fruit. So it was dubbed by Alfred Russel Wallace, traveler in the tropics, contemporary of Charles Darwin. Wallace discovered the principle of natural selection independently of but concurrently with Darwin. But he was not thinking of evolution when he described the durian, of which, as he said, "the more you eat—the less you feel inclined to stop." The taste of durian he likened to "a rich butter-like custard highly flavored with almonds—but intermingled with it come wafts of flavor that call to mind cream cheese, onion sauce, brown sherry, and other incongruities."

No wonder the durian is also the Semang honeymoon tree. Marriage is celebrated only (says Father Schebesta) by the couple's retreat to the forest, a wedding trip, as it were, to the handiest but most secluded durian tree. There they can become acquainted at leisure, without the interruptions of hunting and gathering. The durian provides all the comforts of room service at a seaside resort.

There is scarcely any aspect of life untouched by the vegetal world. Schebesta spoke often of the "plant mentality" of the Semang. They are, rather, the original, natural, and unself-conscious flower children. Each is named for the flowering tree near which he or she was born. After death each expects to go west to live in the shade of a special tree there to do nothing but weave into one's hair the flowers that grow on the tree. Thus live the Immortal Ones, the *Orang Hidop,* in their high home amidst fruits and flowers. From flowers they created the *Cenoi,* those tiny, luminous spirit beings of great beauty. The *Cenoi* go at night to rest in flowers. And in the morning, as the flowers open, they arise and ascend heavenward to assist the *Orang Hidop* in their tasks. Some *Cenoi* live not exclusively in flowers but also in mountains and trees and in some special animals. Some say the *Cenoi* were responsible for creating human beings from their own incestuous alliances. Others say, no, human beings were molded from fruit by the High Ones. But animals were not made from flowers or fruit. They were all human beings once and changed or were changed, no one is quite sure which.

The Semang, it seems, are unsure about a good many aspects of their religious system. Opinions vary from tribe to tribe, from local group to local group, even among individuals in the same camp. Any question about the *Orang Hidop* is sure to set off a lively discussion. This was Schebesta's experience and that of his colleagues as well. A simple life way never guarantees an equally simple world view. Semang religion is formidably complex; it is also open to an astonishing variety of on-the-spot interpretation.

There is general agreement about the High Ones' being two in number with accompanying wives and offspring. There are earth mothers (differently named and envisioned) who are consorts of the High Ones. Of these the most powerful and feared is the Thunderer called *Karei* (or variations thereof). And no wonder. An approaching storm in these regions is a terrifying sight. Sunlight dies beneath a sky instantly black, a blackness split at intervals by lightning which topples trees and bids fair to split the earth itself. Rain falls in sheets, and all the while there is a crashing, shattering din.

Into the teeth of the storm rush the women of the band. Lashed by the wind and rain, they cut their shins with bamboo splinters, catching the blood in bamboo tubes half filled with rain water. They then fling the mixture skyward shouting the while, "You there, Grandmother, climb up and make known to your grandsons, to *Karei* and *Ta Ped'n,* I am paying the debt!" It is an act of atonement, for what they may not know. But the thunder has come. Some rule has, therefore, been broken. Pray that *Karei* may not do worse, may not send the tiger to punish the breaker of taboo. Should a tiger mutilate any one person, then the whole group must pay with blood. Pay for what? Herewith the Semang book of rules:

One must not commit incest.

One must not be adulterous or use obscene language or enjoy one's spouse in the daytime or watch dogs coupling.

One must not converse with one's in-laws or touch them even if they are in mortal danger. (Arthritis punishes the breaking of this particular rule.)

One must not talk loudly or swing a whizzing instrument in the forest. One must not mourn loudly or loudly greet a person returning after long absence. (Indeed, the Semang ignore the new visitor for half an hour until fully accustomed to his presence.)

One must not be disrespectful to elders.

One must not mock or torture animals and insects—not the cicada for it sings to the Thunderer, not the leech for it draws blood for the Thunderer.

One must not offend those animals sacred to, symbolic of the *Orang Hidop.*

The Thunderer is most often described as a giant hairy

gibbon with long arms, a gibbon sometimes thought to live in the sky but just as often located in caves below the earth. (The Semang themselves have a tradition of cave dwelling at one time or another.) *Ta Ped'n,* the other High One, is never pictured as an animal nor made to live underground, and he is always, in Semang thought, benevolent. Sometimes, indeed, he intercedes for them with *Karei,* who is his brother or his father or his other self—opinions vary.

Unlike *Karei,* who seems to represent a foreign power on the celestial scene (the Senoi say so explicitly), *Ta Ped'n* has always been here somehow. Once, some say, he was actually here on earth until, growing weary of human stupidity, he went away into the sky. And yet sometimes the earth mother brings him reports about the misbehavior of earth's children. If the report is bad enough, *Ta Ped'n* may hurl down the bright crystal which causes floods to rise.

In other stories, the tale-carrier is a dragon. The dragon figures often in Semang mythology. It is one of the symbols of the earth mother. The rainbow is seen as a dragon or else as a giant python bathing fearfully and wonderfully in the celestial waters. (One remembers, of a sudden, the Chukchi rainbow snake and wonders whether it traveled northward from these climes.) The dragon appears among the farming folk of Southeast Asia and is a staple theme from first to last in Chinese art and mythology. How, one asks, did such a creature begin? As vision original and unique? Or as vision prompted by, elaborated from some prior earthly form? The persistent seeker can find a hint in the art which decorates Semang blow guns and combs. Often this art is geometric, but now and again it represents mythological figures. One of these resembles nothing so much as the monitor lizard, that ten-foot, 200-pound carnivorous creature found now on the Indonesian islands of Flores and Komodo and on four smaller islands in between. Its range must once have been very much wider. The anthropologist

A. R. Radcliffe-Brown reports the presence of monitor lizards on the Andaman Islands in 1906. There it was addressed by the natives as Ta Petie, Sir Monitor, Grandfather Monitor, the ancestor of humankind. Tales of Sir Monitor, oft repeated and embellished with repetition, may provide us with a prototype of the Asiatic dragon. But that is only a guess.

Among the Semang the earth mother is represented, not only by the dragon, but by the tortoise as well, perhaps in recollection of first beginnings when she floated on the primordial sea along with her children (or was it grandchildren? Just how these offspring came into being the Semang are not prepared to say). Grandmother sent one of them for a stick (from whence?) and, thrusting it into the back of a magical water animal, caused the earth to rise up from the water and dry in the sun. Other sticks, thrust into the new-formed earth, became mountains. One of these bears the sky and is the sacred center of the world (a story which may or may not have trickled down from Cambodia, perhaps by way of those shadowy Semang bowmen who once served there). After this beginning, the world was then divided into layers, one on another. But was it three layers, or was it seven? And was the earth mother really mother after all? Was she male or female or perhaps both at once? More arguments. However much Father Schebesta, with his precise, theological mind, strove to bring order into the celestial chaos of the Semang, chaos persisted.

There were men who might have untangled the web of belief. They were (and are) the Hala, the men of knowledge. But they stood mute. Father Schebesta and his colleagues often never knew exactly who they were. Certainly they never became confidants, informants to these strangers. (No small wonder when one learns that the good Father was willing to open Semang graves in his search for knowledge about the Semang way.) The Hala would stand apart in any case, for it is the rule of their calling to keep secret Semang lore, secret the special language in which the *Cenoi* can be addressed. In this language, Schebesta learned at last, *Karei* has no name and does not exist. It is *Ta Ped'n* alone to whom the *Cenoi* bring messages and *Ta Ped'n* to whom the Hala speaks through the *Cenoi.* He speaks to this celestial being when he heals, when he sends through *Cenoi* the bright objects *Ta Ped'n* loves—the shiny brass and the mirrors in which he, the Hala, is forbidden to gaze. And he speaks to *Ta Ped'n* in the Pano ritual.

For this, women build a special hut, round, with the palm fronds bent inward and tied. To this hut at night comes the Hala with his assistants. They bring torches and fragrant resins on the smoke of which they will ascend the skies. Whether the smoke also brings trance the Hala will not say. Sometimes, it is thought, the Hala grows cobweb shoots from his fingers and toes, shoots by which he grapples the mountains of the four quarters and propels himself upward.

The hut, the night, the fire; the women singing outside; the climb heavenward—all these remind us of the Tungus shaman's journey from his tent. Only the scenery is different: there is heat instead of cold, verdure instead of snowy waste. As in Siberia, the spirits come to the Hala, one by one, and possess his body. First comes the tiger spirit who growls and roars and shakes the hut, speaking the while in an old man's voice. Then appear the others, the *Cenoi* of flowers and trees and animals that love their shade. They sing, and the women outside echo their songs. There is a good deal of affectionate banter, inside and out, for these are familiar spirits, tender ones who, trapping the evil influences that bring sickness and pain, will change them into *Cenoi* of the flowers, turning heavenward with the sun.

The Hala, the special man, becomes so on instruction from *Ta Ped'n,* received in a dream. Or he inherits his position and training from a male relative. Or he finds the Cebuh Stone, inhabited by *Cenoi* who allow the discovery if his position is ordained. Among some Semang it is customary to send new-made Hala to their neighbors, the Senoi (not to be confused with the flower spirits, the *Cenoi*), for training in the good old ways. The bad ones they learn from Malays, from their sorcerers who can inflict harm at a distance. The charms which accomplish these ends are sung in Malay, not in the language of the Semang.

When an ordinary Semang dies he is buried in a niche cut into the side of a deep shaft. With him go bits of wood striped yellow and red to ward off tigers. When the Hala dies, however, his body is deposited in a tree, or, if burial there must be, his head is left exposed. For the Hala turns at death into a tiger, and only when the tiger dies does the Hala's soul go west to the flowers and the shade of the all-encompassing tree.

It is a heaven for the last followers of a way of life once long ago the only way for people of this earth. Yet long ago men like the Semang, simple hunters and gatherers, traveled the land bridges of which only islands remain, rafted over the narrow waters between lands, and slowly penetrated the southern ocean. Perhaps they journeyed in search of game. Perhaps they were pushed by an expansive farming folk. Later still the farmers themselves, the coastal ones, the island ones, the men of southern China's deltas and bays would be pushed in their turn by the march of civilization with its fences and constraints, would take to their boats and, moving from island to island, would people the vast Pacific.

But that venture belongs in another book.

BIBLIOGRAPHY

CHAPTER 1

Cressey, George B. *Asia's Lands and Peoples.* McGraw-Hill, 1963.
Dewey, John F. "Plate Tectonics." *Scientific American,* May 1972.
Dietz, Robert S., and Holden, John C. "The Breakup of Pangaea." *Scientific American,* October 1970.
Hammond Medallion World Atlas, New Perspective Edition. Hammond, Inc., 1969
Hurley, Patrick M. "The Confirmation of Continental Drift." *Scientific American,* April 1968.
Kurten, Bjorn. "Continental Drift and Evolution." *Scientific American,* March 1969.
Newell, Norman D. "The Evolution of Reefs." *Scientific American,* June 1972.
Stamp, L. Dudley. *Asia: A Regional and Economic Geography.* Methuen & Co., 1959.

CHAPTER 2

Anderson, Douglas D. "A Stone Age Campsite at the Gateway to America." *Scientific American,* June 1968.
Brace, C. Loring. *The Stages of Human Evolution.* Prentice-Hall, 1967.
Chang Kwang-Chih. "New Evidence on Fossil Man in China." *Science,* June 1, 1962.
———. "Prehistoric Archaeology in China: 1920–1960." *Arctic Anthropology,* vol. 1, no. 11 (1963).
———. "Archaeology of Ancient China." *Science,* November 1, 1968.

270 BIBLIOGRAPHY

Chard, Chester S. "Archaeology in the Soviet Union." *Science,* February 21, 1969.

Cheboksarov, N. N. "Questions Concerning the Origins of the Finno-Ugrian Language Group." In H. N. Michael, ed., *Studies in Siberian Ethnogenesis.* University of Toronto Press, 1962.

Coon, Carleton S. *The Living Races of Man.* Alfred A. Knopf, 1965.

Corvinus, Gudrun. "An Acheulean Occupation Floor at Chirki-on-Pravora, India." *Current Anthropology,* April–June 1968.

Grigorev, G. P. "A New Reconstruction of Above-Ground Dwelling of Kostenki." *Current Anthropology,* October 1967.

Giddings, J. Louis. *Ancient Men of the Arctic.* Alfred A. Knopf, 1967.

Howells, William. "Homo Erectus." *Scientific American,* November 1966.

———. *Mankind in the Making,* rev. ed. Doubleday, 1967.

Irving, W. N., and Harrington, C. R. "Upper Pleistocene Radiocarbon-Dated Artifacts from the Northern Yukon." *Science,* January 26, 1973.

Jacob, Teuku. "Recent Pithecanthropus Finds in Indonesia." *Current Anthropology,* December 1967.

Klein, Richard G. *Man and Culture in the Late Pleistocene.* Chandler Publishing, 1969.

Lebar, Frank M., Hickey, Gerald C., and Musgrave, John K. *Ethnic Groups of Mainland Southeast Asia.* HRAF Press, 1964.

MacNeish, Richard S. "Early Man in the Andes." *Scientific American,* April 1971.

Mann, Alan. "Homo Erectus." In P. Dolhinow and V. A. Sarich, eds., *Background for Man.* Little, Brown & Co., 1971.

Michael, Henry, ed. *The Archaeology and Geomorphology of Northern Asia.* Arctic Institute of America. Translations of Russian Sources. University of Toronto Press, 1964.

Okladnikov, A. P. "Ancient Populations of Siberia and Its Culture." In M. G. Levin and L. P. Potapov, eds., *The Peoples of Siberia.* Published in translation by the University of Chicago Press, 1964.

———. *The Soviet Far East in Antiquity.* Published in translation by the University of Toronto Press, 1965.

———. "The Petroglyphs of Siberia." *Scientific American,* August 1969.

———. *Yakutia Before Its Incorporation into the Russian State.* Edited by M. N. Michael. Arctic Institute of North America. McGill-Queens University Press, 1970.

Pilbeam, David. *The Ascent of Man.* Macmillan, 1972.

Powers, William Rogers. "Paleolithic Man in Northeast Asia." *Arctic Anthropology,* vol. 10, no. 2 (1973).

Sankalia, H. D. "New Evidence for Early Man in Kashmir." *Current Anthropology,* October–December, 1971.

Simons, Elwyn. *Primate Evolution.* Macmillan, 1972.

Simons, Elwyn, and Ettel, Peter C. "Gigantopithecus." *Scientific American,* January 1970.

Shapiro, Harry L. "The Strange Unfinished Saga of Peking Man." *Natural History* magazine, November 1971.

Solheim, Wilhelm G., II. "Southeast Asia and the West." *Science,* August 25, 1967.

———. "An Earlier Agriculture Revolution." *Scientific American,* April 1972.

Trager, G. L. "Languages of the World," in *Collier's Encyclopedia* (Crowell-Collier, 1970).

Voegelin, C. F., and Voegelin, F. M. "Recent Classification of Genetic Relationships," in *Annual Review of Anthropology,* vol. 2. Annual Reviews, Inc., 1973.

Woo Ju-Kang. "The Skull of Lantian Man." *Current Anthropology,* February 1966.

CHAPTER 3

Anderson. Douglas D. "A Stone Age Campsite at the Gateway to America."
Antropova, V. V., and Kuznetsova, V. G. "The Chukchi." In M. G. Levin and L. P. Potapov, eds., *The Peoples of Siberia*. University of Chicago Press, 1964.
Bogoraz-Tan, Vladimir Germanovich. *The Chukchee*. 3 vols. E. J. Brill, 1904–1909.
———. *Chuckchee Mythology*. Memoirs of the American Museum of Natural History, vol. 12. G. E. Stechert & Co., 1910.
———. "Siberian Cousins of the Eskimo." *Asia*, vol. 29 (1929).
Giddings, J. Louis. *Ancient Men of the Arctic*. Alfred A. Knopf, 1967.
Harner, Michael J., ed. *Hallucinogens and Shamanism*. Oxford University Press, 1973.
Hennigh, L. "Functions and Limitations of Alaskan Eskimo Wife Trading." *Arctic*, vol. 23, no. 1 (1970).
Jochelson, Waldemar. *Peoples of Asiatic Russia*. American Museum of Natural History, 1928.
Kolarz, Walter. *The Peoples of the Soviet Far East*. Praeger, 1954.
Levin, M. G. *Ethnic Origins of the People of Northeastern Asia*. Edited by H. N. Michael. Arctic Institute of North America. Translations of Russian Sources, no. 3. University of Toronto Press, 1963.
———. "The Anthropological Types of Siberia." In Levin and Potapov, *Peoples of Siberia*.
Michael, Henry N. *The Archaeology and Geomorphology of Northern Asia*. University of Toronto Press, 1964.
Popov, A. A. and Dolgikh, B. O. "The Kets." In Levin and Potapov, *Peoples of Siberia*.
Spencer, Robert F. "Spouse Exchange Among the North Alaskan Eskimo." In P. Bohannon and J. Middleton, eds., *Marriage, Family, and Residence*. Natural History Press, 1968.
Stepanova, M. V., Gurvich, I. S., and Khramova, V. V. "The Yukaghirs." In Levin and Potapov, *Peoples of Siberia*.

Reference Note

The quotation on page 48 is from V. G. Bogoras, *The Chukchee*, volume 1.

CHAPTER 4

Batchelor, John. *Ainu Life and Lore*. Kyobunkwan, 1923.
Campbell, Joseph. *The Masks of God: Oriental Mythology*. The Viking Press, 1962.
Coon. *Living Races of Man*.
Egami, Namio. "Light on Japanese Cultural Origins from Historical Archaeology and Legends." In R. J. Smith and R. K. Beardsley, eds., *Japanese Culture: Its Development and Characteristics*. Viking Fund Publications in Anthropology. Aldine Publishing Co., 1962.
Hilger, Sister Mary Inez, and Miyazawa, Eijo. "Japan's 'Sky People,' the Vanishing Ainu." *National Geographic Magazine*, February 1967.
Ishida, Eiichiro. "The Nature of the Problem of Japanese Cultural Origins." In Smith and Beardsley, *Japanese Culture*.
Ivanov, S. V., Levin. M. G., and Smolyak, A. V. "The Nivkhi." In Levin and Potapov, *Peoples of Siberia*.

272 BIBLIOGRAPHY

Jochelson. *Peoples of Asiatic Russia.*

Levin. *Ethnic Origins of the Peoples of Northeastern Asia.*

Meggers, Betty J., and Evans, Clifford. "A Transpacific Contact in 3000 B.C." *Scientific American,* January 1966.

Munro, Neil Gordon. *Ainu Creed and Cult.* Columbia University Press, 1963.

Muramatsu, Konosuke. "The Antlers of Nara." *Natural History* magazine, February 1967.

Noma, Seiroku. "Primitives of Japan: A Legacy in Clay." *Natural History* magazine, March 1963.

Ohnuki-Tierney, Emiko. "Spatial Concepts of the Ainu of the Northwest Coast of Southern Sakhalin." *American Anthropologist,* June 1972.

———. "Shamanism of the Ainu of the Northwest Coast of Southern Sakhalin." *Ethnology,* January 1973.

Okladnikov. *The Soviet Far East in Antiquity.*

Ono, Susumu. "The Japanese Language: Its Origins and Its Sources." In Smith and Beardsley, *Japanese Culture.*

Takakura, Shin'ichiro. *The Ainu of Northern Japan.* Translated by John A. Harnison. Transactions of the American Philosophical Society, vol. 50, part 4, 1960.

———. "Vanishing Ainu of Northern Japan." *Natural History* magazine, October 1966.

Watanabe, Hitoshi. *The Ainu Ecosystem: Environment and Group Structure.* University of Washington Press, 1973.

Watanabe, Masao. "The Conception of Nature in Japanese Culture." *Science,* January 25, 1974.

Watson, William. "Neolithic Japan and the White Race of Today." In Edward Bacon, ed., *Vanished Civilizations.* McGraw-Hill, 1963.

Yawata, Ichiro. "Prehistoric Evidence for Japanese Cultural Origins." In Smith and Beardsley, *Japanese Culture.*

Reference Note

The quotation on pages 52–53 is from Batchelor.

CHAPTER 5

Armentov, M. I. "Frozen Tombs of the Scythians." *Scientific American,* May 1965.

Chang K. C. *The Archaeology of Ancient China.* Yale University Press, 1968.

Eberhard, Wolfram. *Settlement and Social Change in Asia.* Hong Kong University Press, 1967.

Jochelson. *Peoples of Asiatic Russia.*

Lattimore, Owen. *Inner Asian Frontiers of China.* Beacon Press, 1962. (Originally published 1940, 1951 by the American Geographical Society of New York.)

Legge, James, trans. *The Chinese Classics.* Oxford University Press, 1895.

Levin. *Ethnic Origins of the Peoples of Northeastern Asia.*

Maenchen-Helfin, Otto. "Huns and Hsiung-nu and Origin of the Huns." *Byzantion,* vol. 17 (1944–1945).

McEvedy, Colin. *The Penguin Atlas of Ancient History.* Penguin Books, 1967.

———. *The Penguin Atlas of Medieval History.* Penguin Books, 1967.

Okladnikov. "Ancient Populations of Siberia."

———. *The Soviet Far East in Antiquity.*

———. "The Petroglyphs of Siberia."

Phillips, E. D. *The Royal Hordes; Nomad Peoples of the Steppes.* McGraw-Hill, 1965.
Piggott, Stuart. "The Beginnings of Wheeled Transport." *Scientific American,* July 1968.
Potapov, L. P. "The Origins of the Altayans." In H. N. Michael, ed., *Studies in Siberian Ethnogenesis.* University of Toronto Press, 1962.
———. "The Altays." In Levin and Potapov, *Peoples of Siberia.*
———. "The Khakasy." In Levin and Potapov, *Peoples of Siberia.*
Renfrew, Colin. "Carbon 14 and the Prehistory of Europe." " *Scientific American,* October 1971.
Smolyak, A. V. "Certain Questions on the Early History of the Ethnic Groups Inhabiting the Amur River Valley and the Maritime Province." In Michael, *Studies in Siberian Ethnogenesis.*
Ssu-ma Ch'ien. *Records of the Grand Historian of China,* vols. 1 and 2. Translated from the *Shih Chi* and arranged by Burton Watson. Columbia University Press, 1961.
Tokarev, S. A. "On the Origin of the Buryat Nation." In Michael, *Studies in Siberian Ethnogenesis.*
Watson, Burton. *Early Chinese Literature.* Columbia University Press, 1962.

Reference Notes

The poem on page 80 is from James Legge's translation of the *Book of Odes.*
The quotation on page 87 is from Ssu-ma Ch'ien, *Records of the Grand Historian of China,* translated by Burton Watson.
The first quotation on page 89 is from Burton Watson, *Early Chinese Literature.*
The second quotation on page 89 is from Ssu-ma Ch'ien, *Records of the Grand Historian of China.*

CHAPTER 6

Anisimov, A. F. "The Shaman's Tent of the Evenks and the Origin of the Shamanistic Rite." In H. N. Michael, ed., *Studies in Siberian Shamanism.* University of Toronto Press, 1963.
Ivanov, S. V., Smolyak, A. V., and Levin, M. G. "The Nanays." In Levin and Potapov, *Peoples of Siberia.*
Jochelson. *Peoples of Asiatic Russia.*
Kolarz. *The Peoples of the Soviet Far East.*
Lattimore, Owen. *Inner Asian Frontiers of China.* Beacon Press, 1962.
———. *Studies in Frontier History.* Oxford University Press, 1962.
Levin. *Ethnic Origins of the Peoples of Northeastern Asia.*
Levin, M. G. and Vasilyev, B. A. "The Evenks." In Levin and Potapov, *Peoples of Siberia.*
Mirov, N. T. "Notes on the Domestication of the Reindeer." *American Anthropologist,* vol. 47 (1945).
Okladinov. *The Soviet Far East in Antiquity.*
Polo, Marco. *The Adventures of Marco Polo.* Edited by Richard J. Walsh. The John Day Co., 1948.
Shirokogoroff, S. M. *Anthropology of Northern China.* Royal Asiatic Society (North China Branch), 1963. (Published originally in Shanghai, 1923, and in 1968 by Anthropological Publications, Oesterhout N.B., the Netherlands.)
———. *Social Organization of the Northern Tungus.* Anthropological Publications, Oosterhout N.B., 1966. (First published 1929, Shanghai.)

274 BIBLIOGRAPHY

Vasilevich, G. M. "Evenk Concepts About the Universe." In Michael, *Studies in Siberian Shamanism.*

Vasilevich, G. M., and Smolyak, A. V. "The Evenks." In Levin and Potapov, *Peoples of Siberia.*

CHAPTER 7

Aberle, David P. *Chahar and Dagor Mongol Bureaucratic Administration 1912–1945.* HRAF Press, 1953.

Andrews, Roy Chapman. *Across Mongolian Plains.* Blue Ribbon Books, 1921.

Boyle, John Andrew. *The Successors of Genghis Khan.* Translated from the Persian of Rashid Al-Din. University of California Press, 1971.

Burns, John. "Mongolia Still Has a Few Lamas but Mostly as a Negative Example." *New York Times,* July 7, 1973.

Douglas, William O. "Journey to Outer Mongolia." *National Geographic Magazine,* March 1962.

Dundes, Alan. "The Number Three in American Culture." In Alan Dundes, ed., *Every Man His Way.* Prentice-Hall, 1968.

Heissig, Walter. *A Lost Civilization: The Mongols Rediscovered.* Translated by D. J. S. Thomson. Basic Books, 1966.

Kolarz. *The Peoples of the Soviet Far East.*

Krader, Lawrence. *Social Organization of the Mongol-Turkic Pastoral Nomads.* Indiana University Publications. Uralic and Altaic Series, vol. 20. Mouton & Co., 1963.

———. "Buryat Religion and Society." In J. Middleton, ed., *Gods and Rituals.* Natural History Press, 1967.

Lattimore, Owen. *The Mongols of Manchuria.* The John Day Co., 1934.

———. *Inner Asian Frontiers of China.*

———. "Chingis Khan and the Mongol Conquests." *Scientific American,* August 1963.

Phillips, E. D. *The Mongols.* Praeger, 1969.

Polo. *The Adventures of Marco Polo.*

Tokarev. "On the Origin of the Buryat Nation."

Vreeland, Herbert Harold, III. *Mongol Community and Kinship Structure.* HRAF Press, 1953.

Waley, Arthur. *The Secret History of the Mongols.* Allen & Unwin, 1963.

CHAPTER 8

Allworth, Edward, ed. *Central Asia: A Century of Russian Rule.* Columbia University Press, 1967.

Bacon, Elizabeth E. *Central Asians Under Russian Rule.* Cornell University Press, 1967.

Bernshtam, A. "On the Origin of the Kirghiz People." In Michael, *Studies in Siberian Ethnogenesis.*

Debets, G. F. "The Origin of the Kirghiz People in the Light of Physical Anthropological Findings." In Michael, *Studies in Siberian Ethnogenesis.*

Dunn, Stephen P., and Dunn, Ethel. "Soviet Regime and Native Culture in Central Asia and Kazakhstan: The Major Peoples." *Current Anthropology,* June 1967.

Eberhard. *Settlement and Social Change in Asia.*

Forde, C. Daryll. *Habitat, Economy and Society.* E. P. Dutton, 1963.

Giles, Herbert A., trans. and ed. *Gems of Chinese Literature.* Paragon Book Reprint Corp. and Dover Publications, 1965.

Jochelson. *Peoples of Asiatic Russia.*

BIBLIOGRAPHY 275

Krader, Lawrence. *Peoples of Central Asia.* University of Indiana Publications. Uralic and Altaic Series, vol. 23. Mouton & Co., 1966.
Lattimore. *Inner Asian Frontiers of China.*
Maenchen-Helfin. "Huns and Hsiung-nu and Origin of the Huns."
Michaud, Sabrina, and Michaud, Roland. "Winter Caravan to the Roof of the World." *National Geographic Magazine,* April 1972.
Okladnikov, A. P. *Yakutia Before Its Incorporation into the Russian State.*
———. "Ancient Populations of Siberia."
Phillips. *The Mongols.*
Potapov. "The Altays" and "The Khakasy."
Ssu-ma Ch'ien. *Records of the Grand Historian of China.*
Watson, Burton. *Ssu-ma Ch'ien: Grand Historian of China.* Columbia University Press, 1958.

Reference Notes

The quotation on page 127 is from Burton Watson, *Ssu-ma Ch'ien, Grand Historian of China.*
Li Ling's letter, quoted on pages 127 and 128, is from Giles, *Gems of Chinese Literature.*
The quotations on page 130 were cited by A. Bernshtam in his article for *Studies in Siberian Ethnogenesis.*
The quotation on page 131 is cited by A. P. Okladnikov, *Yakutia.*
The quotation on page 132 is cited in Krader, *Social Organization of the Mongol-Turkic Pastoral Nomads.*

CHAPTER 9

Bayard, D. T. "On Chang's Interpretation of Chinese Radiocarbon Dates" and "Reply" by Chang K. C. *Current Anthropology,* March 1975.
Bodde, Derek. "Myths of Ancient China." In Samuel Noah Kramer, ed., *Mythologies of the Ancient World.* Doubleday, 1961.
Campbell. *The Masks of God: Oriental Mythology.*
Chang K. C. *Archaeology of Ancient China.*
———. "Radiocarbon Dates from China: Some Initial Interpretations." *Current Anthropology,* December 1973.
———. "Some Dualistic Phenomena in Shang Society." *Journal of Asian Studies,* November 1964.
Ch'ien Tsun-hsun. *Written on Bamboo and Silk.* University of Chicago Press, 1962.
"A Chinese Minority Grows Bigger." *New York Times,* October 28, 1973.
"Chinese Proverbs Under Party Fire: Classic Confucian Primer Is Termed Poisonous Weed—Class Analysis Urged." *New York Times,* September 1, 1974.
"Confucius's Fame Grows on Taiwan." *New York Times,* August 11, 1974.
Creel, Herrlee Glessner. *The Birth of China.* Frederick Ungar, 1964.
———. *Chinese Thought from Confucius to Mao Tse-tung.* University of Chicago Press, 1953.
Cressey. *Asia's Lands and Peoples.*
Diao, Richard K. "The National Minorities of China and Their Relations with the Chinese Communist Regime." In Peter Kunstadter, ed., *Southeast Asian Tribes, Minorities, and Nations.* Princeton University Press, 1967.
Fairservis, Walter A., Jr. *The Origins of Oriental Civilization.* New American Library of World Literature, 1959.

Galston, Arthur W. "The Chinese University." *Natural History* magazine, August–September 1972.

———. "Education and Science in China." *Science,* January 7, 1972.

Giles. *Gems of Chinese Literature.*

Granet, Marcel. *Chinese Civilization.* Meridian Books, 1958.

Kaltenmark, Odile. *Chinese Literature.* Walker & Co., 1964.

Keesing's Research Report. *The Cultural Revolution in China.* Scribners, 1967.

Latourette, Kenneth Scott. *The Chinese: Their History and Their Culture.* Macmillan, 1965.

Lattimore. *Inner Asian Frontiers of China.*

Legge, James, trans. *The Chinese Classics.*

Lelyveld, Joseph. "Confucius, Target of Chinese Drive, Helped Provide Revolution's Ideology." *New York Times,* February 12, 1974.

Li Chi. *The Beginnings of Chinese Civilization.* University of Washington Press, 1957.

Lin Yutang, trans. and ed. *The Wisdom of China and India.* Random House, 1942.

Mao Tse-tung. *Quotations from Chairman Mao Tse-tung.* Edited by Stuart R. Schram. Praeger, 1967.

Needham, Joseph. *Time and Eastern Man.* Royal Anthropological Institute of Great Britain and Ireland, 1965.

Schram, Stuart R. *Mao Tse-tung.* Simon and Schuster, 1966.

"Soviet Charges China Suppresses Minority Uprisings." *New York Times,* November 8, 1973.

Ssu-ma Ch'ien. *Records of the Grand Historian of China.*

Sulzberger, C. L. "What Happened to the Huns?" *New York Times,* November 3, 1973.

Treistman, Judith. *The Prehistory of China.* Natural History Press, 1972.

———. "The New Archaeology of China." *Natural History* magazine, August–September, 1972.

Wang, William S. Y. "The Chinese Language." *Scientific American,* February 1973.

Watson, Burton. *Ssu-ma Ch'ien: Grand Historian of China.*

———. *Early Chinese Literature.*

Watson, William. *Early Civilization in China.* McGraw-Hill, 1966.

———. *China Before the Han Dynasty.* Praeger, 1961.

Reference Notes

The memorial message quoted on page 153 is cited in Watson, *Early Civilization in China.*

The quotations on page 157 were translated by Lin Yutang and appear in his book *The Wisdom of China and India.*

The translation from *The Book of Documents* quoted on page 161 is by James Legge as are those from *Analects* on the same page.

The quotations on page 162 are from *The Book of Documents* and *The Great Learning* and are translated by James Legge.

The statement of Wu Ti quoted on page 163 was translated by H. A. Giles in his *Gems of Chinese Literature.*

The translations from *The Book of Documents* quoted on page 164 are by Legge.

CHAPTER 10

Baker, Hugh D. R. *A Chinese Lineage Village: Sheung Shui.* Stanford University Press, 1968.

Fei Hsaio-tung. *Peasant Life in China.* E. P. Dutton, 1939.

Gallin, Bernard. *Hsin Hsing, Taiwan: A Chinese Village in Change.* University of California Press, 1966.

Galston, Arthur W. "Down on the Commune." *Natural History* magazine, October 1972.

———. "Peking Man (and Woman) Today." *Natural History* magazine, November 1972.

Gamble, Sidney D. *Ting Hsien.* Institute of Pacific Relations, 1954.

Granet. *Chinese Civilization.*

Hsu, Francis L. K. *Clan, Caste, and Club.* D. Van Nostrand, 1963.

———. *Under the Ancestors' Shadow.* Natural History Library. Doubleday, 1967.

———. "Family System and the Economy." In Robert Hunt, ed., *Personalities and Cultures.* Natural History Library. Doubleday, 1967.

Legge. *The Chinese Classics,* vol. 4: *The Book of Odes.*

Levy, Howard S. *Chinese Footbinding.* Walter Rowls, 1966.

Pruitt, Ida. *A Daughter of Han.* Stanford University Press, 1967.

Yang, C. K. *Chinese Communist Society: The Family and the Village.* MIT Press, 1965.

Yang, Martin C. *A Chinese Village: Taitou, Shantung Province.* Columbia University Press, 1945.

Reference Notes

The quotations on pages 171, 172, and 177 were translated by James Legge and are from *The Book of Odes.*

The spirit message on page 178 is cited by Dr. Hsu in *Under the Ancestors' Shadow.*

The invocation cited on page 180 is from *The Book of Odes,* translated by James Legge.

The spirit message on page 180 is cited in *Under the Ancestors' Shadow* by Dr. Hsu.

The quotations on pages 180–81, 184, and 186 are from *The Book of Odes,* translated by James Legge.

CHAPTER 11

Burrows, Carin. "Fierce and Erotic Gods of Buddhism." *Natural History* magazine, April 1972.

Creel. *The Birth of China.*

Eberhard. *Settlement and Social Change in Asia.*

Ekvall, Robert B. *Fields on the Hoof: The Nexus of Tibetan Nomadic Pastoralism.* Holt, Rinehart & Winston, 1968.

Fa-hien. *A Record of Buddhistic Kingdoms.* Translated and annotated by James Legge. Dover, 1965.

Gorer, Geoffrey. *Himalayan Village,* 2d edition. Basic Books, 1967.

Latourette. *The Chinese: Their History and Their Culture.*

Lattimore. *Inner Asian Frontiers of China.*

Legge, James, trans. *The Book of Documents* in *The Chinese Classics.*

Li An-che. "Bon: The Magico-Religious Belief of the Tibetan-Speaking People." *Southwestern Journal of Anthropology,* vol. 4 (1948).

Norbu, Thubten Figme, and Turnbull, Colin. *Tibet.* Simon and Schuster, 1968.

Pan Ku. *The History of the Former Han Dynasty.* Translated by Homer H. Dubs. Waverly Press, 1955.

Peissel, Michael. "Mustang, Nepal's Lost Kingdom." *National Geographic Magazine,* October 1965.

278   BIBLIOGRAPHY

Pilarski, Laura. "Tibetans in Switzerland." *National Geographic Magazine,* November 1968.

Prince Peter of Greece and Denmark. *A Study of Polyandry.* Mouton & Co., 1963.

Schram, Louis M. J. *The Monguors of the Kansu-Tibetan Frontier.* American Philosophical Society, 1964.

Snellgrove, David, and Richardson, Hugh. *A Cultural History of Tibet.* Praeger, 1968.

Ssu-ma Ch'ien. *Records of the Grand Historian of China.*

Tsung-lien Sheu and Shen-chi Liu. *Tibet and the Tibetans.* Stanford University Press, 1953.

Tucci, Giuseppe. *Tibet: Land of Snows.* Translated by J. E. Stapleton Driver. Stein and Day, 1967.

Reference Note

The quotation on page 195 is from *The History of the Former Han* by Pan Ku, translated by H. Dubs.

CHAPTER 12

Bayard, D. T. "On Chang's Interpretations of Chinese Radiocarbon Dates."

———. "Early Thai Bronzes: Analysis and New Dates." *Science,* June 30, 1972.

Bodde. "Myths of Ancient China."

Chang K. C. "Prehistoric and Early Historic Culture Horizons and Traditions in South China." *Current Anthropology,* December 1964.

———. *The Archaeology of Ancient China.*

———. *Fengpitou, Tapenkeng, and the Prehistory of Taiwan.* Yale University Publications in Anthropology, no. 73. Yale University Press, 1969.

———. "Radiocarbon Dates from China."

Christie, Anthony. "The Sea Locked Lands: The Diverse Traditions of Southeast Asia." In Stuart Piggott, ed., *Dawn of Civilization.* McGraw-Hill, 1961.

Coedes, Georges. *The Indianized States of Southeast Asia,* 3rd edition. Translated by Susan Brown Cowing. Edited by Walter F. Fella. East-West Center Press, 1968.

Dentan, Robert Knox. *The Semai.* Holt, Rinehart & Winston, 1968.

Flannery, Kent V. *The Origins of Agriculture.* Annual Review of Anthropology, vol. 2. Edited by Bernard J. Siegel. Annual Reviews, 1973.

Garrett, W. E. "Pagan, on the Road to Mandalay." *National Geographic Magazine,* March 1971.

Gorman, Chester. "Excavations at Spirit Cave, North Thailand: Some Interim Interpretations." *Asian Perspectives,* vol. 13 (1972).

Groslier, Bernard Phillippe. *Indochina.* World Publishing Co., 1966.

Haskins, John F. "The Cache at Stone-Fortress Hill." *Natural History* magazine, February 1963.

Heine-Geldern, Robert. "Conceptions of State and Kingship in Southeast Asia." *Far Eastern Quarterly,* vol. 2 (1942).

Higham, C. F. W., and Leach, B. F. "An Early Center of Bovine Husbandry In Southeast Asia." *Science,* April 2, 1971.

Lebar, Frank M., Hickey, Gerald C., and Musgrove, John K. *Ethnic Groups of Mainland Southeast Asia.* HRAF Press, 1964.

Legge. *The Chinese Classics.*

Liu, Chungshee H. "The Dog-Ancestor Story of the Aboriginal Tribes of Southern China." *Journal of the Royal Anthropological Institute,* vol. 62 (1932).

———. "On the Dog-Ancestor Myth in Asia." *Studia Sinica,* vol. 1 (1941).

Maspero, Georges. *The Kingdom of Champa.* A translation of Chapter 1 of *Le Royaume du Champa,* Von Oest, 1929. Yale University Southeast Asia Studies. Yale University Press, 1949.

Meynard, Alfred. "The Sacrifice to Heaven and Earth: The Survival at Hue, in Annam, of the Official Worship Once Performed in China." *Asia,* vol. 28 (1928).

Polo. *The Adventures of Marco Polo.*

Pym, Christopher. "The God Kings of Lost Anghor." In Edward Bacon, ed., *Vanished Civilizations.* McGraw-Hill, 1963.

Schafer, Edward H. *The Vermilion Bird: T'ang Images of the South.* University of California Press, 1967.

Solheim, William G. "New Light on a Forgotten Past." *National Geographic Magazine,* March 1971.

———. "An Earlier Agricultural Revolution." *Scientific American,* April 1972.

———. "Northern Thailand, Southeast Asia, and World Prehistory." *Asian Perspectives,* vol. 3 (1972).

Spiro, Melford E. *Burmese Supernaturalism.* Prentice-Hall, 1967.

Ssu-ma Ch'ien. *Records of the Grand Historian of China.*

Voegelin and Voeglin. "Recent Classification of Genetic Relationships."

White, Peter T. "Southeast Asia: Mosaić of Cultures." *National Geographic Magazine,* March 1971.

Wiens, Harold J. *China's March to the Tropics.* The Shoe String Press, 1954.

Reference Note

The quotation on pages 218–19 is from *Le Fou-Nan* by Paul Pelliot as cited in Coedes, *The Indianized States of Southeast Asia.*

CHAPTER 13

Barney, G. Linwood. "The Meo of Xieng Khouang Province, Laos." In Peter Kunstadter, ed., *Southeast Asian Tribes, Minorities, and Nations.* Princeton University Press, 1967.

Condominas, Georges. "The Mnong Gar of Central Vietnam." In George Peter Murdock, ed., *Social Structures of Southeast Asia.* Viking Fund Publications in Anthropology, no. 29. Quadrangle Books, 1960.

———. "The Primitive Life of Vietnam's Mountain People." *Natural History* magazine, June–July, 1966.

———. "Aspects of Economics Among the Mnong Gar of Vietnam: Multiple Money and the Middleman." *Ethnology,* vol. 11, no. 3 (1972).

Dessaint, Alain Y. "The Poppies Are Beautiful This Year." *Natural History* magazine, February 1972.

Garrett., W. E. "The Hmong of Laos." *National Geographic Magazine,* January 1974.

Hickey, Gerald C. "Some Aspects of Hill Tribe Life in Vietnam." In Kunstadter, *Southeast Asian Tribes.*

Kandre, Peter. "Autonomy and Integration of Social Systems: The Iu Mien ('Yao' or 'Man') Mountain Population and Their Neighbors." In Kunstadter, *Southeast Asian Tribes.*

280 BIBLIOGRAPHY

Kunstadter, Peter. "Thailand's Gentle Lua." *National Geographic Magazine,* July 1966.

――――. "The Lua (Lawa) and Skaw Karen of Maohongson Province." In Kundstadter, *Southeast Asian Tribes.*

Keys, Charles F. "Peoples of Indo-China." *Natural History* magazine, October 1970.

La Raw, Maran. "Toward a Basis for Understanding the Minorities in Burma." In Kunstadter, *Southeast Asian Tribes.*

Lebar, Hickey, and Musgrave. *Ethnic Groups of Mainland Southeast Asia.*

Lehman, F. K. "Ethnic Categories in Burma and the Theory of Social Systems." In Kunstadter, *Southeast Asian Tribes.*

Lin Yueh-hua. *The Lolo of Liang Shan.* Translated by Ju-shu Pan. Edited by Wu-chi Liu. HRAF Press, 1961.

Manndorff, Hans. "The Hill Tribe Program of the Public Welfare Department, Ministry of Interior, Thailand." In Kunstadter, *Southeast Asian Tribes.*

McAlister, J. T., Jr. "Mountain Minorities and the Viet Minh." In Kunstadter, *Southeast Asian Tribes.*

Osborn, G. M. T. "Government and the Hill Tribes of Laos." In Kunstadter, *Southeast Asian Tribes.*

Ling Shun-sheng and Ruey Yih-fu. *A Report on an Investigation of the Miao of West Hunan.* Academica Sinica. Translated by Laen-en Tsao. HRAF Press, 1963.

Sochurek, Howard. "Vietnam's Montagnards: Caught in the Jaws of a War." *National Geographic Magazine,* April, 1968.

Ssu-ma Ch'ien. *Records of the Grand Historian of China.*

Voeglin and Voeglin. "Recent Classification of Genetic Relationships."

Reference Note

The quotation on page 242 is from Ssu-ma Ch'ien, *Records of the Grand Historian of China.*

CHAPTER 14

Auffenberg, Walter. "Komodo Dragons." *Natural History* magazine, April 1972.

Coon. *The Living Races of Man.*

Dentan. *The Semai.*

Evans, Ivor H. N. *The Negritos of Malaya.* Cambridge University Press, 1937.

Lebar, Hickey, and Musgrave. *Ethnic Groups of Mainland Southeast Asia.*

Radcliffe-Brown, A. R. *The Andaman Islanders.* Free Press of Glencoe, 1964.

Schebesta, Paul. *The Negritos of Asia,* vols. 1 and 2. Translated by Frieda Schutze. HRAF Press, 1962.

Sebeok, Thomas. "The Languages of Southeastern Asia." *Far Eastern Quarterly,* August 1943.

Voeglin and Voeglin. "Recent Classification of Genetic Relationships."

Von Fuer-Haimendorf, C. *Morals and Merit.* University of Chicago Press, 1967.

Wallace, Alfred Russel. *The Malay Archipelago.* Dover Public Reprint, 1962. (Originally published by Macmillan & Co., 1869.)

Weaver, Robert W. "Through Unknown Thailand." *Natural History* magazine, June 1956.

Williams-Hunt, P. D. R. *An Introduction to the Malayan Aborigines.* Malaysian Government Press, 1952.

――――. "A Lanoh Negrito Funeral." In de G. Sieveking, ed., *Federation Museums Journal,* Museum Department of Malaya, 1954–1955.

INDEX

Afghanistan, 23, 135
Africa, 7, 8, 9, 255; early man in, 11, 13, 14, 15, 16
Ainu, the, 22, 26, 52–68, 97, 106; ancestors of, 67, 68; appearance of, 56, 57; arrow heads poisoned by, 57; and bear sacrifice, 52–54, 56; clothing of, 57; and descent, counting of, 64–65; eye shape of, 56; and *Fuji-Kamui,* 62, 63, 64; and Japanese, 58–60; and Jomon people, 67–68; and *kamui,* belief in, 62, 63, 64; language of, 56–57; and *Shiramba-Kamui,* 62, 63; village life of, 62

Akha, the, 238
Alaska, 19, 29, 35, 37, 40, 50
Aleutian Islands, 35
Altai Mountains, 5, 75, 86
Altai region, 81, 82, 84, 89, 90, 126, 129, 131, 133
Altan Khan, 209
Amur, the, 84, 85
Amur River, 5, 6, 56, 84
Analects (Confucius), 158, 160, 161
Anatolia, 82
Andaman Islands, 255, 265
Angkor, 24, 232, 233
Arabian Desert, 6, 74
Armenia, 77
Armor, invention of, 84

Arntynov, S. A., 37
Asia: anatomy of, 3–9; early man in, 12–19 *passim*, 21
Asoka, King, 229
Attila, 90, 93
Australia, aboriginal peoples of, 21–22
Australoids, 57
Australopithecines, 13, 14, 15, 16
Austroasiatic languages, 24, 243, 245, 254, 257
Avars, 90

Bacon, Elizabeth E., 136
Baikal, Lake, 20, 72, 75, 86, 105, 112, 115, 126
Baker, Hugh, 172, 179
Bamboo, uses of, 260
Bassbeg (warrior), 131
Batchelor, John, 54, 62, 63
Battle-ax People, The (Vlahos), 24
Battle-ax people in steppes, 71–94
Bayard, D. T., 226
Bear, homage paid to, 52–55, 106
Benedict, Paul, 227, 242
Bering Strait, 20, 29, 35, 38, 68
Bernshtam, A., 133
Black-Headed People, 155, 171
Black Sea, 24, 75, 77, 90
Blow gun, 257, 259
Bogatyr (warrior hero), 131
Bogoras, Vladimir, 30, 31, 33, 34, 35, 38, 40–50 *passim*

Borneo, 254
Bourtai (wife of Genghis Khan), 119
Bronze, earliest use of, 226
Buddhism, 93, 115, 117, 121, 122, 158, 165, 167, 174, 175, 200–208 *passim*, 229, 230, 231, 243, 244
Buffalo, sacrifice of, 248
Bulgaria, 124, 131
Buret' site, 20, 21
Burma, 229, 230, 231, 233, 238, 243, 254, 255

Cambodia, 24, 219, 230, 231, 233, 234, 241, 256, 265
Cannibalism, 18
Caribou, 37
Caspian Sea, 77
Caucasus, 5, 77, 90, 129
Cavalry, raids by, 81–82
Central Asia, 8, 19, 24, 81, 136
Ceylon, 229
Champa, kingdom of, 217, 218, 219, 230–34 *passim*, 241, 256
Chang, K. C., 145, 146, 148, 224, 227
Chao T'o, 216, 217, 237
Chariot, war, 77
Chenla, kingdom of, 230
Chiao-chou (Hanoi), 212, 214, 217, 222
Ch'in Dynasty, 87, 152, 164, 214, 216, 217
Ch'in Shih Huang-ti (Chinese emperor), 164, 213–14

INDEX

China, 5, 8, 9, 12, 21, 24, 58, 66, 78, 79, 81, 84, 86, 87, 90–94 *passim,* 104, 109, 121, 122, 123, 130, 205, 227, 234, 242; Communist rule in, 168, 169; Cultural Revolution in, 169; early man in, 12–19 *passim,* 21; ethnic groups in, 167; Great, *see* Great China; village, *see* Village China

Chinese Revolution (1911), 110, 210

Ch'ing (Manchu) Dynasty, 109, 152, 210

Chopper (tool), 17, 19, 65, 222

Choris site, 37, 38

Chou Dynasty, 79, 80, 87, 148, 150, 152, 153, 155, 156, 164, 171, 214

Choukoutien, 12, 13, 17, 18

Christianity, 91, 92, 121, 131, 165, 174, 175, 203, 244

Ch'u domains, 214–15, 216

Chuang, the, 26, 166

Chuang Tsu, 157

Chukchi, the, 20, 26, 29–51, 55, 58, 61, 97, 100, 106, 109, 264; as Americanoids, 40; appearance of, 29–30; dogs cherished by, 32; dwellings of, 33, 41; and Eskimos, 35–36, 38; family titles among, 41, 42; fishing by, 33; group marriage among, 44, 45, 46; as herders, 31, 32, 34, 36, 41, 42; as hunters, 31, 32, 33, 34, 36, 41; and *ke'let,* 47, 48; reindeer domesticated by, 32, 42; rituals of, 46–47; and Russian Revolution, 50, 51; scapulimancy used by, 38; sexual folkways of, 44–45; shamans of, 49, 50; "Soft Men" among, 44; and spirits, belief in, 47, 48; sturdiness of, 29; suicides among, 48; as warriors, 34–35; women's position among, 42–44

Chulalongorn, King, 256

Cimmerians, 82

Coedes, Georges, 255

Columbus, Christopher, 9

Condominas, Georges, 245, 246, 247, 248, 250

Confucius, 158–62 *passim,* 164, 168, 174, 175

Continents, origin of, 7

Coon, Carleton, 21, 68

Creel, H. G., 193

Darwin, Charles, 10, 11, 261

Deer of Nara, 61

Dentan, Robert, 225, 258

Dnieper River, 74

Domestication of animals, 73–74

Don River, 5, 20

Dong-son, bronzes of, 217, 221, 226

Dragon, in art and mythology, 264, 265

Dubois, Eugene, 12, 13, 14

INDEX

Durian, 261
Dzungarian Gates, 8, 23, 82, 86, 122

Egami, Namio, 66, 85
Ekwall, Robert, 195, 197, 198, 200, 211
Eskimo, 20, 26, 35, 36, 37, 38, 40, 46
Eskimo Kinship Terminology, 41
Estrada, Emilio, 68
Ethnogenesis, 111
Eurasia, 4, 7, 8, 9, 10, 14, 15, 16, 19, 24, 71, 75; languages of, 23, 24, 26
Evans, Clifford, 68
Evans, Ivor H. N., 256, 257
Everest, Mount, 4

Fei Hsiao-tung, 174, 181
Fergana, and Wu Ti, 165
"Fertile Crescent," 73
Figurines, early, 20–21, 65
Finns, 22, 26
Fuji-Kamui, 62, 63, 64
Funan, kingdom of, 218–19, 229, 230

Galston, Arthur, 189
Gamble, Sidney D., 172, 174, 182, 183
Ganges River, 5
Gathering folk, 253, 254, 255
Gems of Chinese Literature (Giles), 142
Genghis Khan (Timuchin), 22, 93, 112–23 *passim,* 125, 133, 134, 208
Georgia, Soviet, 77
Ger (Mongol housing), 114
"Ghost marriage," 181
Giddings, J. Louis, 37, 38
Giles, Herbert, 142
Gilyak, the, 26, 56
Girdle-descent, counted by Ainu women, 64, 65
Gobi Desert, 5, 6, 84
Golden Horde, 93
Gorman, Chester, 222, 223, 244
Granet, Marcel, 154
Great China, 115, 141–70, 207; and August Ones, 151; cities of, 149, 150, 151, 152, 212; Classics of, 159–60, 161, 163, 164, 166, 168, 189, 190; and Confucius, 158–62 *passim;* and conquests by Wu Ti, 165–66; dynasties of, 152 (table); family in, 153–54; feudal lords of, 155–56; Five Rulers of, 151, 161; *Four Books* of, 160, 162; Great Wall completed in, 164; history of, beginnings of, 151–52; and language, 141–45; Mandate of Heaven in, 160, 161, 164, 165; Middle Kingdom of, 151, 193, 194, 201; religions and philosophies in, 157–58, 201, 202, 229; and writing, ideographic, 143–45
Groslier, Bernard, 231

Hainan Island, 242
Hakka, the, 179
Halpern, Joel, 244
Han Dynasty, 80, 86–90 *passim*, 128, 129, 152, 158, 160, 162, 164, 165, 166, 167, 175, 194, 195, 213, 216, 217, 227
Heine-Geldern, Robert, 231
Hennigh, L., 46
Hill people, 236–51
Himalaya Mountains, 4, 5, 24
Hindu Kush Mountains, 4, 5
Hinduism, 229, 231
Hoabinhian complex, 222, 223, 255
Hokkaido, 54, 57, 58, 59, 60, 64, 66
Homo erectus, 14, 15, 17
Homo sapiens, and *Homo Erectus*, 14
Hong Kong, 172, 174
Honshu, 59, 66
Howells, W. W., 21
Hsia Dynasty, 151, 152, 153, 161, 166, 194
Hsiang, King, 80
Hsiung-nu, the, 87, 88, 89, 90, 92, 118, 120, 125, 126, 129, 133, 155, 165, 194
Hsu, Francis L. K., 175, 176, 177, 185, 187, 188
Huang, the, 242
Hungary, 23, 26, 71
Huns, 90, 129, 131
Hunting folk, 31, 32, 33, 34, 36, 41, 253, 254, 255, 256, 259–60
Hwang Ho River, 5, 8

Ice Age, 36, 40, 55, 56, 96
Ideographic writing, 78, 143–44
India, 5, 7, 8, 9, 15, 19, 23, 77, 93, 201–207 *passim*, 210, 228, 230, 244
Indians, American, 21, 22, 33, 36, 38, 44, 54, 60
Indo-European languages, 23, 24, 142, 228
Indonesia, 218, 264
Indus River, 5, 6, 226, 228
Ipoh tree, 257, 260
Iran (Persia), 23, 73, 82, 86, 88, 120
Irrawaddy River, 230, 255
Islam, 92, 121, 135, 136, 165, 167, 175, 205, 230

Jakun, the, 254, 255
Japan, 4, 22, 26, 34, 84, 85, 121, 123, 146, 165; Ainu in, *see* Ainu
Jarai, the, 241
Java Man, 12, 13, 14, 15, 18
Jimmu Tenno, 58, 59
Jochelson, Waldemar, 40
Jomon people, 65–66, 67, 68
Juan-Juan, the, 90, 91, 119, 129
Juchi (son of Genghis Khan), 133
Jung people, 80, 155
Jurchens, 92, 109, 119

Kachin, the, 238, 243
Kalmucks, 122
Kamchadal, the, 26, 35
Kamchatka, 4, 35
Kami, 61
Kamui, 62, 63, 64
Kao-tsu (Chinese emperor), 87, 88, 160, 162, 217
Karakorum, 4, 123
Karen, the, 238, 243, 244
Kashmir, 135, 208, 211
Kazakh, the, 135, 136, 137
Kazakhstan, 137
Ket, the, 33, 55
Khazar Khanate, 92, 129
Khitans, 91, 92, 119, 133
Khmer, the, 230, 232, 233, 256
Khmu, the, 244, 245
Kipling, Rudyard, 3
Kirghiz, the, 91, 124–37; appearance of, 128; in China, 137; clans of, 135; clothing of, 133; economy of, 132; graves of, 131–32; Great Khan of, 130, 132; great ladies of, clothing of, 133; and jinns, belief in, 135; marriage among, 132, 136; mullahs of, 135, 136; as raiders, 135; records of life and times of, 131; rituals of, 136; shamans of, 135, 136; shelter for, 133; and Soviet Union, 136; yaks owned by, 134–35
Koenigswald, Ralph von, 13, 15
Koko Nor, Lake, 194, 195, 207, 208

Kolarz, W., 51
Korea, 26, 66, 67, 89, 165
Koryak, the, 26, 35, 40
Krader, Lawrence, 115
Ku women of Miao-Yao, 241
Kuang, among Mnong Gar, 248, 249
Kuan-Kung, 174
Kublai Khan, 116, 117, 121, 209
Kumiss, 115
Kunstadter, Peter, 244
Kurile Islands, 54, 57, 60, 67
Kushan, kingdom of, 88, 201
Kwangsi Province (China), 214
Kwantung Province (China), 214
Kyul-Tegin, 130, 131
Kyushu, 59, 66

Languages, 23, 24, 26, 35, 36, 85, 91, 119, 141–42, 230, 242, 245, 254, 257
Laos, 230, 233, 237, 240, 242, 244
Lao-tze, 156–57
Lapps, 22, 26, 72, 107
Lattimore, Owen, 109, 118, 126
Lawa, the, 244
Lena River, 5, 36, 72
Leonowens, Anna, 234
Levin, M. G., 29
Levirate, 45
Lhasa, 207, 208
Li Kuang, 126, 128
Li Ling, 126, 127, 128
Liao lineage, 179
Lin Yueh-lua, 237
Linton, Ralph, 141

Lisu, the, 238
Lizard, monitor, 264, 265
Lolo, the, 166, 236, 237–38
Lu (Chinese empress), 217
Lung-shan culture, 149, 221, 227

Magyars, 26, 92
Mak, the, 242
Malayo-Polynesian languages, 24, 67, 218, 241, 254
Malays, 254, 257, 258, 267
Malaysia, 223, 254, 256
Mal'ta site, 19, 20, 21
Mammoth hunters, 20
Man people, 236, 238
Manchuria, 71, 96, 101, 102, 104, 105, 107, 110, 120, 122, 123
Manchus, 26, 93, 94, 105, 122, 166, 188, 210
Manichaeism, 165
Mao Tse-tung, 168, 169
Massagetae, the, 82, 86
Mediterranean Sea, 7, 8
Meggers, Betty, 68
Mekong Delta, 229, 230
Mekong River, 5, 225, 233, 242
Mencius, 164
Merkits, 112
Meru, Mount, 231
Mesopotamia, 8, 10, 73, 76, 78, 143
Miao, the, 166, 214, 227, 236, 238, 240, 241, 243, 244, 245
Middle East, 77, 81, 82, 146
Mi-mo clans, 215

Min, the, 236
Ming Dynasty, 93, 121, 152, 183, 209, 220
Mnong Gar, the, 245–50
Modun, 87, 88, 89, 93, 125, 194, 201
Mo-ho, the, 92
Mon, the, 230, 231, 232
Mongkut, King, 234, 256
Mongolia, 5, 19, 84, 87, 90, 104, 117, 119, 121, 122, 123
Mongoloids, 21, 57, 76, 256
Mongols, 22, 26, 91, 92, 93, 94, 100, 104, 111–23, 125, 126, 133, 134, 136, 166, 209, 220, 232, 233; animals owned by, 114–15; Buryat, 112, 115, 117, 119, 122, 123; clans of, 112–13, 117–18; clothing of, 113; conquests by, 119–21; extended families among, 118; Great Khan of, 115, 116, 117; as herders, 114, 115; homes of, 113–14; as hunters, 114; and Manchus, 122; marriage among, 113; Oirat, 119, 121; shamans of, 112, 115, 117; and spirits, belief in, 115; and thunder, fear of, 116; white-black dichotomy among, 117; wolves honored by, 114; women's position among, 113
Monguor, the, 122, 208
Mon-Khmer language, 243–44, 245, 254

Montagnards, 246
Munro, Neil Gordon, 54, 58, 65
Muong, the, 245

Nan Chao, kingdom of, 220, 232, 233, 237
Nan Shan Mountains, 194, 195
Nanais, 104, 105
Neanderthal Man, 11, 19, 55, 56
Negritos, 255–56
Nen River, 108
Nepal, 202, 204, 205, 207, 211
New Guinea, 255
Nicobar Islands, 254
Noin Ula tombs, 126, 134
Non Nok Tha site, 225, 226, 227
Nosu, the, 237, 238
Nuclear family, 41, 42, 250
Nung, the, 242
Nurhachi, 109

Oc-eo, 229
Ogedai (son of Genghis Khan), 116
Okladnikov, A. P., 36, 72, 85, 131
Ono, Susumu, 67
Opium, 240
Ordos Desert, 6, 84, 117, 121
Orkhon River, 131, 132

Pagan, kings of, 232, 233
Paintings, rock, 72, 74
Pakistan, 24, 226
Paleoasiatic languages, 26, 57
Paleoasiatics, 57, 105
Palestine, 73, 93

Pamir Mountains, 4, 86, 128, 134
Pangaea, 6, 7
P'an-ku ("dog of many colors"), 151, 227, 228, 241
Panthalassa, 6
P'an-yu (Canton), 194, 214
"Parthian shot," 81
Pazyryk tombs, 84, 86, 96, 126
Peking Man, 13
Philippines, 254, 255
Phillips, E. D., 75, 82, 125
Piggott, Stuart, 76
Pithecanthropus allalus, 12
Pithecanthropus erectus, 12
Polo, Marco, 9, 108, 112, 120, 121, 233
Polyandry, 198–99
Pontus, 5
Pottery, 65, 66, 67, 68, 75, 145, 146, 147, 149, 222, 224, 226, 227
Pruitt, Ida, 175
Pygmies, African, 255, 257
Pyu people, 230, 232

Radcliffe-Brown, A. R., 265
Rashid-ad-din, 116
Red River Delta, 217
Reindeer, 31, 32, 33, 34, 36, 38, 42, 72, 73, 101, 107, 108, 109
Rhade, the, 241
Rice, early domesticated, 226–27
Russia, 20, 71, 74, 75, 77, 84, 93, 120, 121; *see also* Soviet Union

Sahara Desert, 74
Sakas, 73, 82
Sakhalin Island, 22, 54, 56, 58, 60, 63, 109
Samoyeds, 22, 26, 32, 72, 96, 104, 107
Sanskrit, 230, 232
Sarmatians, 82
Sayan Mountains, 107, 108
Scapulimancy, 38, 238
Schafer, Edward, 214, 220
Schebesta, Paul, 256, 259, 261, 262, 265, 266
Scythians, 82, 84
Selenga River, 131, 132
Semang, the, 223, 224, 225, 256–67 *passim;* and book of rules, 263; as "flower children," 261–62; *hala* among, 265, 266, 267; as hunters, 259–60; mythology of, 262–67 *passim*
Senoi, the, 225, 254–58 *passim*, 264, 267
Serveyev, D. A., 37
Shamans, 49, 50, 96–102 *passim*, 104, 112, 115, 117, 135, 136, 231, 249
Shan, the, 243
Shang Dynasty, 78, 79, 81, 86, 149, 150, 151, 152, 153, 155, 161, 162, 193, 214
Shang Ti (god), 151, 155
Shanghai sites, 226
Shantung Province (China), 172, 175

Shinto, 61
Shiramba-Kamui, 62, 63
Shirokogoroff, S. M., 102–106 *passim,* 112
Shishkino, 72, 96
Shom Pen, the, 254
Shun (Chinese emperor), 151
Siberia, 5, 8, 17, 19, 20, 22, 26, 30, 38, 40, 49, 50, 56, 57, 58, 67, 102, 105, 108, 110, 124, 266; Chukchi in, *see* Chukchi
Sinanthropus pekinensis, 13
Sinkiang (Chinese Turkestan), 5, 90, 122, 137, 165, 167
Sino-Tibetan languages, 24, 26, 238
Siva (god), 230, 231
Smith slaves, Turkic, 129
Sochurek, Howard, 247
Soghdians, 129
Solheim, William G., 17, 222, 225, 226
Songsten-gampo, 204, 205, 207
South Africa, 13
Southeast Asia, 5, 8, 11, 12, 17, 21, 22, 57, 58, 121, 146, 165, 201, 205, 222, 227–38 *passim,* 242, 254, 255, 258, 264; crops grown in, 224–25
Soviet Union, 30, 50, 51, 101, 123, 136; *see also* Russia
Spencer, R. F., 46
Spirit Cave, 222, 223, 224, 225, 244
Ssu-ma Ch'ien, 80, 86, 87, 89, 127, 151–55 *passim,* 158, 160,

162, 163, 164, 166, 168, 214, 215, 236, 242
Stag, in mythology, 72
Sui Dynasty, 152, 201, 219
Sumatra, 254, 255
Sung Dynasty, 93, 119, 121, 152
Szechwan Province (China), 216, 237

Taiwan, 222, 224
Taklamakan, 4, 6, 9, 121, 129, 165, 207
T'ang (Chinese conqueror), 152, 160, 163
T'ang Dynasty, 86, 112, 128, 129, 130, 132, 152, 182, 201, 207, 208, 212, 213, 214, 219, 220, 237, 242
Taoism, 157–58, 174, 175, 201
Tarim Basin, 5, 6, 86, 122, 201, 208
Tasadays, 254
Tatars, 111
Technocomplex, 222
Thai languages, 242
Thailand, 223, 227, 229, 230, 231, 233, 234, 240, 244, 254, 256, 257
Thubten Figme Norbu, 203, 205, 206
Ti people, 79–80
Tibet, 4–5, 24, 91, 93, 122, 125, 166, 167, 193–211, 228, 229; Bon in, 202, 203, 204, 205, 208; Buddhism in, 200–208 *passim*; Ch'iang (shepherds) of, 193, 194, 195, 216; Communist China's invasion of, 210; Dalai Lama in, 206, 207, 209, 210; Gelupka order in, 209; High Pasture Nomads of, 195, 196, 197, 200, 211; kings of, early, 206, 207; marriage in, 198, 199; Mongol rule of, 208; polyandry in, 198–99; polygyny in, 199; Sakya Monastery in, 208, 209; tent group families in, 198; in war with Great China, 207–208; women of, 198, 199, 200
Tien, kingdom of, 165, 166, 215, 216, 220, 237
Tien Shan Mountains, 4, 5, 128, 133, 134
T'in, the, 245, 253
Ting-ling, the, 86, 91, 125, 126, 128, 133
Toba Wei Dynasty, 201
Tocharians, 23, 86, 125
Tools, early, 16, 17, 19, 72, 222, 226
Tripolye people, 74–75
Tseng-sun, 174
Tsong Khapa, 209
Tucci, Giuseppe, 198, 207
Tumen, 87, 88, 125
Tung-hu, the, 88, 92
Tung-pei, peoples of, 91, 92, 109
Tungus, the, 26, 32, 33, 38, 49, 56, 72, 85, 92, 95–110, 111,

112, 113, 114, 117, 125, 126, 166; clans of, 101–104; as hunters, 105, 106; marriage among, 103; origin of, 104–105; and reindeer, 107, 108; shamans of, 96–102 *passim,* 104; and Soviet Union, 101, 110

Tunhuang, 195, 204, 207

Turkey, 26, 124

Turkic peoples, 26, 90, 91, 92, 94, 119, 124, 129, 131, 135; *see also* Kirghiz

Turko-Tatar languages, 91

Turks, 90, 91, 104, 111, 124, 125, 208, 213; *see also* Kirghiz

Uigur script, 120, 121, 123, 208

Uigurs, 91, 129, 135, 166, 208, 213

Ural-Altaic languages, 26, 32, 91, 137

Ural Mountains, 3, 8, 24, 56, 107

Usatova, graves of, 75

Viet Cong, 246

Vietnam (Nam Viet), 24, 165, 214, 219, 220, 221, 226, 230, 232, 233, 234, 240, 241, 242, 245, 246

Village China before 1911, 171–88; age honored in, 179–80; ancestors honored in, 176, 177, 178; bride's duties in, 184–85; clans in, 178, 186; and club membership, 188; Communist rule contrasted with, 188–90; craft shops in, 187–88; crops grown in, 173; family unity in, 186–87; footbinding in, 182–83; funeral rituals in, 176; and God of Earth and Grain, 171, 172, 173; Kitchen gods in, 174; marriage in, 181–82, 183–85; religions in, 174–75; Sheung shui in, 172, 179, 240; and Ting Hsien complex, 174, 183; West Town in, 175, 176, 177, 178, 180, 185; women's position in, 185–86

Vishnu (god), 230, 231

Volga River, 5, 121

Vreeland, Harold, 113

Wa, the, 243

Wallace, Alfred Russel, 261

Wang, William S. Y., 143

Weapons, early, 16, 75

Weaver, Robert W., 254

Wen (Chinese emperor), 88, 153, 162, 217

Whale hunters, 31, 32, 36, 37

Wheel, invention of, 76–78

Williams-Hunt, P.D.R., 256

Wolf, honored by Mongols, 114

Wu-sun, the, 86, 88, 90, 125, 126, 133

Wu Ti (Chinese emperor), 88, 126, 127, 158, 162, 163, 165, 169, 213, 216

Yak, 114, 134–35, 196–97, 200
Yakut, the, 33
Yamato Dynasty, 67
Yang, C. K., 172, 173, 174, 180, 183, 188
Yang, Martin C., 172, 173
Yang-shao culture, 146–48, 149
Yangtze River, 5, 174, 214, 217, 222, 227, 238
Yao, the, 238, 240, 241, 245
Yao (Chinese emperor), 151
Yayoi, the, 66, 67, 68
Yellow River, 73, 105, 137, 146, 152, 155, 194
Yenesei River, 33, 55, 75, 105, 106, 107, 129, 131, 133, 134
Yesugei, 112, 119
Yin ruins, 152–53
Yu (Chinese emperor), 161, 166, 194, 242
Yuan Dynasty, 93, 121, 152, 209
Yueh, the, 214, 216, 217, 236, 240, 242
Yueh-chih, the, 86, 87, 88, 90, 125, 126, 194, 201
Yukaghir, the, 26, 33, 36, 37, 40, 55, 58, 105, 109
Yumbri, the, 245, 254, 255
Yunnan Province (China), 165, 175, 216, 232, 237
Yurt, 114, 133, 136